CW00763360

SEVENTEENTH CENTURY ENGLAND: TRADERS AND THEIR TOKENS

SEVENTEENTH CENTURY ENGLAND: TRADERS AND THEIR TOKENS

GEORGE
BERRY

LONDON

To Barbara, my wife, for her patience and understanding,
Deirdre Long for her excellent typing,
Wendy Long for her help and encouragement.

First published 1988

Typeset by Servis Filmsetting Ltd, Manchester
and printed and bound in Great Britain
by Oxford University Press
for the publishers
B.A. Seaby Ltd
8 Cavendish Square
London W1M 0AJ

Distributed by
B.T. Batsford Ltd
P.O. Box 4, Braintree, Essex CM7 7QY

British Library Cataloguing in Publication Data

Berry, George
Seventeenth century England: traders and their tokens.
1. Tokens — Great Britain — History
I. Title
737'.3'0941 CJ5056

ISBN 1-85264-003-0

CONTENTS

ACKNOWLEDGEMENTS

I am grateful to John Mussell for allowing me to use a considerable amount of material from articles originally appearing in *Coin and Medal News*.

I would also like to acknowledge the help I have received over many years from the staffs of the Coin and Medal Department at the British Museum and the Heberden Coin Room, Ashmolean Museum, Oxford.

I should like to thank the following for permission to reproduce copyright illustrations:

Ashmolean Museum, Oxford	3.4, 3.5, 4.1, 4.2, 4.4, 12.6
British Museum	11.1, 12.8, 12.9, 15.1, 15.2, 15.3, 15.4, 16.1
Alan Cane	6.3
Glendinings	8.2, 8.3, 12.1
Museum of London	12.7, 16.2, 16.6
National Museum of Wales, Cardiff	6.4, 7.1, 8.4
Society of Antiquaries of London	6.1
Yorkshire Museum, York	6.2

PREFACE

The vast number of tokens that appeared in the seventeenth century between the years 1648 and 1672 provides a unique insight into contemporary Engish life and trade. Tokens were issued by innkeepers and alehouse women, grocers and cheesemongers, doctors and chemists, carriers and chapmen, wool merchants and weavers, hatters and cappers, carpenters and glaziers, clock and watch makers, booksellers and stationers, goldsmiths and pewterers, postmasters and coffee houses, prisons and work houses, opticians and jewellers, cutlers and bell founders, boat men and horse hirers. Few aspects of life in this fascinating age are not touched upon by contemporary tokens.

Most writers on this series of tokens have concentrated on the numismatic detail of the pieces themselves. I have attempted instead to explore the background of the issuers, enter their homes, meet their families, observe their eating and drinking habits, their smoking, their shopping, their travel, their clothing, their reading, their sport, their medical care, their treatment of the poor and even their religion.

INTRODUCTION

THE UNDERLYING NEED FOR TOKENS AS SMALL CHANGE

Thomas Snelling, an early London coin dealer and prolific writer, wrote in 1766, 'in all well-regulated governments it is found to be as requisite that there should be money of small value for the use of the market and the poorer sort of subjects, as of the larger species for the other purposes of trade and commutation; and what the value of the smallest piece should be, is pointed out by the proportion the price of provision bears to that of labour, and the abilities of the lower class of people to purchase them'.

There is little doubt that tokens have been used in Britain as small change for the 'lower class of people', as Snelling puts it, from the thirteenth century onwards. More than 2,000 pewter tokens were found in a cess pit in Winetavern Street, Dublin, which could be fairly closely dated to the years 1250–75. Lead tokens were part and parcel of the commercial life of Tudor England; Erasmus in his *Adagia* (c. 1500) speaks of 'plumbeos Angliae'. Budelius in *De Monetis et Re Numeria* (1591) suggests that lead and tin money were stamped by grocers, chandlers and tavern keepers as currency for the poor. He adds, however, that as they could only be used in the shop from which they had been received, 'the loss to the poor was most grievous'. This is one of the reasons why town councils in the seventeenth century favoured municipal issues rather than tokens issued by private individuals.

Dickinson reminds us that between 1540 and 1560 prices generally doubled. In consequence there was a further increase in the amount of 'Leaden money' in circulation as farthings and half pence. The long and prosperous reign of Elizabeth witnessed a steady growth in trade both at home and overseas. An increasing number of farmers and landowners were paying wages in cash rather than in kind. The number of market stalls, small shops and taverns in the high street doubled and trebled. It became clear that there was a need for some form of base currency. In 1574 a coinage of base silver was proposed, but suppressed on account of the Queen's disapproval. The silver half pence and farthings already in circulation were far too small for convenient handling.

In 1578 the City Council of Bristol, then England's second city, took the initiative of obtaining a licence to issue copper tokens for use as change within a radius of ten miles of the city. The first striking of 28,000 pieces failed to satisfy demand, and eventually over 100,000 copper farthings were struck. They were square, with the city arms (ship and castle) on the obverse and the letters C.B. (Civitas Bristollie) on the reverse. They were considered official currency, as they were authorized by the Queen, and clearly circulated far beyond the legal ten mile limit, as they were accepted in London.

James I knew the value of a copper coinage of low denomination, having issued 'turners' as King of Scotland, in 1597. These coins imitated the French double tournois, and came to be widely used as farthings in England in the early years of the seventeenth century. The wily monarch granted a patent in 1613 to Lord Harrington, one of his favourites, to strike copper farthings. James calculated that 100,000lb of farthings would cost just over £24,000 and bring him in £90,000. Of the £65,000 profit, under the terms of the patent, £25,000 would go to the patentee and the rest to the monarch. After Harrington's death the fraudulent patent continued in other hands. The unpopularity of Harrington and Maltravers farthings may be seen in numerous contemporary pamphlets, including a tract of 1644 entitled *A Remedy against the loss of the Subject by Farthing Tokens*. The anonymous author of the tract bemoans the fact that thousands of pounds worth of tokens issued under royal patent were forced on to merchants, traders and labourers, not to ease circulation but purely to provide profit for the patentee, and that forgers and counterfeiters also flooded the market to the detriment of the poor. The year 1644 saw the removal of these fraudulent patents and an official regal copper currency was agreed upon. The Civil War and the execution of Charles I not only deferred this scheme but caused the shortage of small change to become even more acute. Traders had no alternative but to resort to the issuing of their own private half pence and farthings.

THE TOKENS

Values

Michael Dickinson lists more than fourteen thousand major varieties in his *Seventeenth Century Tokens of the British Isles*, including three thousand in London. The vast majority of tokens issued during the period 1648–72 were farthings and half pennies, struck on rounded flans in copper or brass. The earliest are dated 1648. If these were struck after the execution of Charles I on 30 January 1648, as seems likely, they must have been issued during Feburary and March, as the following year 1649 traditionally began on 25 March.

All tokens bearing dates between 1648 and 1656 were farthings. The half penny made its first appearance in 1656, but remained the scarcer denomination until the Restoration. After 1664 half pennies became commoner than farthings. Dickinson points out that this is not an indication of inflation, but was due to the disappearance of the fairly common silver half pence in 1661 on the demonetization of the Commonwealth coinage commonly dubbed 'breeches' money, as the two shields on the obverse resemble a pair of breeches. An extract from the proclamation reads, 'many thousands of pounds of good sterling silver were coyned into syngle pence and Two pences, that so there might be good money current among the poorest of our subjects'. Boon observes that from small beginnings the production of halfpenny tokens swelled to several hundred a year during the years 1666 until 1670.

Tokens valued at a penny made their first appearance in North Wales in 1663. It is significant that the use of the penny at this early stage is confined to very few areas including North Wales and Cheshire, as the higher denomination was needed to meet the expense of importing goods by sea in the first instance. The first dated Cheshire penny was struck at Chester in 1666 by Thomas Minshull (*W*26), giving no indication of his trade. In the following year, similar pennies were struck in Chester for seven tradesmen: Thomas Heath an apothecary, Robert Hewitt a grocer, Will Hewitt, James Knowsley, John Salmon a haberdasher, Peter Stringer, and Henry Williams an ironmonger. The year 1668 saw seven more, 1669 six more, and 1670 four more. Pennies are extremely rare elsewhere. They appeared in Shropshire, Lancashire and Yorkshire in the north and in London and Southwark in the south. Most London pennies were issued by coffee house proprietors.

The vast majority of tokens were made of copper or brass. A few issuers had tokens struck from the same dies in both metals, including a Beaumaris farthing issued by two mercers, Ben Jones and John Worsley. A few tokens were struck on flans of one metal with a central plug of the other. A number of lead pieces are known, including a 1656 farthing of Stephen Dagnall, an Aylesbury bookseller, and a farthing of Watford, issued jointly in 1653 by T. Jerman and I. Burgess, who also issued a brass halfpenny in 1669. Larger lead tokens appeared in London, two at Three Cranes Wharf, Thames Street – issued by Edward Burford and Coates and Biddle respectively. Thomas Harman issued a lead piece at the Chequer Inn, Dowgate. All these tokens bear no mark of value.

A handful of London tokens were struck in leather, including three for the Chapter Coffee House. Unfortunately there is no indication of locality. They are all extremely rare, and all known examples are now housed in the British Museum Collection.

Size and shape

Tokens vary considerably in size. One would expect farthings to be the smallest, yet they vary in diameter from 14mm to 22mm. The town farthings for the poor tend to be larger. As Dickinson points out, halfpennies tend to be the most consistent in size, ranging from 17mm to 20mm. Pennies vary from 14mm to over 25mm. The denomination is not always clear on a token, so an educated guess is sometimes necessary.

The vast majority of seventeenth-century tokens were circular. Those which differed from the norm would certainly have caught the eye. About a hundred or so octagonal pieces were struck, eighty heart-shaped tokens, twenty square and a mere handful of diamond-shaped pieces. Octagonal and heart-shaped pieces were striking, and also allowed more information to be given than was possible on smaller round tokens.

HOW THE TOKENS WERE MADE

The tokens were struck by means of a simple mill and screw press, like that which was used on the regal coinage from 1662 onwards. Dr Samuel Pegg wrote in a *Gentleman's Magazine* of 1757 of a press for coining the tokens of Edward Wood, an apothecary of Chesterfield in Derbyshire, and his son Richard.

Although Samuel Pegg had a coin die of Edward Wood in his possession, it has now disappeared, but several token dies are still in existence, including a pair of dies for the half penny token of Samuel Bacon of Kineton in Warwickshire, to be found in the Ashmolean Museum, Oxford. This is, of course, the token of a private trader. The Ashmolean Museum also possesses the pair of dies for the corporation half penny of Henley on Thames. The Gloucester Museum has the obverse die for the farthing token of Mayor Thomas Price.

Some tokens were struck on strips of metal and then stamped with a ringed punch, but many were struck on individual blanks. Most of the dies were manufactured in London. We can identify only one die maker, David Ramage, who produced farthings during the Republic and early Restoration period. He died in 1662. Ramage was an official engraver of dies at the Tower Mint at this time. State papers record that on 14 March 1649, 'Rainage' and three other 'moneyers' raided the premises of one Reeves of Whitecross Street and seized the tools used 'in making copper farthings unlicensed, which if made at all should be done in the Tower'. Peck discovered another fascinating reference to Ramage in a tract of 1660, 'one Ramage farthing maker in the Tower, whose aime in all this business is to suppress all tools for making farthings but his own, the said Ramage having proffered a large weekly sum to be paid to one party, if all the presses for making farthings may be but taken away about London but only his, so that he may have the sole trade in his hands'.

The characteristics of Ramage-struck tokens include a five-point mullet mark, an outer border of labels and lozenge shaped stops. Peter Preston Morley and Harry Pegg point out that after the Restoration a small open cinq foil replaced the mullet as the mintmark.

There are certain common characteristics of later tokens (1662–72). Boon observes that a damaged six-point rosette stop employed on no less than thirty-four tokens dated between 1666 and 1672, was also used extensively in the English series. He notes Bedales (Yorkshire) and Ashburton (Devon) as random examples. The London series also witnessed its widespread use. It has not been possible yet to identify any of the post-Ramage engravers.

It is generally agreed that the first striking of a token issue would take place centrally in London. It seems likely that the die would be given to the issuer for subsequent use, thus some tokens could well have been struck locally. Boon writes, 'as for local striking, the different die-alignments are a strong indication and the existence of overstrikes on other tokens is proof positive that dies were sooner or later sent down from London'.

Design

Seventeenth-century tokens normally carry the name of the issuer, the town or village where his trade is practised, the arms or symbol of his trade, and the initials of the issuer and his wife. More than half are dated and frequently the value is given, especially if it is a half penny or penny.

A typical piece of a Hertford ironmonger (*W*107) reads, ABRAHAM RVTT Ironmongers' Arms/OF HARTFORD 1666 A.M.R. Spelling was not standardized in the seventeenth century, so one can find Hertford, for example, spelt in four different ways on as many tokens. The initials A.M.R. in the form of a triangle stand for Abraham Rutt and his wife Martha. It is very helpful to have the initial of the issuer's wife's Christian name on tokens, as this often gives a positive identification of the issuer. This triangle of initials, a seventeenth-century custom, can sometimes be seen on buildings of the period.

A typical London token (*W*1759) reads, AT THE WHIT LYON A lion rampant/NEIR LONDON BRIDGE T.A.C. The name of the issuer is missing here; only the initials provide a clue. In this case he has not yet been identified. London tokens rarely include the name of the city in the legend; it is assumed that they will not circulate outside the city. Usually they give the name of a street or a district, whereby the locality of the issuer's business can easily be recognised. Thus we find on *W*2002: WALTER RANDELL IN YE STRAND/NEERE YE NEW EXCHANGE 64 HIS HALF PENY or (*W*3112) AT THE horseshoe IN THAMES STREET/NERE THE OLD SWAN GROSER P.N. (The Old Swan refers to the Stairs, not to a tavern.)

The principal feature of the design is a pictorial device. The arms of the appropriate guild company of London are frequently used both on metropolitan and provincial pieces. The Mercers' Arms are especially popular. Signs and symbols of all kinds appear on the tokens to indicate the issuer's trade. Thus we find clock dials, hammers, guns, fans, lasts, lobsters, malt shovels, pole axes, saddles, shin bones, shuttles and swords. The list is endless.

HOW THE TOKENS WERE USED IN EVERYDAY LIFE

It has traditionally been assumed that seventeenth-century tokens had an extremely limited circulation. Evelyn's off-quoted words add weight to this assumption, 'the tokens which every tavern and tippling house (in days of late anarchy amongst us) presumed to stamp and utter for immediate exchange as they were passable through the neighbourhood, which though seldom reaching further than the next street or two . . .' Evelyn wrote this in 1697, when they would still have been remembered by everyone over the age of thirty.

It should be remembered, however, that the diarist was referring to tokens issued in London. Seventeenth-century London both before and after the Fire was a maze of narrow streets and alleys. Will Hinton's half pence issued at his tavern of the Golden Fleece in Cornhill would find their way into the tills of other innkeepers and tradesmen of all kinds in Cornhill, Threadneedle Street, Lombard Street, Poultry, and all the adjoining alleys (there could well have been a hundred shops or more within a radius of a few hundred yards of his tavern!). Hinton's coins would be accepted by all those who knew him and trusted him to redeem them. Most Londoners had their favourite places of refreshment, seldom venturing into unknown territory. Their wives did their shopping in their own and adjoining streets, and no doubt the circulation of tokens followed this pattern. Few London tokens would wander far from their place of issue. If you had tokens from a distance that were unacceptable in the district, you could always go to Drury Lane and change them at the premises of Richard Rich, who described himself as a Changer of Farthings. He issued his own farthing and half penny (*W*880); the latter reads, RICHARD RICH IN LITEL/DRVRY LANE CHANGER OF FARTHINGS. An intriguing obverse device consists of a bird perched on a sheaf of corn. A figure 2 is placed on each side of the sheaf, standing for 2 farthings. It is not known exactly how his tokens were used and how they circulated.

It can be surmised, however, how most tokens were used. If you bought some groceries from Edward Davis, a grocer in Fenchurch Street, he would give some of his own farthings in change. You could then spend them elsewhere, perhaps buying candles from James Waggoner a few doors away, or a book from John Young, or even visiting Samuel Pepys' favourite tavern, the Mitre. By the time you returned to the grocer's you might have tokens of Edward Davis, James Waggoner, John Young and the Mitre. He would accept them all, and exchange some of his own for coinage of the realm if asked. Traders and tavern keepers kept sorting trays on their counters so that when a sufficient number of any one type had been received they could be redeemed by the appropriate tradesman.

In small towns and villages the system of token usage was similar, except that the tokens travelled further. We have seen evidence that Watford tokens were known and used in Bushey, five miles away, and that Lincoln town pieces could be spent in Spalding, forty miles away. We know that one Devon token circulated in at least three villages. A half penny of John Lethbridge (*W*307) reads, JOHN LETHBRIDGE OF SOVTH I.M.L./TAWTON CHAGFORD AND MORETON HIS HALFE PENNY. He also issued a token at another village, Zeal; thus he conducted business in four separate village stores. There is little doubt that municipal issues carried considerable prestige. Bristol farthings, in particular, set the weight standard and were accepted over a wide area. The numerous Bristol issues of 1652, 1660, 1662 and 1670 fulfilled the needs of the citizens so completely that only six private tradesmen felt compelled to issue their own. It remains a mystery why the city of London did not similarly issue an official coinage.

SUPPRESSION AND DISAPPEARANCE

Numerous petitions were made during the Commonwealth period for a copper coinage in farthings or half pennies but to no avail. Patterns were actually struck in 1658, bearing the Protector's portrait, but he died in the same year. Oliver Cromwell's successor, Richard, agreed to a copper coinage in April 1659, but he was compelled to retire prematurely from government shortly afterwards. Despite pressure from all quarters during the first decade following the Restoration, the much needed copper currency of farthings and half pence was not introduced until August 1672. The King's *Proclamation for making Current His Majestie's Farthings and Half Pence of Copper and forbidding all others to be used* begins, 'Whereas of late several persons and Corporations, upon pretence that there wanted small moneys to be currant in low and ordinary payments amongst the poorer sort, have presumed to cause certain pieces of Brass, Copper and other Base Metals to be stamped with their private stamps; and then imposed those pieces upon our poor subjects for Pence, Halfpence or Farthings, as the makers thereof were pleased to call them, whereby our subjects have been greatly defrauded, and our Royal authority and the laws of our Kingdom violated . . .'

Offenders were threatened with severe penalties. Even so we read in a *London Gazette* of 23 February 1673/4, 'divers retailers and shop keepers, in several cities, towns and corporations of this kingdom do continue to utter in exchange and payments, pence, half pence and farthings of their own making in contempt of his Majesties Proclamation'. A further proclamation of 5 December 1674 stated that 'several persons and corporations remote from London have forborne to call in their private farthings and do still presume to make use of and other the same . . .'

These proclamations had their effect; the law was enforced and tokens disappeared from circulation. We can be quite sure that many people were unable to redeem the tokens that they still had.

UNDERTAKING RESEARCH

A good deal can be discovered about the men and women who issued tokens – their family background, social standing, political and religious leanings. Possible sources are parish registers, hearth tax records, borough archives, wills and inventories and records of the Free Churches.

Printed records

Records of Quarter Sessions often reveal useful information concerning issuers who have appeared before the magistrates. Nonconformists were frequently fined for non-attendance at church.

Borough archives such as the Burford Records (1920) and the Ledger Book of High Wycombe (1956) provide invaluable information concerning the contribution of issuers to civic life.

Phillimore's Parish Registers often give details of marriages, but omit baptisms and burials.

The County Inventories of the Royal Commission on Historical Monuments give details of most interesting buildings which were in existence in towns and villages at the time of compilation. I have frequently discovered vital information concerning inns in these inventories, and also in local trade directories which date back to Victorian times.

Manuscript sources

It is even more exciting to make discoveries at first hand. Numerous seventeenth-century documents may be studied. The handwriting can be mastered without too much difficulty, after a little practice.

Here are some suggestions for records which you might consult.

1. Wills and inventories are often to be found in county record offices, as well as at Somerset House.
2. Parish registers giving details of baptisms, marriages and burials may be in the care of county record offices or individual parish priests.
3. Hearth tax returns and lay subsidy returns may be consulted at the Public Record Office in London. The unpopular hearth tax introduced by Act of Parliament in 1662 brought in revenue of two shillings a year on each fire hearth or stove. Householders had to inform the constables of the number of hearths and stoves they possessed. The hearth tax accounts give a good indication of the size of a man's house or inn, for instance David Gascoigne of the Bull at Nettlebed (*W*108) paid tax on ten hearths, whereas Thomas Austin of the Red Lion at Adderbury (W Oxon. 1) only paid for one hearth.

The hearth tax caused much ill feeling, especially as the constables were authorized to enter and search houses. Chimneys were walled up and false returns were submitted. Larger houses were subdivided into tenements. Cottagers complained bitterly that they had to pay two shillings a year for a stone 'not worth two pence which the Chimney villains call a hearth'. Ironworkers, including smiths, braziers and pewterers, were liable unless they could prove that their hearths were used solely for the purpose of their work.

CHAPTER 1

INNS, TAVERNS AND ALEHOUSES

The cultivation and fermentation of barley to satisfy men's thirst has been going on for thousands of years. It has been suggested that the Persians were the first people to discover brewing, and the ancient Egyptians were also past masters of the art. The commonest drink in Roman Britain was ale; Pliny the Elder commented, 'the natives who inhabit the west of Europe have a liquid with which they intoxicate themselves made from corn and water'. Alehouses were well known in Saxon Britain, and an eighth-century edict decreed that no priest was to eat or drink in a tavern. A law passed in Edgar's reign (957–75) restricted the number of alehouses to one per village. Many church and social festivities witnessed brewing on a large scale. There were church ales, midsummer ales, lamb ales, bride ales and tithe ales, to celebrate the appropriate occasion.

The Normans, on the other hand, chiefly drank wine. From the Conquest of 1066 until the end of the Hundred Years War, large quantities of duty-free wine were imported from France. Throughout the Middle Ages wine and ale were both consumed, the former by the aristocracy and merchants, the latter by country peasants and poorer townsfolk. Each alehouse and inn brewed its own ale. It was the Dutch who introduced beer made from hops to Britain in the early fifteenth century, as the rhyme has it:

Hops, Reformation, Bays and beer
Came to England all in one year.

Hitherto, beer had been simply another term for ale. There was no clear-cut distinction between alehouses and taverns at this time. Michael Brander suggests that the former provided ale and entertainment, and the latter food and wine in addition. Brander also provides a neat distinction between the inn and the tavern, affirming that the tavern provided wine but no lodging, whilst the inn provided lodging but no wine. The sixteenth century witnessed a considerable number of inns, taverns and alehouses, on account of trade expansion under the Tudors. In 1553, an Act was passed to limit the amount of wine sold, by restricting the number of taverns in major towns and cities, as follows: London 40; York 9; Bristol 6; Cambridge, Canterbury, Chester, Exeter, Gloucester, Hull, Newcastle on Tyne and Norwich 4 each; Colchester, Hereford, Ipswich, Lincoln, Oxford, Salisbury, Shrewsbury, Southampton, Westminster and Worcester 3 each. A census of 1557 shows the following figures for England and Wales: 14,202 alehouses, 1,631 inns and 329 taverns.

Shiploads of sherry, brandy, and sack were beginning to cross the Channel. William Vaughan warned in 1600, 'sack doth make men fat and foggy and therefore is not to be taken of young men'. Claret was the most popular wine.

Most places of refreshment in England were well run throughout the sixteenth century. William Harrison reports in 1563, 'every man may use his inn as his own house in England.' Fynes Morison, writing half a century later, comments, 'there is no place in the world where passengers may so freely command as the English inns and are attended for themselves and their horses as well as if they were at home and perhaps better'. Three soldiers from Norwich taking part in a lightning tour of twenty-six counties in 1634 were similarly complimentary about the service that they received.

However, the Civil War and the ensuing Commonwealth period of Cromwellian rule, made life difficult for many an inn keeper and tavern holder. Brander quotes from a Government order of 1656 to the Justices of Hertfordshire, 'For as much as His Highness the Lord Protector of the Commonwealth hath token special note of the mischiefs and great disorders which daily happen and are committed in Taverns, Inns and Ale houses . . . The Justices of this country of Hertford are adjoined to take special care for the suppressing of all such ale house keepers as are or shall be convicted of the profanation of the Lord's Day by receiving into their houses any company or of swearing, drunkeness, suffering tippling, gaming or playing at Tables, Billard Table, Shovel Board, Cards, Dice, Ninepins or of keeping a Bowling Alley or any of them or any other games'.

In the seventeenth century, unlike Victorian times, there was no stigma attached to being an innkeeper. Many innkeepers were respected members of the community, holding high office in local government. Although the Puritans objected to drunkenness, swearing and gaming, they did not object to inns and taverns as such, provided that their customers refrained from 'profanities'. Isaak Walton in his *Compleat Angler* of 1653 paints a delightful picture of an inn during the Protectorate, 'I'll lead you now to an honest ale house, where we shall find a cleanly room, lavender in the window and twenty ballads stuck about the wall'.

A large number of inns, taverns, and alehouses issued tokens from 1648 to 1672. More than a thousand are known for London alone, and inn tokens are prolific also in the provinces. Twenty-four Buckinghamshire inns issued them, including eight at High Wycombe and six at Colnbrook.

COACHING INNS

The typical coaching inn of the mid seventeenth century was an impressive Tudor timber-framed building with a spacious courtyard, overhanging galleries, stabling for a dozen horses and barns for their fodder. A large communal room on the ground floor served many purposes including the feeding and entertainment of the guests. The bedchambers were usually to be found on the first floor, whilst the servants slept in the garrets. Fynes Morison provides an interesting insight into the dining arrangements of a contemporary inn, 'if he will eat with the Host or at a common table with the others, his meals will cost him 6D or in some places 4D, but if he will eat in his chamber he commands what meat he will, according to his appetite, yea the kitchens are open to him to command the meal to be dressed as he best likes. If he have desire he shall be offered musick . . .'

The King's Head at the top of the market square in Aylesbury, the county town of Buckinghamshire, is still very much a thriving concern. A record of 1455 refers to 'the messuage called the Kings Hede' – shop, cellar and cottage. The building retains a number of its original fifteenth-century features including a large hall and window, and is now owned by the National Trust. I once looked through an inventory of its furniture, in Birmingham Public Library of all places. The inventory of about 1650 is of particular interest in that the inn was then held by William Dawney who issued three farthings there. W12 reads, AT YE KING'S HEAD/IN AILLSBVREY 1657 W.D.E. The initials stand for William Dawney and his wife Elizabeth. Dawney married Elizabeth Horwood in 1637 when he was twenty-four years old, so he must have been forty-four when this token was circulated. One of his sons, Thomas, received serious head injuries whilst sitting in the gallery of St Mary's Church with other school children, listening to a Saturday morning lecture, on 11 December 1658. There is a graphic account of it in the church records, 'There happened to fall in the sermon a great stone, which wayed three or four score pounds and there was then present in their seats near a hundred schoolers, which stone did break two of their heads and part of the gallery where in they sat. So through the providence of God there was none other hurt done . . . Thomas Dawney and Robert Brayon were the two schoolers which were hurt'.

William Dawney was church warden in 1665 but allowed his reputation to suffer fourteen years later when fined at the Quarter Session the sum of a shilling for 'not doing his service to the amending of the high wayes in the parish of Aylesbury'. This is rather ironical since a coaching inn depended upon good highways.

Another celebrated Buckinghamshire coaching inn which is still thriving is the Ostrich at Colnbrook. Three hundred years ago the high street of Colnbrook was bustling with coaches, carts, and packhorses from dawn until dusk. Colnbrook was the second stage out of London on the busy road to Bath. More than a hundred horses would be stabled each evening in the yards of the ten or so inns overlooking the main thoroughfare, no less than six of which issued tokens: the White Hart of Thomas Burcombe, the Bear of John Forest, the Bell of Alice Goad, the Ball of Susan Homes, the Angel of John Hosey, and the Ostrich of Samuel Mills. Only the Ostrich still plies its original trade, although the White Hart was an inn within recent memory, but now leads a quieter existence as a private house.

The token of Samuel Mills, innkeeper of the Ostrich, bears the landlord's name and a peculiar creature supposed to resemble an ostrich. The reverse reads IN COOLBROOKE 57 S.M.M. The number represents the date 1657 whilst the initials stand for the innkeeper and his wife, Margaret. The piece, being small and insignificant, is, of course, a farthing, the price of a pint during the Commonwealth period. The spelling of Colnbrook is no surprise, as the town is spelt in almost as many ways as there are tokens: Colbrooke, Covlbrough, Covlbroke, Coalbrvck, Colebrook and Coolebrooke. Colnbrook takes its name from the River Coln, but it will be noticed that none of the seventeenth-century spellings contains the letter N. Spelling was not standardized at that time, and no one version was more correct than any other.

Even in 1657 the Ostrich was quite ancient. A substantial part of the surviving attractive timber work is Elizabethan or even earlier. It is certain that an inn existed on the site in the 1400s, but the statement that the inn definitely dates back to 1106 must be treated with caution. It may well, however, have historical links with a hospice. The Ostrich today is a very handsome black-and-white timbered building with a tiled roof. It has a projecting upper storey with a gable at each end, and the original gateway is still to be seen. Throughout the nineteenth century a fascinating flap existed, which could be let down from a bedroom window to enable coach passengers to enter their bedroom directly from the stagecoach.

However, the inn's main claim to fame is its fourteenth-century landlord named Jarman, who took a sadistic delight in murdering his guests in quick succession. They were tipped out of their beds through a trap door into a bubbling cauldron to be burned alive before drowning. An account of the Ostrich murders first appeared in a fifteenth-century book by Thomas Delaney; a later version appeared in a Victorian romantic novel, 'At the Sign of the Ostrich' by Charles James.

Samuel Mills, the landlord during the Commonwealth period, was fined in 1646 the sum of ten shillings 'for selling ale by illicit measures to the prejudice of the inhabitants'. To add insult to injury the court hearing took place in his own inn. It was common practice for court sessions to be held in taverns or inns when public buildings were unavailable. Mills married twice. His first wife, Margaret, died in 1662, just six years after her husband had issued his farthing with her initial on it. His second wife, Alice, survived her husband who died in 1672.

The White Hart was situated at the London end of the village on the same side of the road as the Ostrich. Although now a private house with an attractive Georgian frontage, one can still discern traces of its former life, for example the coaching entrance. Some seventeenth-century timber-work still survives. Thomas Burcombe's attractive farthing token is undated but bears all the hallmarks of David Ramage's pre-1660 period, including the five point mullet initial mark and outer border of labels and lozenge stops. A lively-looking hart is featured on the obverse, looking over its shoulder. The initials T.D.B. on the reverse stand for the issuer and his wife, Dorothy, who died in 1674. Her husband was church warden at the parish church of Horton. The church records show that Thomas Burcombe put in new timbers and a new dormer window in the church in 1629. He was appointed receiver of tolls to repair roads and bridges in 1653.

An interesting ballad reputed to have been composed at the White Hart in 1658 and thus contemporary with the token, reads,

'There were three cooks of Colebrook
And they fell out with our cook.
And all was for a pudding he took
From the three cooks of Colebrook.'

The ballad is said to relate to three apprentices, Sparks, Bedborough and Tollitt, who were engaged at the White Hart in quick succession.

Joseph Finch is mentioned as innkeeper of the White Hart in Pigot's *Directory* of 1830. Only the Ostrich and the White Hart of our seventeenth-century inns are referred to in this directory. The other four, the Ball, the Bear, the Bell and the Angel had all disappeared by then. Yet the George, the King's Arms and the Catherine Wheel, all inns of note in the seventeenth century, still appeared although no tokens of any of them have come to light. The George, incidentally, is still flourishing today, like the Ostrich.

John Hosey's token issued at the Angel not only depicts the inn sign, but includes its name in the legend. The initials I.I.H. appear on the reverse. The issuer's wife, Joan, died in 1668 just two years after the death of her husband. The token is early in style and belongs to the 1650s. The Angel lay about half a mile to the west of the Ostrich. The Session Records of 1699 relate that the highway was to be repaired from the bridge near the Angel Inn to the west of the Ostrich Inn. Hosey's token is quite rare; only two specimens are known.

John Forise's token farthing issued at the Bear in 1667 is also scarce. Little is known about the issuer or his inn. The date 1667 is late for a farthing, due to the inflation consequent upon increased trade which accompanied the Restoration. The Parish Register tells us that Forise died in 1674, just seven years after the issue of his farthing.

The final two token-issuing innkeepers in Colnbrook were both women. Alice Goad was the only trader in the village to issue a halfpenny. It is dated 1669, quite late in the series, and was not known by Williamson. It reads, ALCE COAD AT THE BELL/IN COLBROOKE 1669 HER HALF PENY. One of her rare tokens has been dug up in the village. Again the spelling is much nearer the original Colebrok (1146) than the present Colnbrook. An extremely large bell dominates the obverse of Alice Goad's halfpenny, but like John Hosey of the Angel, the issuer has also included the name of the inn in the legend. Alice was the widow of William Goad, a doctor, who died in 1658. She survived her husband by eighteen years. A wall tablet in the north aisle of Horton Church is inscribed, 'Near ye place Lyes ye Body of William Goade ye Father and William, his son, both late of Colebroke, Physitians'. William's brother, George, also issued a halfpenny token of smaller size than that of his sister in law, but bearing the same date, 1669. This may well be more than a coincidence. George's token was issued at Horton in the township of Colnbrook. It gives no clue as to the occupation of the issuer, but the value of the piece is made quite clear in the legend, HIS TOKEN FOR A HALF PENY. George Goad, like Thomas Burcombe, was church warden at the parish church in Horton.

The remaining innkeeper's token, W. Devon 45, reads, WIDOW HOMES AT YE/BALL IN COALBRVCK S.H. A large ball is featured on the obverse. All we know is that her name was Susan, as the initial on the reverse, and that she died in 1682.

The county of Buckinghamshire possesses many old coaching inns, not a few of which, like the King's Head in Aylesbury and the Ostrich in Colnbrook, issued tokens. The Greyhound in Chalfont St Peter is another fine example. A genuine stage coach stood outside it until the landlord was forced to sell it some years ago on account of its vulnerability to vandalism. The first known record of the Greyhound appears in the will of William Duke (3 March 1592) 'And I doe give unto John Tyelye the fower and twentye pounds which I lent him when he toke the Greyhound'. Two tokens, a farthing and a half penny, were struck at the Greyhound by successive innkeepers. Jarvis Good's farthing depicted the inn sign and the initials J.M.G. Unfortunately we do not know his wife's Christian name, which began with M. He was born in 1626 according to the register of births, whilst the burial register records his death in January 1673 at the age of fifty (obviously the parish clerk was no mathematician). Like William Dawney of Aylesbury,

1.1 Half penny token of John Bennett of the Greyhound Inn, Chalfont St Peter.

Jarvis Good was a churchwarden. The Church of St Peter at Chalfont St Peter is conveniently close. An amusing tale is told of Good's father, also called Jarvis. On Christmas Day 1635, as constable, he arrested someone for debt in the church during the communion service. On being challenged for unlawful arrest, he denied that he had arrested him in the church itself, claiming that he only whispered in his ear, then took him to nearby Gerrards Cross and arrested him there.

The second token issued at the Greyhound was struck in the name of John Bennett. This was a half penny token, bearing the date 1668, just three years after the Plague when John Milton took refuge in neighbouring Chalfont St Giles and two years after the Fire of London, when it is recorded that charred wood and paper was picked up in the gardens of Chalfont St Peter villagers. Bennett's token also shows a greyhound with the initials I.O.B. He was probably married twice for the register of 21 September 1630 records the marriage of John Bennett and Susanne Butterfield. I have not found evidence of his second wedding to O. He died in November 1675 in his seventies, so he must have been in the middle sixties when his token appeared.

Interestingly, Bennett is described as a tailor in his will. It was quite customary for tradesmen to have two occupations. It seems clear that he took over the Greyhound quite late in life and may well have devoted most of his active life to tailoring. The details of his will are quite intriguing:

To Thomas Bennett, his eldest son, one shilling
John Bennett, his second son, £5
Arthur Bennett, his third son, £5
Robert Bennett, his son, all other goods and chattels.

One wonders why his eldest son had been 'cut off with a shilling'.

No less than eight innkeepers issued tokens at High Wycombe. The sites of all eight inns are known and five of the original buildings are still standing – those of the Wheatsheaf, Red Lion and Antelope in the High Street, the Chequers at the corner of Church Street and White Hart Street, and the Greyhound in Easton Street. The largest and most important inn in Wycombe in the seventeenth century was the Red Lion. Richard Lucas, thrice mayor, was its innkeeper. The chief claim to fame is that it was the forerunner of the Royal Military College of Sandhurst during the years 1799–1813 when the whole of Europe lay under Napoleon's shadow.

Few people realise that the Royal Military College at Sandhurst began in the upstairs room of an inn close to the centre of High Wycombe. The

1.2 Greyhound Inn, Chalfont St Peter.

building still exists, but no longer dispensing ale to thirsty officer cadets; it now consists of a jeweller's shop conjoined with a grocery business. The Georgian frontage of the upper storey, behind whose façade young British army officers learnt map reading and battle strategy, can still be seen today. The roof tells us that the fabric is considerably earlier. It is known that the inn was flourishing in the seventeenth century for Robert Whitton issued a farthing token in the 1660s, displaying a quaint creature faintly resembling an antelope on the obverse and the initials RWK on the reverse, representing the landlord and his wife, Katherine. Mr Ogilby in his *Tables of Measured Roads* (1692) observes, 'High Wycombe contains near 200 houses with several good inns as the Antelope and Catherine Wheel'. We must be careful not to confuse Whitton's inn with the present Antelope at the corner of the High Street, close by the parish church. This Antelope was formerly known as the Royal Oak.

A print of a painting by William Hannon in 1772, showing the broad high street, is accompanied by a fascinating contemporary description by the artist of the persons who figured in his painting. The description concludes, 'Mr Hutchinson of the Antelope speaking to a post boy. The maid servant at the window with her broom'. One wonders if the Mr Hutchinson seen chatting to a post boy was still landlord of the Antelope when General Le Marchant first visited the premises in 1799 to see if it was suitable for housing a school for army officers. The general's comment on seeing the building was characteristically terse and to the point, 'it is an old place but it will do to begin with'. In the event the college occupied the Antelope for fourteen momentous years. Over thirty officers enrolled at the academy when it opened at High Wycombe on May 4, 1799. Le Marchant was nominated Commandant and Jarry his Director of Instruction. The cadets were taught geometry, trigonometry, French and military strategy, embracing fortifications, siege-warfare, bombing and the calibre and range of guns.

1.3 Farthing token of the Antelope issued by Robert Whitton.

1.4 Eighteenth-century print showing the Antelope, High Wycombe.

Much more could be written about Buckinghamshire inns and their tokens, but I will end with a cautionary tale. One of the treasures in my collection is a half penny of William Willis of Beaconsfield (*W*24). It reads, WILLIAM WILLIS 1668/AT BECKINGSFEILD HIS HALF PENY W.F.W. A lively bull is featured on the obverse. There is a Bull Farm at London End, Beaconsfield, and I had long assumed that Willis's token had been issued there, especially as there is a coach entrance to the property. I had thought that the farm was named after the seventeenth-century inn. Recently, however, a local historian discovered that the George in Wycombe End was named the Bull during the 1660s and 70s. It was originally known as the George, became the Bull in the seventeenth century, reverting to the George again in the eighteenth century, named after the monarch of the day. The George it has remained ever since.

Two tokens were struck for the Bull/George by successive innkeepers, the half penny of William Willis and an earlier farthing of Joseph Grimsdale (*W*23), which reads, IN BECKONSFEILD I.M.G./IN BVCKINGHAMSHIRE B. 1658.

Joseph Grimsdale, the issuer, married Mary Gibbons at the parish church of High Wycombe in 1652.

Hertfordshire too had its fair share of coaching inns, which issued tokens. One of the most celebrated was the Reindeer at Bishop Stortford, kept by Edward Aynsworth (*W*41). His token reads, YE RAINEDEARE IN/BISHOP STARTFORD E.E.A. A reindeer is depicted on the obverse. The initials stand for Edward Aynsworth and his wife Elizabeth.

The landlord's wife, Betty, wore the trousers. She was a female Falstaff. Stories of her crude songs and jests were told with relish in inns and taverns throughout the eastern counties. She had been banished from Cambridge for running a brothel. When the Vice Chancellor and numerous college dignitaries unwittingly stopped at the Reindeer one night on their way to London, they were royally entertained and fed off silver plate. In the morning she refused to accept any payment, claiming that by expelling her from Cambridge they had made her fortune.

Samuel Pepys knew her well, as the entry in his diary for 7 October 1667 confirms 'And before night came to Bishop Stortford whither Lowther and his friend did meet us again and carried us to the Raynedeere where Mrs Aynsworth, who lived here to fore at Cambridge and whom I knew better than they think for, do live. It was the woman that, among other things, was great with my cozen Barnston of Cottenham, and did use to sing to him, and did teach me full forty times over a very lewd song, a woman they are all well acquainted with and is here what she was at Cambridge . . . but there was so much tearing company in the house that we could not see the landlady, so I had no opportunity of renewing my old acquaintance with her'.

The diarist also had occasion to dine at the Reindeer the following year. He wrote on 23 May 1668, 'up by four o' clock . . . I with my boy Tom . . . away to Bishops Stortford. Dined and changed horses and coach at Mrs Aynsworth's but I took no knowledge of her . . . I hear Mrs Aynsworth is going to live at London but I believe will be mistaken in it, for it will be found better for her to be chief where she is than to have little to do at London'. Pepys seems to have been mistaken for she continued to live in Bishop Stortford until her death in March 1685.

Another story concerning this notorious landlady is to be found in a contemporary pamphlet entitled *Boteler's Case*. It seems that she was implicated in the murder of Captain Wood, a Hertfordshire gentleman, at Manuden in Essex. A man named Boteler was convicted of the murder, and executed at Chelmsford on 10 September 1667. Mrs Aynsworth was tried as an accessory before the fact, but was acquitted through lack of evidence, though on her way to jail she attempted to throw herself into the river.

The Reindeer has long since disappeared, but a number of Hertfordshire token-issuing coaching inns survive, including the Red Lion at Barnet, the Dimsdale Arms of Hertford, and the Rose and Crown at Tring. The Red Lion at Barnet was originally the Cardinal's Hat in the fifteenth century. It became the Antelope in 1553, and changed to the Red Lion at the end of the seventeenth century, after its tokens appeared. *W*21 reads PEETER BLACKWELL AT YE HIS HALFE PENY/ANTELOPE IN BARNET 66 P.A.B. In the eighteenth century it was a large Georgian building with a magnificent porch. There was stabling for more than a hundred horses. In 1771, a general's wife, considerably younger than her husband, was overtaken there after eloping with his aide-de-camp.

1.5 Farthing token of the infamous Betty Aynsworth of the Reindeer, Bishop Stortford.

The Dimsdale Arms at Hertford has changed its name several times. In the seventeenth century it was the Red Lion. William Thorne kept it in 1621. It had become the Half Moon and Stars by 1719. Throughout the eighteenth century its licensees kept the county jail, which stood opposite the present Corn Exchange. One of them named Isaac Oxinton is reputed to have hanged an inmate from his sign. Caesar Saunders was also asked to take charge of the Hertford bridewell. In 1828 the Half Moon changed its name again to the Duncombe Arms after Thomas Slingsly Duncombe, Member of Parliament for Hertford from 1826 until 1832, the only radical ever to gain a seat there. In 1833 it changed its name again to the Dimsdale Arms when it was bought by the Dimsdale family. It was well known as a coaching inn, running its own coach as well as acting as a staging post for other coaches. Its off-licence, now the Talbot Arms, used to be the Chequers. A token issued there reads THOMAS PRATT/IN HERTFORD T.M.P. (*W*106). The Chequers was widely known for its cockpit.

The earliest documentary evidence of the Rose and Crown at Tring refers to an inn kept by Thomas Robinson in 1621 but the building dated from the previous century. A half penny was issued there in 1668 by William Axtell, reading, WILLIAM AXTELL HIS HALF PENY/OF TRING 1668 (*W*194). This busy coaching inn, situated on the road from London to Watford, was used for many purposes apart from catering for the needs of hungry and thirsty travellers. The Justices used to meet there regularly, especially when dealing with highway affairs. From the seventeenth to the nineteenth centuries it housed the excise office, and it was later used by the London and North Western Railway Office as a booking office.

LONDON TAVERNS

It is not often realised just how small the city of London was before it began to spill over its ancient boundaries in the early eighteenth century. I have spent many a pleasant Sunday evening wandering along the quiet streets of the city in the footsteps of Samuel Pepys as he wended his way from the Navy office where he worked to the taverns where he spent his evenings in congenial company with his friends and office colleagues. May I recommend the pastime, although there are far fewer places of refreshment to visit than in Pepys' day. It is possible to traverse the City boundaries from Temple Bar to the Tower and back in a single evening. Samuel Pepys would recognise some of today's street patterns, but would be completely lost around St Paul's.

The next time you walk along Fleet Street look out for the diarist's haunts: the Crown, the Devil, the Hercules Pillars and the Mitre. Go a little further along Cheapside and search for the Bull Head, the Feathers, the Mitre (another one), the Star and the Nag's Head. If you go in the spirit of Pepys you will find them, although of course the actual buildings have long since disappeared. A large number of London taverns issued tokens and many of them have an exciting tale to tell, but unfortunately limitations of space mean I can only describe a handful.

Our journey starts not in the city itself but just across the river in Southwark at the Bear at Bridge Foot – so called because it lay at the southern end of London Bridge. The Bear issued two tokens, a farthing (*W*198) and a half penny (*W*197). The former reads, CORNELIVS COOKE AT THE/BEARE AT THE BRIDGE FOT C.A.C. The half penny reads, ABRAHAM BROWNE/BRIDG FOT SOVTHWARK HIS HALF PENY.

There was only one bridge spanning the river when these tokens circulated so traffic jams were frequent. He waited patiently in his coach for half an hour and then got down to look for his friends' coach. He discovered that they had gone into the Bear and so he hurried to join them. When he finally emerged to look for his coach, it had gone without him. 'So I fain to go through the dark and dirt over the bridge and my leg fell in a hole broke on the bridge, but the constable standing there to keep people from it, I was ketched up otherwise I had broke my leg – for which mercy the Lord be praised.'

The following year saw Pepys crossing the bridge, on foot this time, because there were no coaches running on account of the plague. He called in at the Bear for a biscuit, a piece of cheese and a gill of sack. Bar snacks existed even in the seventeenth century! Two years later (3 April 1667) the diarist records the elopement of the Duke of Richmond with Mrs Stewart, the society beauty who is reputed to have modelled for the Britannia reverse on the contemporary coinage. Charles II was extremely displeased with the proposed match, so they stole away by night to the Bear, where a coach was waiting to take them to a secret hideout in Kent.

Pepys mentions the Bear a dozen times in his diary, so he obviously knew it well. He knew both the tavern keepers who issued tokens there, Cornelius Cooke and Abraham Brown, although he does not actually mention their names. The former was vintner there in 1648. He had been an active Parliamentarian during the Civil War, becoming a colonel in Cromwell's army. Abraham Browne took over the tavern in 1666, after his previous inn, the White Horse in Lombard Street, had been burnt down in the Great Fire. Earlier in the year Samuel Pepys had visited the White Horse and noticed what an ill-assorted pair the landlord and his wife were. He writes: 'here by chance I saw the mistresse of the house I have heard much of, and a very pretty woman she is endeed, and her husband the simplest-looked fellow and old that ever I saw'. Abraham Browne's first wife, Penelope, had died fourteen years previously. His beautiful second wife, Frances, did not enjoy her life with her ageing husband, for shortly after the move to the Bear 'she did fling herself into the Thames and drownded herself' (24 February 1667). Five years later Abraham Browne himself died at Charleton in Kent. The Bear meanwhile continued to flourish and ended its 500 years' existence in 1761 when the bridge was widened.

The Borough High Street in Southwark contained numerous inns and taverns cheek by jowl. The lone seventeenth-century survivor is the George, rebuilt after a disastrous fire in 1687, which has the distinction of being the last galleried inn in London.

The Bull Head in Cheapside, like the Bear at Bridge Foot, was an integral part of the fabric of London's history for many centuries. Two farthings were issued there, one in 1650 and the other in 1665. The earlier piece (*W*573) bears the legend, THE BULL HEAD TAVERNE/IN CHEAPSIDE 1650 T.E.B. The later farthing (*W*594) reads, GEORGE PEIRCE/IN CHEAPSIDE 1665 G.M.P. Both farthings depict a bull's head. Like the Bear, the Bull Head was venerable even when Pepys knew it. An Elizabethan ballad recalls

'The Mitre at Cheap and then the Bull Head
And many like places that make noses red'.

It appears in records as early as 1307. In 1553 it was one of no less than six Cheapside taverns which were allowed by Parliament to stay open – the others being the Mitre, the Goat, the Eagle, the Nag's Head and the Star.

At the time of the King's Restoration in February 1660, General Monk retired to the Bull Head in order to arrange billets for his troops, after dining with the Lord Mayor and City Council. Pepys refers to Monk's visit in his diary, 'And so we went to the Star Tavern, Monk being then at Benson's'. Thomas Benson was, in fact, the issuer of the first farthing. Samual Pepys enjoyed several meals at the Bull Head, proclaiming one to be the second best meal he ever had. It consisted of a venison pasty, which must have been enormous, for six or seven men were unable to demolish it at one sitting and returned three days later, on 4 September 1660 to be precise, to eat the remains.

The Hercules Pillars in Fleet Street was visited no less than twenty-three times by Pepys between 1660 and 1669, usually in company with friends and colleagues. An early token (*W*1095) circulated from this tavern, reading, THE HERCVLVS PILLERS/IN FLEETE STREET I.M.S. We do not know for certain the identity of the issuer although Dr Rogers suggests that it might have been John Symons. He must have left the inn before 1657, since Edward Oldham's name appears in the ward mote returns of that year. Oldham issued a half penny token in the 1660s. The diarist often called in at this Fleet Street tavern after visiting the theatre. On 22 February 1669 he treated his friends to 'the best supper I could and pretty merry, and so home between 11 and 12 at night and so to bed'. His supper would undoubtedly have been served by Edward Oldham. The Hercules Pillars was built during the reign of James I and stood on the south side of Fleet Street, nearly opposite St Dunstan's Church.

The tavern known best of all to Samuel Pepys and which he visited most often was the Mitre in Fenchurch Street. Only one token is known to have been issued there (*W*994), reading, AT THE MITETR IN/FENCHVRCH STREETE D.M.R. The initials are those of Daniel Rawlinson and his wife Margaret. Samual Pepys rarely refers to the Mitre by name, preferring simply to call it Mr Rawlinson's. Rawlinson was a close friend of his, and he was extremely upset by his friend's double misfortune – losing his wife in the plague and his home in the Fire. In August 1666 we read 'so homeward and hear in Fenchurch Street that now the mayde also is dead at Mr Rawlinson's so that there is three dead in all, the wife, a manservant and maidservant'. Just over a year later (8 September 1667), 'And hear it comes into my head to set down what Mr Rawlinson (whom I met in Fenchurch-street on Friday last, looking over his ruins there) told me . . .' Daniel Rawlinson took over the Mitre in 1641 and kept it until his death in 1679. His son Thomas also became a tavern keeper. He became interested in local politics, however, was eventually knighted and became Lord Mayor of the city in 1706.

The Mitre has a most interesting history. It was known as the Bishop's Mitre in Queen Elizabeth's reign. An inventory of 1615 gives each room of the tavern a colourful name such as Phoenix Rose, Primrose, Swan or Spreadeagle. The Mitre in Fenchurch Street witnessed the start of the official procession to Lord Lovat's execution on Tower Hill in 1747. The sheriff's officers and executioner set out from the tavern. This was the very last occasion in this country when decapitation was carried out as a legal punishment.

Pepys' cousin, Anthony Joyce, kept the Three Stags in Holborn. He issued a farthing there (*W*1427) reading, ANTHONY JOYCE/AT HOBORN CONDED A.K.I. Three stags appear on the reverse. The initials represent Anthony Joyce and his wife Katherine. The diarist mentions numerous visits to his cousin's house before and after he took up his position as an innkeeper. He was rather fond of Anthony's wife, Kate, whom he describes as a 'comely fat woman'. He saw his cousin's house on fire on 5 September 1666 and was later asked by Kate for a loan of £350 to cover his losses. He writes on 3 December 1666, 'Thence at noon home and there find Kate Joyce who dined with me. Her husband and she are weary of their new life of being an inkeeper, and will leave it, and would fain get some office, but I know none the fool is fit for'.

It seems clear that Anthony Joyce is not cut out to be an innkeeper. In January 1666 he attempted to take his own life. Pepys gives a most graphic description of the episode, 'And while at the office comes news from Kate Joyce that I must come presently . . . and find him in his sick bed, but his breath rattled in his throat and they did lay pigeons to his feet . . . But the sorrow is that it seems that on Thursday last he went sober and quiet out of doors in the morning to Islington and behind one of the inns, the White Lion, did fling himself into a pond, was spied by a poor woman and got out by some people binding up hay in a barn there and set on his head and got to life'. Anthony Joyce died shortly afterwards. Pepys personally entreated the King to grant the estate to his widow. He did not attend the funeral as he did not have a suitable black cloak to wear, but went to the theatre instead. Incidentally, a half penny token was issued at the White Lion, Islington, in 1668, in the same year that Pepys' cousin drowned himself close by.

Sometimes the actual word TAVERN appears on a token, as on a piece of Wood Street (*W*3527), AT YE MITER TAVERNE/IN GREAT WOOD STREET W.E.P. This landlord became a victim of the plague, as the following diary extract shows, 'In the meantime there coming a citizen thither with his horse to go over that told us he did come from Islington this morning, and that Proctor the vintener of the Miter in Woodstreet, and his son, is dead this morning there – of the plague. He having laid out abundance of money there – and was the greatest vintener for some time in London for great entertainments'. (31 July 1665).

The baptismal and burial registers of St Michael's, Wood Street, contain several references to the children of the issuer and his wife Elizabeth. They had no less than ten children born between 1639 and 1654.

Another tavern whose farthing token actually bears the word 'tavern' is the Mouth in Bishopgate Without (*W*323). The token reads, AT THE MOVTH TAVERN/WITHOUT BISHOP GATE R.K.S. The initials on the farthing have not yet been identified, although we know the names of the two previous keepers of the tavern – George Hitchcock and Edward Pettit.

There were a dozen and more Mitre taverns within the confines of the city of London, almost all of which issued tokens. Probably the two most celebrated were the Mitres in Fleet Street and Cheapside. William Paget, a keen musician, issued an undated farthing (*W*1092) at the Fleet Street tavern during his tenancy (1658–60), which reads, WILL PAGET AT THE/MITER IN FLEET STREET W.E.P. Paget had a music room built upstairs, to which Pepys refers in his diary. He later moved to another Mitre in St Paul's Churchyard, which also possessed a music room. Several widows kept the Mitre in Fleet Street at various times; Widow Baly who occupied it in 1640 was brought before the magistrates for 'having company in her house at unlawfull times'. Its heyday was undoubtedly the middle of the eighteenth century. Johnson's Hebridean tour was planned there. A plaque on the building now occupied by Messrs Hoare, Bankers, 37 Fleet Street, marks the site of the original tavern.

The Mitre in Cheap was one of the oldest taverns in London, vying with the Bear at Bridge Foot, the Swan in Old Fish Street and the Cardinal's Hat in Lombard Street. Its token (*W*579) reads, AT THE MITR IN CHEAP/SIDE FORGET NOT T.D. The initials stand for Thomas Dudley, taverner from 1627 to 1642, and again from 1648 to 1650. The token must have been issued during his later tenancy. Thomas Dudley married Bridget, the servant girl of a previous tavern keeper, Henry Fryth. She died in 1637, so her initials do not appear on the farthing.

The Mitre had an important position overlooking the route of the great pageants of medieval, Tudor and Stuart Britain, and was situated close to the halls of two great city companies – the mercers and the grocers. It was a most popular tavern and is mentioned in a number of contemporary plays.

There were almost as many Mermaids in London as Mitres. Undoubtedly the most celebrated Mermaid tavern was the one in Bread Street, which issued two tokens, a farthing in 1657 and a half penny in 1665. The initials T.M.D. appear on the farthing and I.S.C. on the half penny. Neither set of initials has been identified with any certainty, although Kenneth Rogers claims that the half penny may well have been struck for John Chitrey, who was a searcher of the Vintners' Company in 1663 and whose name appeared in the parish of St Mildred, Bread Street at the time of the Fire.

There are frequent references in contemporary literature to city taverns bearing the name 'Mermaid', but few specify the location. One of the few which do is an epigram of Ben Jonson:

'At Bread Street's Mermaid, having dined and merry,
Proposed to go to Holborn in a wherry'.

Rogers reminds us that such a trip was then possible – from the Thames by the Fleet River. The Mermaid was undoubtedly the scene of many hilarious evenings. Beaumont declares to Jonson,

'What things have we seen,
Done at the Mermaid! heard words that have been
so nimble, and so full of subtile flame'.

Thomas Coryat, the eccentric 'legstretcher' of the time who once walked nearly all the way to Venice and back, has provided indisputable evidence of the Jacobean drinking and dining club which met regularly at the Mermaid Tavern in Bread Street. He informs us that the club meetings were presided over by a High Seneschall. Other officers included a Bedellus or Peodle, a post occupied by Coryat himself, and a Clerk of the Purse. The members were graded into *socii*, *fratres* and *alumni*, or fellows, brothers and probationers. Coryat's last and most remarkable journey commenced in 1612. He travelled by ship to Constantinople and then on by land to India, where he died of dysentry four years later.

ALEHOUSES AND ORDINARIES

Alehouses brewing their own beer multiplied in the later Middle Ages. Retailing was forbidden, and strict control was exercised over prices, measures and quality. Many towns employed an ale taster. A large number of unlicensed alehouses carried on business all over London. A contemporary observer claimed in 1613 that there were over a thousand alehouses in the city. Strangely enough Samuel Pepys refers to only two alehouses by name – the Cock at Temple Bar and the Rose and Crown at Tower Stairs. The Cock was a notable place of refreshment, frequented by the greatest in the land, so by 1650 the term alehouse seems to have no significance. The farthing issued at the Cock in 1655 (*W*3037) reads, THE COCK ALEHOVSE/AT TEMPLE BARR 1655 H.M.C. The name of the house is extremely appropriate, as cock is an old word for tap. The Cock stood near St Dunstans Church on the north side of Fleet Street, close to its junction with Chancery Lane. Pepys visited the alehouse four times during his diary period. On his last visit on 23 April 1668 he wrote, 'Thence by water to Temple, and there to the Cocke alehouse and drank and eat a lobster and sang and mighty merry. So almost night I carried Mrs Pierce home . . .'

We do not know the identity of the token issuer. He may well have been the same man who put an advertisement in the *Intelligencer* at the time of the plague, 'this is to notify that the master of the Cock and Bottle commonly called the Cock Ale House at Temple Bar hath dismissed his servants and shut up his house for this long vacation, intending (God willing) to return at Michaelmas next so that all persons whatever who have any accounts, with the said master or farthings belonging to the said house are desired to repair thither before the 8th of this instant July, and they shall receive satisfaction'.

The second alehouse referred to by the diarist is not mentioned by name. We read on 4 September 1665, 'my finding the Angell tavern at the lower end of Towerhill shut up and more than that, that the person was then dying of the plague when I was last there, a little while ago at night, to write a short letter there, and I overheard the mistress of the house sadly saying to her husband some body was very ill, but did not think it was of the plague – to hear that poor Payne my waterman hath buried a child and is dying himself . . .'

The dying alehouse keeper was surely Morgan Cowarne, who issued two tokens there, a farthing (*W*3185) and a half penny (*W*3176), both undated. The farthing reads, THE ROSE AND CROWN/AT TOWER STAIRES M.H.C. and the half penny, MORGAN COWARNE HIS HALF PENY/IN THE TOWER. The Rose and Crown was one of a number of taverns and alehouses nestling around Tower Hill. Pepys' favourite was the Dolphin in Tower Street, which he mentions no less than forty-five times, and which issued a token in 1650. Further along Tower Street was the King's Head, which he seems to have visited only once. He steered clear of it after an unfortunate visit on 25 April 1661, when he records 'At noon Mr Moore and I went to an ordinary at the King's Head in Tower Street and there had a dirty dinner. Afterward home'.

CHAPTER 2

LONDON COFFEE HOUSES

A seventeenth century token of uncertain attribution bears the legend A COFFEE PENNY FOR NECESARY CHANGE. The token shows a contemporary coffee pot and cups on the obverse, and a stove to keep the drink warm on the reverse. About eighty different types of token – pence and half pence – were issued during the mid 1660s and early 1670s by the newly opened and popular coffee houses of London. Although tradesmen's tokens were issued as early as 1648, the first dated coffee house token appeared in 1664.

The heyday of the coffee penny was the brief period from 1669 to 1671. Almost half of the London coffee house tokens were issued during this period. About twenty were valued at a penny, and very few were farthings, which had become unfashionable by 1664. (One of the exceptions is Richard Askew's undated farthing issued at Ironmonger Lane.) Thus the majority of coffee house pieces are pence or half pence.

The earliest known coffee house in England was the Angel in Oxford, which opened in 1650. Two years later Christopher Bowman started the first London coffee house, known as *Pasqua Rosee*, in St Michael's Alley, Cornhill. Bowman had been coachman to a 'Turkey merchant' named Hodges, who set him up in business. Although no tokens of Bowman's original shop are known, there exists a fascinating piece issued by his successors at St Michael's Alley. This must have appeared after Bowman's death from consumption in 1663, for it was struck in the names of Stephen Hayward and George Backler, and bears the device of a hand pouring coffee into a cup. Bowman's wife left the house to George Backler in 1664 and the latter must have teamed up with Hayward shortly afterwards. There are not many recorded instances of such partnerships in the seventeenth century. The reverse legend on this token actually refers to Bowman's period of occupation: AT THE OVLD COFFEE HOUSE IN ST. MICHAELLS ALLY FORMERLY BOMANS ½. The hearth tax records of 1668 contain the joint assessment of George Backler and Stephen Hayward on eight hearths.

The siting of this first London coffee house at Cornhill is significant; it was near both the Royal Exchange and the early London post houses. Numerous coffee houses were set up in this neighbourhood, shortly afterwards becoming the meeting places of writers, journalists, businessmen and foreign merchants. Token-issuing coffee houses in this locality include Robert Halton's in Cornhill, Morat's in Exchange Alley, the Globe at the back of the Royal Exchange, and the Sultaness at Sweetings Rents, Cornhill.

The diarist Samual Pepys, lover of good conversation and liquid refreshment, almost certainly visited all of them, although his diary references are at times rather obscure. He writes on 10 December 1660, 'He and I in the evening to the coffee house in Cornhill, the first time that ever I was there. And I find much pleasure in it through the diversity of company – and discourse'. Strangely enough, Bryan Lillywhite's authoritative work *London Coffee Houses* fails to mention any seventeenth-century coffee house in Cornhill. Undoubtedly Pepys' visit was to the coffee house which issued an undated farthing in the name of ROBERT HALTON. It is an attractive piece, featuring a servant pouring coffee into a cup held by his master.

On 19 August 1663 the diarist visited the Globe to meet his friends. He writes, 'And to the great coffee house against the Exchange where we sat a good while talking . . .' Significantly, the token issued there reads, AT THE GLOBE COFFEE HOVSE/ ON THE BACK SIDE OF THE ROYALL EXCHENG (*W*969). A globe on a stand is depicted. Pepys actually mentions the Globe by name in a diary entry three years later, when he refers to 'a boy from the Globe Coffee House'. The Globe was originally a tavern, but by 1663 had become a coffee house. The *Intelligencer* newsheet for December of that year contained the following information: 'there is a parcel of coffee berry to be put to publique sale on Wed. 23 instant at 6 o clock at the Globe Coffee House'.

Morat's Coffee House in Exchange Alley was probably the most celebrated of all, but the proprietor's name has not yet been discovered. His business was certainly prosperous, and issued no less than four tokens – three pennies and a half penny. The name comes from that of an almost contemporary Turkish sultan, Morat IV (1623–40), whose head appears on all four tokens. Morat, or Amurath to give him his correct name, seems to have fascinated Englishmen in the 1660s, for his head appears on a good number of the thirty or so London coffee house tokens which feature a Turk's head. He was in fact a cruel tyrant with no redeeming qualitites, who eventually committed suicide.

Morat's house in Exchange Alley is known to have opened in 1662, as a newspaper of that year announced that free coffee would be available at the sign of the Great Turk at the new coffee house in Exchange Alley. Coffee houses were not only places of refreshment, they also functioned as shops. At Morat's one could buy coffee powder at 4s to 6s per pound, 'turkie berry' at 3s per pound, East India Berry at 20d per pound and obtain a free set of instructions for its preparation with each purchase. Sherbets perfumed with lemons, roses or violets cost from 6s to 60s per pound.

The penny tokens issued there advertise not only the coffee and sherbet sold, but other items too. *W*965 reads, MORAT Y GREAT MEN DID MEE CALL/ WHERE EARE I CAME I CONQVERD ALL *Coffee Tobacco Sherbet Tea and Chocolat retal'd in Exchange Ally*. The Sultan is shown full face on the obverse. Morat's coffee house was burnt in the Great Fire, and not rebuilt.

An undated half penny token was issued at the Sultaness coffee house at Sweetings Rents. An amusing reference to the Sultaness in the *London Gazette* confirms that beverages other than tea were sold in coffee houses: 'That Excellent and by all Physitians approved, China tea, called by the Chineas Tcha and other nations Tay alias Tee is sold at the Sultaness-head, a coffee house in Sweetings Rents by the Royal Exchange'.

2.1 Halfpenny token of Morat's Coffee House in Exchange Alley, visited by Samuel Pepys.

2.2 Coffee house token of the Turks Head, Laurence Lane, London.

The close relationship that often existed between coffee houses and post offices may be seen in following the fortunes of Henry Wellington. Wellington was originally the proprietor of a coffee house in Chequer Yard, Dowgate. In 1665, he issued a halfpenny token there showing a hand pouring coffee from a pot. A post office, or letter office as it was then called, run by one James Hickes, was close by in Cloak Lane, Dowgate.

At that time newspapers hardly circulated outside the coffee houses in London, where, as in the provinces, their distribution was in the hands of the letter office. Both coffee house and post office at Dowgate were consumed in the Fire. Yet within twelve months we find coffee man and post-master re-established as close neighbours in Bishopsgate. Wellington issued a post-Fire token at his new coffee shop. The legend, beginning on the obverse and continuing on the reverse, reads HEN WELLINGTON NEAR YE POST HOVS IN BISHOPSGATE STREET COFFEE HOUSE W.H.W. 'Ye post house' was, in fact, occupied by his friend Hickes and was in Sir Samuel Bardistan's house in Bishopsgate. It is likely that the Anglo-Portuguese Bank at 9 Bishopsgate occupies the site of both coffee house and post office. Wellington and twelve other coffee men, including another token issuer, Silvester Dean who issued his token in Broad Street in 1667, found themselves in serious trouble with the authorities. A warrant was issued against them by the Secretary of State in September 1667 for publishing and dispensing false news.

St Paul's Churchyard was another popular place for buying books and newspapers, so it is not surprising to find a coffee house established there in the early 1660s. Samuel Pepys visited it twice during his diary period. On 11 January 1661 'at night walked to Paul's churchyard and bespoke some books against next week; and from thence to the coffee house – where I met Captain Morrice the upholster', and again on 20 March 1663, 'Thence homeward and meeting with Mr Kirton's kinsman in Paul's churchyard, he and I to a coffee house . . .' The penny token issued there reads, THE COFFEE HOVSE AT

THE/WEST END OF ST PAUL'S LONDON. The usual Turk's head is featured on the obverse (*W*2730). It is strange to find the word 'London' actually appearing on a token.

A contemporary fire decree gives the exact location of the coffee house, as follows: 'the Lord Bishop of London leased to John Hayes in 1662 a tenement being a coffee house known by the sign of the Turk's Head, then in the possession of Luke Pethey, abutting south on a tenement called The Three Bibles, to the north on a tenement called The Miter then in the possession of William Paget, towards the east on a tenement called the Peter and Paul and towards the West upon the street'. All these properties, including the coffee house, would have been consumed in the Great Fire. The coffee house was certainly rebuilt, for the undated penny token is of the post-Fire period, but we do not know if John Hayes was still the proprietor. Mr Kirton, the bookseller referred to by Pepys, lost the whole of his stock, valued at £8,000, in the Fire.

Like a number of other coffee houses, the Rainbow in Fleet Street started life as a tavern, and a barber named James Farr took it over as a coffee house in 1656. A year later he was brought before the Justices 'for making and selling of a drink called coffee where by in making the same he annoyeth his neighbores by evil smells, and for keeping a ffier for the most part night and day . . .'

By the Restoration (1660) coffee houses had become respectable, although a statute of 1663 made licensing obligatory. Farr issued a token depicting the sign of the house, a rainbow, and obviously had a thriving business, for in 1666 he employed three apprentices and in 1674 he was assessed on twenty-four hearths. The Rainbow is the sole survivor of the Stuart coffee houses of London, although the present coffee house, standing on the original site, was erected in 1859.

The Rainbow and Nando's next door were typical coffee houses of the period, i.e. 'gossip shops' where men of all classes and creeds could discuss the news of the day. The news would be read aloud for those who could not read. Coffee houses were exclusive only in that women were not permitted to enter; no honest man with a penny in his pocket was refused admission. His penny, regal or token, purchased far more than a cup of coffee. A contemporary observer commented:

So great a Universitie
I think there ne'er was any
In which you may a scholar be
For spending of a penny.

Although London was the real home of seventeenth century coffee houses, they became quite popular in the provinces too, but unfortunately few issued tokens. An Aylesbury coffee man, William Burgess, issued two half pence in 1670. One (*W*8) reads, WILLIAM BVRGAS IN/AYLSBVRY 1670 HIS HALF PENY and is round. A Saracen's head appears on the obverse. The other is square with a similar obverse legend in script, whilst the reverse shows a Turk pouring from a coffee pot into a bowl. The site of the coffee house is 13–15 Temple Street. A deed relating to this building records that the property was purchased by William Burgess, licensed victualler, from Richard Prior, and that it joined the house of John Dossett of Cobblers Row, now George Street, and the stables of the King's Head.

2.3 Farthing token of Laurence Short of Oxford.

An octagonal coffee house token was issued in Derby in 1667 by Luke Neyld. A harp is featured on the reverse whilst the Turk's head appears on the obverse, together with the word MORAT.

2.4 Octagonal token of Luke Neyld of Derby.

CHAPTER 3

GROCERS AND FOODSELLERS

GROCERS

A very large number of grocers issued tokens: Williamson lists 445 bearing the Grocers' Arms, and no less than thirty-seven had tokens circulating in the city of Norwich. This reflects their importance in shaping the eating habits of Europe.

The Arms of the Grocers' Company of London: 'Argent chevron gules between 9 cloves sable' allude to the early medieval fraternities of pepperers and spicerers. Pepper was a vital preservative of meat, but by the middle of the seventeenth century grocers sold a wide range of spices, brought to Europe by sailing vessels of the new merchant companies. A patent roll of 1447 refers to 'ginger, succade, cloves, cinnamon and mace fruits, cardonums, dates, senna, turpentine, ammonia, prunes, anniseed, carraways, comfits and rice'. The grocer of the seventeenth and eighteenth century dealt also in tea, coffee and chocolate which had recently been introduced to England, and also lined his shelves with chocolate, raisins, currants, prunes, figs and almonds. He was also expected to stock 'soap, starch and blues of all sorts' (Campbell). Some grocers dealt in spirits such as rum and brandy. No grocers, however, stocked fresh foodstuffs such as bread, meat and butter; these were the province of the butcher, the baker, and the dairymaid or cheesemonger.

Grocers' tokens did not predominate in all parts of England and Wales; Boon points out that only nine grocers produced tokens in the entire Welsh series as compared with fifty-eight mercers. He claims with considerable justification that many of these mercers also assumed the role of grocer, citing an inventory of Griffith Wyn, a Caernarvon mercer, which contains not only cloth and haberdashery but a wide range of grocery goods. Few Welsh grocers actually describe themselves as grocers on their tokens; one exception struck a half penny in Carmarthen (*W*23), which reads, JOHN WILLSON GROCER IN CARMARTHEN 1669/HIS HALF PENNY. The token carries no other sign of his trade. Edward Williams of Mold, on the other hand, shows the Tallow Chandlers' Arms. He probably included candles in his wares, although it is unlikely that he made them.

A Salisbury grocer also shows part of the Tallow Chandlers' Arms on his tokens: a dove with an olive branch. He issued no less than four farthings, in 1656, 57, 58 and 67 respectively. Another Salisbury grocer depicts a fanciful coat of arms on his farthing, *viz.* a chevron between three scallop shells (*W*225). Rowe believes that this implies a pun on the issuer's surname. The token farthing reads, HENRY SEWARD OF/SARVM GROCER H.M.S.

It is significant that few grocers in rural counties actually put the word GROCER on their tokens. Only one token issued in Buckinghamshire, for example, actually has the word GROCER in its legend, as compared to nine bearing the description MERCER. Milne was very cautious when dealing with mercers, grocers and drapers, as he considered that many tokens bearing the Grocers' Arms were issued by mercers, for example the token of Alexander Johnson of Woodstock. One grocer in Woodstock, however, clearly put his trade on one of his farthings (*W*251) which reads, THOMAS WOODWARD/IN WOODSTOCKE GROCER T.W. Woodward seems to have been in comfortable circumstances; in 1662 he paid tax on four hearths in his dwelling house and five on a house he did not live in. He became a freeman of Woodstock in 1629, served as Alderman from 1645 to 62, being elected mayor in 1652, and was termed a gentleman in his will.

There are a number of cases where two grocers issued a token jointly. Symon Walburgh and Anthony Manton, for instance, had a farthing struck featuring the Grocers' Arms at Stamford in Lincolnshire (*W*252). It reads, S WALBVRGH A MANTON/OF STAMFORD S.W. A.M. The issuers were admitted to their Freedom on the same day in 1655. Walburgh took an interest in local politics, serving as constable the same year and becoming a capital burgess and alderman in 1662. He was elected mayor in 1665 and served as a coroner the following year. He died in 1674, and is referred to in the parish records as Simon Walburgh, gentleman. Anthony Manton only survived eight years after gaining his Freedom, and does not seem to have played any part in local affairs.

It is beyond the scope of this book to give a full account of grocers' tokens throughout the country, but a brief look at those of Norwich may help to provide some kind of picture. There were thirty-seven grocers in the City of Norwich who circulated tokens, including one woman. Twenty-six of the tokens bear the Grocers' Arms and just twelve the word GROCER. In one case, a father and son, both grocers, each issued a token, and there are several examples of token-issuing grocers being followed later by their apprentices.

Of these thirty-seven grocers, several took a keen interest in local affairs, with nine acting as churchwardens, four as mayor, six as sheriff, five as overseer and one as a Member of Parliament. It is interesting also to note that the eighteen dated tokens span a period of twenty-five years: 1652, 53 (2); 1654, 55, 56, 57, (2); 1658 (2); 1659, 60, 62 (2); 1664 (2); 1667 (2).

Let us now look at one or two of the Norwich series of grocers' tokens. Augustine Bridges was the grocer who became a Member of Parliament. His token (*W*123) reads, AVGUSTINE BRIDGS/IN NORWICH GROCER A.B. The family emblem, a cock, is featured on the obverse. Bridges was born in 1617, and admitted to his Freedom in 1644. A staunch supporter of the King, he was made sheriff in Restoration Year and mayor ten years later. He died in 1684 at the age of sixty-seven.

Thomas Green's token (*W*146) reads, THOMAS GREEN IN/NORWICH 1658 T.S.G. The obverse bears the ubiquitous Grocers' Arms. The Grocers' Company, once known as the 'Pepperers Grossers and Apothecarics' was first

3.1 Square half penny of William Doggett, Grocer, of Ipswich.

incorporated under the name of Grocers in 1345. It included grocers, confectioners, druggists, tobacconists and sugar refiners. Two monarchs accepted high office in the Company, Charles II becoming Master in the year of his Restoration, and William III in 1689. The Apothecaries became independent in 1617. The company was the second of the first twelve livery companies in order of precedence.

Thomas Green was apprenticed to Benjamin Baker and admitted to his Freedom just six years before his token was struck. He was elected churchwarden at St Peter Mancroft in 1665 and buried there in 1683. His son Thomas entered the church, becoming Bishop of Norwich in 1721.

A farthing was issued jointly in 1658 by John Lawrence and Lawrence Goodwyn, both grocers (*W*164). More is known about the latter, who was apprenticed to Thomas Wilson and admitted a citizen in 1632. He became sheriff in 1659 and mayor ten years later. It is likely that they had a shared business, for the city records reveal that salt was provided to the council in 1672 under their joint names. Their farthing reads, JOHN LAWRENCE 1658/L GOODWIN IN NORWICH $^{\text{IL}}_{\text{LG}}$. The die sinker did not have room for Goodwyn's Christian name on the reverse legend.

Ann Munford was the sole woman grocer in Norwich to issue a token, which simply bears her name, her initials, the place of issue and the company arms. Williamson states that 'the widow Munford was rated in St Peter Mancroft from 1659 to 1664 being buried there in 1681'. It is conceivable that the George Munford who issued a similar token dated 1657 was her late husband.

Francis Morley issued an early but undated token (*W*173). He was admitted Freeman in 1628 and was buried at St Peter Mancroft in 1658. Thomas Warren and William Witherby, both token issuers (*W*217 and 219), were apprenticed to him. Unfortunately neither token is dated. Interestingly, Daniel Toft and his son Benjamin, both grocers, issued tokens within eleven years of each other. Daniel's farthing appeared in 1653 and his son's in 1664. Williamson informs us that Daniel was admitted Freeman in 1645 and his son in 1661, and that the family lived in St Clement's parish where they had a house close to the church. Daniel died in 1660 at the comparatively early age of forty-seven.

Edward Woodyard issued a farthing in 1656 reading, EDWARD WOODYARD/NORWICH GROC 1656 E.M.W. (*W*222). The obverse depicts a sugar

3.2 A wine jar made for Edward Woodyard, Grocer, and his wife Margaret, bearing the same initials as their token.

loaf and two cloves, a device linked to the grocer's trade. Woodyard was admitted Freeman in 1630, and lived in the parish of St Peter Mancroft with his wife Margaret. I have illustrated a fine wine jar specially made for E. and M. Woodyard bearing the same initials as the token. The jug is dated 1649.

FISHMONGERS AND POULTERERS

Fish was obviously an important food commodity in the seventeenth century, as the company of Fishmongers was ranked fourth in order of precedence. The company gained the first of its twenty-four charters as early as 1272. Its most celebrated Warden was Sir William Walworth who killed Wat Tyler at Blackheath in 1381, thus saving the city from the rebel mob. The Arms of the Company: azure three dolphins naiant, embowed in pale argent, finned, toothed and crowned or between two pairs of stockfishes in saltire argent, over the mouth of each fish a crown or; on a chief jules three pairs of keys of St Peter in saltire or, are depicted on several fishmongers' tokens, including those of William Birtby of Clare Market, London (*W*643) and Francis Mabberley of Farnham in Surrey. William Birtby's half penny reads, WILLIAM BIRTBY IN CLARE/MARKET FISHMONGER HIS HALFE PENNY 1667. One would expect fishmongers to have stalls on the market place. Another London market holder was Mark Lawn of St James' Market, whose token (*W*2539) reads, MARK LAWN FISHMONGER 1667/IN ST JAMES MARKET PLACE. The unusual reverse features a plough. Francis Mabberley did not have a market stall at Farnham. We know that he was charged on seventeen hearths in the

3.3 Farthing token of Nicholas Orum, Fishmonger, of Oxford.

3.4 Half penny token of William Robinson, Fishmonger, of Henley.

Hearth Tax of 1664, so he must have occupied exceptionally large premises. Two Oxfordshire fishmongers issued tokens; Nicholas Orum in Oxford and William Robinson at Henley on Thames. The first displays a lobster and the second a dolphin, which is of course not a fish at all! William Robinson was elected bailiff in 1668 and 1669, becoming Henley's first citizen in 1690. Milne tells us that he never married, and died in 1698, thirty years after his token appeared. His house was appropriately in Fisher Road, and his estate reveals that he was a wealthy man. He was the sort of fishmonger that Campbell had in mind when he wrote, 'the fishmonger is a tradesman calculated for the great and wealthy. His profits are without bounds'.

Campbell also likened the fishmonger to the poulterer, whom he describes in these terms, 'he is purveyor for the great. He furnishes their tables with fowl and game of all sorts, and has the secret of making them pay very dear for what they have of him. If they pay their bills the nobleman is bit, but if they do not, as frequently happens, the poulterer is bit'. Poulterers' tokens are scarce. Two were struck for London tradesmen: Edmund Warner at Newgate Market (*W*2031) and John Puller in the Strand. Edmund Warner's token reads, EDMVND WARNER POVLTERER IN NEWGATE/MARKET HIS HALF PENNY 1666. The Poulters' Company of London had its first ordinance in 1368, and it is known that poulters were active in business in the city even earlier. In 1475 they lined the Poultry, where they practised their trade, to watch the coronation procession of Edward IV. Melling notes that during the seventeenth century the Poulters' Hall was situated in Stinking Lane, later Chicken or Fowl Lane, and obviously connected with the poultry trade.

MEALMEN AND OATMEAL MAKERS

Many women baked their own bread from the flour they bought from the mealman. He was usually a middleman, buying flour from the miller and selling to the baker or housewife. In some cases he made his own meal. Several tokens hint at this, for instance a Reading mealman's token shows a mill cramp on the obverse and a sack of flour on the reverse (*W*74). It reads, THOMAS BYE OF/READING MEALMAN T.L.B.

A London farthing shows a malt shovel, a tool of the trade (*W*1919). This token was struck for a woman, who does not describe herself as a mealman but rather gives her address as a meal shop. Her token reads, MARY CRAGGE A MEALE/SHOP IN THE MINERYS M.C.

Another London token (*W*388) circulated from a meal shop reading, AT THE BLACK TALBVT/BOWE LANE MELE SHOP. The trade sign of the business is depicted on the obverse – a talbot dog in collar and chain, but the shopkeeper's name is not given.

Most mealmen's tokens, however, use a wheatsheaf as the sign of their trade, including those of Joseph Fossey of Bishopsgate Without, Will Tew of Eastcheap, Nicholas Hawett of Holborn, John Allcock of Maiden Lane, John Smith of the Minories, I.E. of the New Crane in Wapping and Ralph Alexander of Bow in Middlesex. Will Tew's halfpenny features three sheaves and Nicholas Hawett's piece depicts three birds perching on his sheaf. You will have noticed that all these tokens were issued in London; however, several mealman outside the capital had tokens struck, including three in Essex: Thomas West of Barking who also describes himself as a chandler, John Corie of Plaistow and Robert Bradley of Stanstead Mountfitchet. Tokens were issued by three Kent mealmen: Richard Cresswell of Chatham, Richard Jefry and James Waters of Debtford. A pair of scales is shown on the latter piece. Strangely mealmen's tokens seem to be restricted to London and the eastern Home Counties; none are known in East Anglia and the West Country.

Specialist makers of oatmeal issued tokens, but these are quite unusual and appear in widely scattered places such as Hitchin in Hertfordshire, Norwich, Bury St Edmunds and Farnham in Surrey. The Norwich token reads, MATHEW SOVLTER IN NORWICH/OATMEALE MAKER M.B.S. (*W*202). Williamson gives us a considerable amount of information about Matthew Salter. His name occurred in the overseers' book during the period 1666–83. The initial B on the token stands for his wife, Bridget, who bore no less than twenty-two children. Probably he fed them all on porridge oats! The Mayoral Court Book of 19 May 1666 records 'it is ordered that ye oatmeale house of Math. Salter in St Ethelred's parishe shall be shutt up by the Overseers of ye parrishe and the constables to assist them', as the plague had overtaken the city. It is obvious that Matthew Salter frequently supplied oatmeal to the poor.

Danial Hurst of Hitchin put a man using a sieve on his token; Edward

Worton of Bury St Edmunds has a cogwheel. Robert Friar of Farnham simply uses a flower emblem, a fleur-de-lys, to advertise his business (*W*74). His token reads, ROBERT FRIOR OF FARNUM/OATMEALEMAKER R.I.E. The issuer was probably the Robert Friar who was elected Vicar's Warden in 1682. A contemporary account book contains numerous records in his name during the period of his office including the following items,

Payd the appariter for bringing the proclamation how ye Royal ffamely should be prayed for	01 – 00
Payd for Ringers when the rebels were beaten	11 – 00
Payd for Ringers when the King (James II) was proclaimed	10 – 00
Payd Goody Jeffrey for mending and washing the surplices	06 – 00

CHEESEMONGERS

There are few cheesemongers' tokens to be found outside London, probably because most country housewives made their own cheeses in the seventeenth century. An interesting halfpenny was issued by a Canterbury cheesemonger (*W*42): THO BAKER CHEESMONGR/OF CANTERBVRY 1667 HIS DVBBLE TOKEN. The issuer dubbed it a double token because most tokens issued hitherto were farthings. The device on the obverse was a hand holding a pair of scales.

More than twenty cheesemongers' tokens of London and Southwark are known. Undoubtedly the cheeses were made on the premises and not transported from the country. Numerous dairies functioned within the city bounds. The commonest trade sign of the London cheese seller was a dairymaid working a churn. She appears on a cheesemongers' token issued in St Katherine's Lane close by the Tower (*W*2630), which reads, AT THE DEARY MADE/IN S KATHARNS 1653 W.S.W. The initials have not been identified. The dairy maid is seen on numerous other London and Southwark tokens, including those of Will Bonner of Newgate Market, Thomas Pagett in St James's Market Place, Will Horsley at the Strand, Isaac Hickman of Limehouse and Sam Abery of Southwark. It is significant that two circulated in market places.

Another market token issued at Westminster reads, JOHN HOOKE IN YE MARKET/PLACE WESTMINSTER I.A.H. (*W*2534). A cheese taster is featured on the obverse. A cheese knife appears on a halfpenny of John Plater of Shadwell Dock, Middlesex. A pile of cheeses is depicted on the reverse of a farthing of John Hammond struck in 1667 (*W*754), which reads, JOHN HAMMOND CHEES MONGER/AT COW CROSS 1667 I.H. A year later, a John Hammond issued a cheesemonger's token of Norton Folgate. This time the initials I.S.H. and the unexpected device of a tobacco roll appear. One wonders if the two men were related.

Other seemingly inappropriate trade signs appearing on tokens of cheese sellers include the Tallow-Chandler's Arms (Thomas Batcheler of Bedford Street) and the Pewterers' Arms (Robert Bristow of Wapping Wall).

Campbell reminds us that cheesemongers also sold other farm products such as butter, eggs and bacon. He observes, 'it is a pretty precarious business and liable to a great many accidents – their cheeses lose in their weight, their homes stink and their bacon rusts'.

OILMEN

Even in the seventeenth century oil had four main uses in society – heating, lighting and cleaning homes and supplying some food requirements. Campbell reminds us that oil shops were not just stocked with oil, but supplied customers with soap, salt and even ham; however, oilmen regarded themselves chiefly as providing oil for lamps and lanterns. We find a lantern bravely casting its light across the obverse of a halfpenny of Jonathan Smith of Chiswell Street, London (*W*627). This oilman's token reads, JONATHAN SMITH OYLEMAN/IN CHISWELL STREET HIS HALFE PENNY 1667. Three tongues of flame are appropriately depicted on John Baker's token of Fenchurch Street.

The specialist oilman seems to be confined to the capital, at any rate we do not find oilmen's tokens outside London or Southwark. In the provinces, no doubt, other tradesmen such as grocers and apothecaries supplied their customers with their oil requirements.

Oil was obtained from sunflower seeds, hence the number of tokens which depict sunflowers. Joseph Man's farthing (*W*2745) reads, JOSEPH MAN NEARE/THE SAVOY OYLMAN HIS HALF PENY 1667. Both the sunflower and the sun as the source of all light appear on the obverse. Henry Quelch's halfpenny shows a sunflower and a barrel of oil (*W*318). It reads, HEN QUELCH OYLEMAN AT Y^E/WITHOVT BISHOPGATE HIS HALF PENEY. This is undated, but seems to have been struck after the Fire. Quelch may well have moved premises as a result of the Fire, as he issued an earlier farthing in Leadenhall Street, showing a barrel but not the sunflower. Three tuns or barrels also appear on William Parkes' token of Mark Lane. Ship's captains stocked up with large quantities of oil for long voyages, so it is appropriate that Philip Reilley, an oilman of Russell Street, Covent Garden, should feature a ship on his token.

A Fleet Street oilman who issued two farthings, *W*1099 dated 1653 and the other undated, was hauled before the magistrates on St Thomas's Day, 21 December 1644, 'for selling his goods by lightweight'. The dated farthing reads, THOMAS TISBERY OLE/MAN IN FLEET STREETE 1653.

Two oilmen's tokens bear devices completely unconnected with oil. The farthing of John Amyes of Leadenhall Street illustrates three arrows and a farthing of John Tyler of Fenchurch Street shows a woolpack. Both are, of course, punning devices on the issuers' names!

Finally, no brief survey of oilmen's tokens would be complete without reference to a Princes Street piece (*W*2280). It reads, THOMAS SNELLING OYLMAN HIS HALFE PENNY/IN PRINCES STREET. The Bakers' Arms appear on the reverse. Williamson speculates that the issuer was an ancestor of Thomas Snelling, the celebrated eighteenth-century antiquary and numismatist.

COOKS AND CONFECTIONERS

A number of cooks' tokens are known. Most of the issuers were Londoners, including Thomas Dansell of Aldergate Street, Edward Woodward of Paul's Chain, John Peck of the Savoy, John Reynold of Shipyard, Temple Bar, and Thomas Chub of Sweetings Rents. Sometimes they worked for the aristocracy or the swelling ranks of professional men in the civil service, sometimes they were employed by an institution such as a school or hospital, or even a town council. Thomas Green who issued a halfpenny in Doncaster was appointed Cook to the Corporation of Leeds in 1662 'as a testimony to his ability in the mystery of cooking'. His half penny (*W*71) reads, THOMAS GORST OF HIS HALF PENY/DONCASTER COOK. The reverse features the Cooks' Arms: argent, a chevron engrailled sable between three columbine flowers azure.

Campbell has some scathing comments concerning the French influence on the culinary art. He writes, 'in the days of good Queen Elizabeth when mighty roast beef was the English food our cooking was plain and simple as our manners. It was not then a science or a mystery. But we have of late years refined ourselves of that simple taste and confirmed our palates to meals and drinks after the French fashion. The natural taste of fish or flesh is become nauseated to our fashionable stomach . . . All the earth must be ransacked for spices, pickles and sauces, not to relish but to disguise our food'.

It was customary for professional men to hire cooks to prepare special meals at home, or to take their own cook with them when having a meal out. On 13 March 1668, Samuel Pepys tried to get hold of a cook with a good reputation but without success. He then tried a Mr Gentleman who was not available, and states that Mrs Stone would not let her man Lewis come. He was desperate, 'I was at a mighty loss what in the world to do for a cooke'. After trying to obtain the services of two more he was directed to a Mr Levitts, 'who would not come, at last Levett as a great kindness did leave his business and came himself which set me in great ease in my mind'. William Levett ran the Ship Inn in Bartholomew Lane, and was famed for his culinary skill. His inn token (*W*133) reads, WILLIAM LEVETT/IN BARTHOLMEW LANE W.M.L.

A number of specialist pastry cooks worked in London. Campbell comments, 'he is nice at making all manner of pyes, pasties, tarts and custards and is skilled in the architecture of paste and charging his pyes with all manner of sculpture and statuary'. At least two London pastry cooks had tokens struck: an unidentified cook issued a farthing (*W*2802) in Shoe Lane in 1667, PASTRY COOKE 1667/IN SHOO LANE I.H.R. A crown is featured on the obverse. Robert Cryer issued a half penny in Rosemary Lane a year later (*W*2399), ROBERT CRYER PASTRY COOK/IN ROSEMARY LANE 1668 HIS HALF PENY R.S.C.

The art of confectionery was becoming popular by the middle of the seventeenth century. Campbell describes their trade, 'the confectioner is a sweet-tooth'd tradesman. He makes all manner of sweet meats, preserving all manner of fruits and is the architect of a desert. He builds walks, castles and pyramids of sweet-meats and sugar-plumbs. He disguises many things. He makes sour things sweet and sweet things sour'. Most confectioners' tokens appeared in London. Typical examples are those of Joseph Higgs of Gray's Inn Gate (*W*1234) and Anthony Goldstone of the Strand (*W*2978). The former reads, JOSEPH HIGGS CONFECTIONER I.A.H./AGAINST GRAIS INN GATE IN HOLBORN HIS HALF PENY, and the latter ANTHONY GOLDSTON AT Y[E]/STRAND CONFECTIONER A.G. Four cloves are depicted on the reverse as a symbol of his trade. Grocery and confectionery had much in common, so it is not surprising to find Will Noble of Bread Street describing himself on his half penny of 1666 CONFECTIONER AND GROCER. His token features the Grocers' Arms on the reverse.

However, not all confectioners' tokens appeared in the metropolis. Samuel Heath issued an attractive heart-shaped token valued at a penny in Chester in 1660. He must have been quite young when he issued his penny, for he was elected a Town Councillor in 1698, and died ten years later. *W*145, a

Norwich token reads, L. GOODWY CONFECTIONER IN NORWICH/AT THE GOLDEN CAMELL 1660. The trade sign of a camel, symbolizing the influence of the East, is depicted on the reverse. Williamson recorded that Lawrence Goodwyn was apprenticed to John Lawrence and admitted to the Freedom of the City in 1661. Lawrence was the grocer who struck a joint token in 1658 with Lawrence Goodwyn who was still serving his apprenticeship (*see* Grocers above). John Lawrence had been practising his trade since 1632. He was active in local politics, serving as sheriff in 1659 and mayor ten years later. Goodwyn followed in his footsteps, becoming sheriff in 1682 and mayor in 1697. Ten years previously he had been one of the city aldermen who was ejected by James II. The Norwich confectioner died in 1725 at the ripe age of ninety-two, and was buried in the nave of St Andrew's Church.

Godfrey Foliambe's half penny describes him as a 'comfitt maker' (*W*1030). His token reads, GODFRY FOLIAMBE 1664 COMFITT MAKER/AT FILDE LANE CORNER G.H.F. Comfits were sugar-coated sweets, normally encasing a nut. The word comfit, known as early as the fifteenth century, is derived from the Latin 'confectum', something made, with the same root as 'confectionery'.

FRUITERERS AND GARDENERS

Only one token is known bearing the actual word FRUITERER, that of JOHN BVTLER FRVITERER/WITHOUT TEMPLE BARR HIS HALF PENY (*W*3036). The term 'greengrocer' was unknown in the seventeenth century, although numerous men traded in fruit and vegetables. The fruiterer was probably the nearest counterpart to the modern greengrocer, but there were numerous gardeners, several of whom also issued tokens, chiefly in London. Campbell describes them thus, 'about London their skill lies in the kitchen garden and their dexterity in bringing the best and earliest garden products to market'. The fruiterer and the gardener were very often one and the same. It is not surprising to find a Banbury gardener's token bearing the Fruiterers' Arms on the obverse, for example *W*21 of MATHEW SMITH GARDNER/IN BANBERY 1669 HIS HALFE PENY M.S.M. Milne informs us that he was the son of a Matthew Smith who was buried in January 1666, and that he had six children baptized between 1682 and 1701. His token must have been issued early in his working life, for his will was proved in 1716, forty-seven years after his token had been struck (Ill. 3.5).

Most of the tokens bearing the Fruiterers' Arms bear London addresses, including those of Thomas Edinburgh of Queen Street, Edward Reade of Rosemary Lane, John Ashton of Russell Street, Covent Garden (a particularly appropriate location!) John Bewer of Wellclose Stile, Richard Joyce of Blowbladder Street, Ann How of Drury Lane, and William Richardson of Cow Cross. An intriguing example is *W*2246 of WILL VESEY AT THE GARDEN/HOVSE NEARE PICCADILLY HIS HALFE PENNY W.S.V. The Fruiterer's Arms containing the tree of paradise and the serpent between Adam and Eve appears on the obverse. A Thomas Street token actually bears the address AT THE ADAM AND EVE. At least two fruiterers' tokens were issued in Ireland, both pennies, one by Edmund Yeomans in Charleville, Cork and the other by Nic Delone at Lazy Hill, Dublin. Both depicted the Fruiterers' Arms. An Oxfordshire fruiterer with the unusual name, Manasses Plumton,

3.5 Half penny token of Matthew Smith, Gardener, of Banbury.

had two farthings struck in Banbury in 1653, one depicting the Fruiterers' Arms and the other a fruit tree. Milne observes that the issuer was taxed on three hearths in 1662 and was buried on 4 September 1667. He notes that the fruiterer and his wife were earlier presented at the Peculiar Court for not kneeling whilst receiving the Sacrament.

Gardeners preferred to have the name of their profession in the legend of their tokens. They also used a variety of devices for their trade, including a tree, a spade and a bunch of grapes. *W*208, a Thame token, reads, ISAAC WEEKES 1667/GARDENER IN THAME HIS HALFE PENNY. A tree figures on the obverse.

A Dublin seedsman, Elnathan Brocke, issued no less than four tokens during a period of three years, from 1654 to 57. They all depict a fleur-de-lys, an appropriate emblem for his trade. *W*285, the latest, struck in 1657, was valued at a penny and reads, ELNATHAN BROCKE SEEDMAN ID/IN HYGHE STREETE DVBLIN ID 1657.

Seed shops often had nursery gardens attached. Campbell observes, 'the seed shopkeeper sells all manner of garden and grass seeds, gardener's tools, matts, and some of them are nurserymen and furnish gentlemen with young trees, both fruit and forest and with flower-roots'.

3.6 Penny token of Nic Delone, Fruiterer, of Lazey Hill, Dublin.

LIME MEN

Lime-burning had been practised since Elizabethan times, especially in East Anglia. Lime was required in considerable quantities for the production of marl, a mixture of clay and lime or chalk and lime. The *Concise Oxford Dictionary* defines marl as a soil consisting of clay and carbonate of lime, a valuable fertilizer. Lime is defined as a white, caustic alkaline earth (calcium oxide) produced by burning limestone, used for fertilizing. John Standbrooke, a lime man, issued a token for the use of his gardening customers at Millbank, London, reading, IOHN STANDBROOKE LYME MAN/AT MILBANCKE HIS HALF PENY I.E.S. (*W*1909). A workman is shown carrying a sack of lime.

CHAPTER 4

THE BUTCHER, THE BAKER, THE CANDLESTICK MAKER

The three tradesmen in this nursery rhyme were undoubtedly among the favourite shopkeepers of children in the seventeenth century, completely capturing their imagination. Hearing the rhyme recently on a children's radio programme I was drawn to look at some of the tokens issued by the butcher, the baker, and the candlestick maker when the jingle was in its infancy. Large numbers of tokens were struck for bakers and chandlers during the period of token popularity (1648–72); surprisingly few, however were issued by butchers. The following figures from three adjoining counties reflect this discrepancy.

	Oxon	Bucks	Herts
Chandlers	11	7	16
Bakers	3	5	7
Butchers	2	0	0

BUTCHERS

Butchers' tokens are fascinating, despite their scarcity. Nicholas Langford, a Watlington butcher, issued both a half penny and a farthing. The latter is considerably earlier than the dated half penny (1670) and shows the tools of his trade – a chopper and a knife – whereas the half penny more dramatically illustrates a butcher about to slaughter a bull with a pole-axe. The letters N.L.G. on both tokens represent the issuer's initials, together with that of his wife, Grace. J.G. Milne discovered from parish registers that Nicholas Langford died in 1704, nine years after the death of his wife. He had to pay tax on only two hearths in 1662, and in the same year he was elected constable of the parish.

Derbyshire boasts three butchers' tokens – two of them in the same village, Bonsall. These half pence of John Balme and Henry Hille significantly appeared within a year of each other, in 1670 and 1671 respectively; in a competitive society Henry Hille would not wish to be outdone by his rival. John Balme's half penny depicts the Butchers' Arms – crossed pole-axes between three cattle heads – whilst his neighbour's farthing shows the tools of the trade.

4.1 Farthing token of Nicholas Langford, Butcher, of Watlington.

4.2 Half penny token of Nicholas Langford, Butcher, of Watlington.

Butchery was a difficult and messy business. R. Campbell, writing in 1747, emphasizes this: 'the butchers generally require more skill to learn their trade than any other victualling branch. They must not only know how to cut up and dress their meat to advantage, but know how to buy a bullock, sheep or calf. They must judge of his weight and fatness by the eye. Butchers are necessary, yet it is almost the last trade I should bind a lad to. It requires great strength and a disposition in no way inclined to the coward'.

Both tokens of the Bonsall butchers clearly state their issuer's occupation. The third Derbyshire piece circulated at Higham. It is a heart-shaped half penny dated 1669 and bears the Butchers' Arms.

Two butchers' tokens appeared in Salisbury, Wiltshire, namely a farthing of Roger Godfrey (*W*190) and a half penny of Edward Penny (*W*215). The farthing reads, ROGER GODFREY IN/NEW SARVM 1666 R.E.G., and shows a butcher's knife above a whetstone, used for sharpening. Rowe notes that Roger Godfrey's farthings are of an unusually yellow brass. Edward Penny's token reads, EDWARD PENNY IN/SARVME 1671 HIS ½ TOKEN. The obverse features the Butchers' Arms. Rowe suggests that the issuer was probably sensitive about his surname and preferred to have ½ TOKEN put on the piece rather than ½ PENNY. Butchers' tokens also appeared at Leicester, Chiswick and Ipswich.

4.3 Heartshaped half penny of John Lowe of Higham, Derbyshire.

BAKERS

Bakers' tokens are quite common. The majority of them bear the Bakers' Arms, but some show a wheatsheaf and others a sugar loaf. The illustrated token was issued by John Alexander in the village of Great Tew, Oxfordshire. The Bakers' Arms are depicted on the obverse. Alexander's wife's initial is added to his own (Milne has identified her as Ann). John Alexander followed in his father's footsteps as a baker. His mother, Widow Alexander, must have been running the business in 1662, for she paid tax on three hearths in that year. Three years later her son John, the token issuer, was in charge, for he paid the tax in his own name. As confirmation, the token, although undated, is late in style, probably appearing later than 1664.

Bakers' shops were an established feature of both towns and villages. In Buckinghamshire, for example, bakers' tokens are known in Iver, Ivinghoe and Lavendon, all tiny villages in the seventeenth century. Emerre Bradley issued a farthing in the county town of Hertford in 1668, bearing a wheatsheaf as his trade sign. He was probably not married when his token appeared, for only the initials E.B. are shown. He certainly married later, for his widow was summoned before the magistrates in 1685 for having a dangerous brewhouse chimney. Bakers needed a roomy chimney!

Another Hertfordshire baker issued a token at Furneaux Pelham, reading, THOMAS PHIPPE IN T.P. 1671/FVRNISH PELLVM HIS TOKEN (*W* 84). The die sinker had understandable difficulty with the place name. The Quarter Sessions Records of 21 April 1666 have an entry 'Thomas Phipps of Furnex Pelham, husbandman, traded as a baker, without having been duly apprenticed'. This may account for the fact that there is no clue as to the issuer's occupation on the token itself. Phipps was also in trouble for using bad language many years later. The Sessions Records of 7 April 1784 read, 'Thomas Phipps, the elder, of Furnex Pelham, to be bound over for speaking seditious and scandalous words of a justice's warrant for the laying of conventicle money'.

Campbell points out that the baker, unlike some tradesmen, could not make huge profits for he was 'so much under the direction of the magistrate . . . the poor are more at his mercy than the rich, small families more than great, for in rolls, two penny loaves and three penny loaves there is no check

4.4 Farthing token of John Alexander, Baker, of Great Tew, Oxon.

upon him . . .'. Campbell also comments on the peculiar fact that bakers preferred a customer who ran a tally with them rather than the 'ready money' customer, although he cannot refrain from pointing out the opportunity for cheating afforded by the tally system. He slyly observes, 'the ill-natured part of the world allege that they take opportunity of making Dead Men, as they phrase it, that is of cutting double strokes on their tally, which makes a large amends for the lying out of their money'.

Two interesting bakers' tokens were issued in London. John Snow of Ironmonger Lane issued two farthings, the second of which refers to him as a WHIT(E) BAKER. Another Londoner, Richard Alder of Battle Bridge, Southwark, issued a half penny in 1669, showing a baker's peel (*W*142). It describes him as a specialist baker: RICH ALDER GINGER BREAD BAKER/ SOVTHWARK NEAR BRIDG HOVS 1669.

CHANDLERS

Chandlers' tokens are legion, like those of bakers. They normally depict a man dipping candles in the tallow, as seen on a half penny of Charles Lord of Little Brickhill, a small village in Buckinghamshire, and an early farthing of Richard Godfrey of Royston in Hertfordshire. Sometimes only the stick of candles appears, as in Henry Tripp's half penny of Beaconsfield. These chandlers were, of course, tallow chandlers as distinct from wax chandlers. Campbell describes their manufacture in the *London Tradesman*. 'In order to make the common store candles, the tallow is first rendered and strained from the skin, and all impurities in the fat. The wickers are made from cotton spun for that use. The workmen cut them into proper lengths. The tallow is melted and put into a vat of boiling water, which keeps it in constant flow. The wicks are ranged five or six upon a stick and placed upon stands near the fat. The candle maker makes one of these sticks by both ends, plunges it into the fat and takes it out again. This he lays down upon the stands and takes up another until he has dipped them all. Then he begins with the first and dips it again, and continues dipping them one after another, until they are of the thickness wanted . . .'

Campbell continues, 'it is a nauseous greasy business, but the profits attone

4.5 Half penny token of Charles Lord of Little Brickhill, Bucks.

for that inconvenience. Yet pthisicky people, not used to it, find much difficult to breathe near the scent of a tallow-chandler's workhouse'. We are reminded that his place of business was a workshop rather than a shop as we would think of it in modern times.

Candlestick makers were, of course, the electricians of the seventeenth century. Their workshops could be found in town and country alike. Two chandlers' tokens were put into circulation in Aylesbury, the county town of Buckinghamshire, an undated farthing by William Welch and a half penny by John Hill in 1665. Both show a man candle dipping, and state the issuer's occupation in full, TALLOW CHANDLER. William Welch's farthing does not even bear his name. Only the initials W.W.I. are recorded. The I stands for Jane Michael, his second wife, whom he married in 1657. Welch was a Nonconformist, a loyal member of the local Baptist church. During a period of office as constable in 1678 he was understandably indicted for neglecting his duties, which included selling the goods of convicted Nonconformists! He was hauled before the magistrates on numerous occasions for absenting himself from church. Welch was one of the twelve Aylesbury Baptists sentenced to death under the Conventicles Act, but later reprieved (see Chapter 7).

Much less is known of Henry Tripp, issuer of the Beaconsfield half penny (*W*21). The token reads, HENRY TRIPP 1668/OF BECKONESFEILD HIS HALF PENY H.A.T.

A stick of candles is featured on the obverse. No contemporary references to the Tripp family are to be found in the parish registers, and so I have been unable to discover the identity of Henry's wife A. . . although I have traced the burial of a son, Amborne Tripp, on 12 April 1672. Tripp is an old Beaconsfield surname. A lovely old seventeenth-century cottage in Aylesbury End is still in the family's possession. Perhaps Henry Tripp carried on his business there. Who knows?

Chandlers were often highly respected, even comparatively well-off members of society. One flourishing Hertfordshire chandler, John Rotherham, issued no fewer than four separate tokens at Barnet between 1653 and 1655. He was a governor of the celebrated Queen Elizabeth School in the town from 1651 until 1665.

Although I have failed to find a butcher's or baker's token issued by a woman, there were several female tallow chandlers who issued tokens, such as Ann Keimpton, whose workshop was in the tiny village of Little Munden in Hertfordshire. Her token reads, ANNE KEIMTON OF/LITTLE MONDEIN 65. A.K. (*W*139). A stick of five candles is depicted on the reverse, whilst the unusual obverse shows a monkey dressed as a woman.

Wax candles were made in quite a different way from tallow candles. They were not dipped but rolled and drawn. Wax chandlers made other products such as sealing wax. They were considered superior in status to the tallow chandler. Only two tokens of wax chandlers are known, both by the same man. Unfortunately both his identity and his workplace are still obscure. One of the tokens reads, WAX CHANDLER IN G.E.H./SMCLATCH. A bull's head is featured on the reverse. This token and its companion have puzzled numismatists for centuries.

SOAPBOILERS AND STARCHMAKERS

Several tradesmen, describing themselves variously as soapboiler, soapmaker or soapman, issued tokens. Two Londoners, Iam Smith of St John Street and Edward Leader of Tooley Street, Southwark, and a Welshman, John Webb of Carmarthen, put their trade as 'sopeboyler'. Webb's half penny (*W*21) reads, JOHN WEBB SOPE BOYLER/IN CARMARTHEN 1669 HIS HALF PENY. The three doves from the Tallow Chandlers' Arms are featured on the obverse.

Another Londoner, Thomas Leader of Ratcliff Highway, possibly related to the Southwark soapboiler with the same surname, describes himself simply as a soapmaker. His token (*W*2353) reads, THO LEADER SOPE MAKER/AT RATCLIFF HEYWAY HIS HALF PENY. A whale and three harpoons form the device on the obverse, reminding customers that soap is chiefly made from oil and fat. Yet another London tradesman, Francis Richardson of Wapping, issued a half penny in 1666, describing himself as a 'sope man'.

Campbell describes the process of soapmaking as a 'laborious nasty business'. He writes 'soap is composed of lime, salt of vegetables and the fat of animals. A lee of lixivium is made of kelp, that is the salt of seaweed obtained by burning into which is added a quantity of lime water. When the lee has stood long enough in the fats to extract all the salts from the ashes it is then drained off and put into a boiler with a proportion of tallow (if for hard soap) or of oil (if for soft soap) where it is allowed to boil until the tallow or oil is sufficiently incorporated with the strong lee and is become of one thick consistence. It is then taken out with the ladles and poured into chests. Before it is cool they pour over it some blue, which penetrates through the mass. When it is cold it is taken out of the chests and cut into lengths with a wire and laid up to dry'.

A solitary starchmaker's token is known – that of Hercules Cox of Lambeth (*W*161). His half penny reads, HERCVLIS COX STARCH/MAKER IN LAMBETH 69 HIS HALF PENY H.E.C. The obverse device comprises a wheatsheaf and three birds. The issuer paid hearth tax on seven hearths in his house in 'Lambeth towne'. Starch was obtained from grain and potatoes, and Campbell states that starch was chiefly made in country districts from the finest flour soaked in water and then dried. Cox's starch would be used by countless washerwomen in Lambeth and Southwark.

CHAPTER 5

THE SKILLED CRAFTSMAN

Nowadays, we no longer expect the things of everyday life, such as buckets, pots and pans, knives, cups and saucers to be fashioned by hand, but there are still a few specialist craftsmen: potters, woodcarvers and workers in brass who produce hand made articles. Seventeenth-century towns and villages contained the workshops of countless such craftmen. Quennell comments, 'there are several interesting books of trades published about 1680 (Van Vliet and others) – workers making pottery or baskets, painting, printing, turning on the lathe, and busily engaged in dozens of other crafts'. As we shall see, the trade tokens of the mid-seventeenth century reflect this multifarious activity.

CLOCK AND WATCHMAKERS

Prior to the seventeenth century few families possessed a clock or watch of their own; villages and townsfolk alike depended upon the regular hourly striking of the church tower clock. In the late seventeenth century, however, a growing band of clock makers, working chiefly in Oxford and London, changed the situation.

Joseph Knibb of Oxford and London was one of their number. His token is a charming piece with the obverse legend *Joseph Knibb Clockmaker in Oxon* in four lines, inscribed in a beautiful hand. The reverse features a clock face with the hands at half past twelve. The initials I.K. appear on either side. Knibb's farthing is undated, but its style indicates that it must have appeared about 1670. It is unlikely that it circulated before 1668, however, for he was in frequent conflict with the authorities for carrying on his trade within the city liberties without being a freeman of the city. He was finally admitted freeman in 1668.

It is significant that no wife's initial appears on his token. His will, dated 23 August 1697, refers to his wife Elizabeth and one son, Thomas, who had not yet reached his majority. He probably married in later life after his token had been struck.

A close inspection of the Roman numerals on the reverse reveals that the die maker had difficulty in fitting in the numbers VII to XII. Consequently the numbers VIII, IX and X are merged and appear thus VIIIX. Leeds suggests that

5.1 Farthing token of Joseph Knibb, Clockmaker, of Oxford.

Knibb might have made the dies for the token himself; I rather doubt this. It is much more likely that the dies were centrally made in London.

Joseph Knibb was the most celebrated of a notable family of clock makers. His father was a yeoman, however. Joseph was born in 1640 at Claydon in Buckinghamshire. As a youth he was apprenticed to a cousin, Samuel Knibb, who practised the art of clock-making at Newport Pagnell. Samuel left Newport Pagnell in 1662, moving to Threadneedle Street in London. Although only three of his clocks are known to have survived, all three are of extremely fine workmanship, bearing designs reminiscent of Ahasverus Fromanteel. One of the three belonged at one time to the Royal collection at Windsor Castle. Lee suggests that Samuel may well have supplied the clock to Charles II.

Joseph decided to start work on his own account in Oxford in 1662. His early years in Oxford were far from easy since he was regarded as a 'foreigner'. Knibb made several unsuccessful attempts to become a freeman before resorting to devious methods. An entry in the city archives relates, 'under pretence of being a gardner to Trinity Colledge, Joseph Knibb had within the liberties of the city . . . it is agreed that he should suddenly shutt down his windows and remove either to St. Clements or else to some other place out of the city liberties . . .' Fortunately this was not necessary as Joseph was admitted a freeman for a fee of twenty nobles and a leathern bucket. His house was situated on the south side of Holywell, quite close to the corner of Broad Street. His brother John later occupied the same premises, also practising as a clock maker.

Joseph's stay in Oxford, although short, has a significant place in the development of the craft of clockmaking. Early in the century clocks had begun to compete with their Continental counterparts regarding quality of appearance, but they were unreliable time-keepers. Christian Huygen, a Dutchman, first used the pendulum as a method of controlling clockwork in 1656. Fromanteel, working in London, was the first man to make use of this discovery in England. Joseph Knibb was one of just a handful of makers during this exciting decade (1660–70) to put Huygen's invention to full use, and to improve upon it. As R.A. Lee reminds us, really accurate time-keeping was only made possible by the inventions of the anchor escapement and a seconds beating pendulum. Traditionally Clement was credited with producing the first escapement in 1671, but it now seems certain that Joseph

Knibb made anchor escapements before this. He fitted one to the turret clock of St Mary the Virgin in 1669 and another to the Wadham College clock in the same year. He also fitted a seconds-beating pendulum to an ebony long case clock in Oxford at about the same time. These successes probably contributed to his decision to move to London in 1670.

Quite a number of Joseph Knibb's Oxford clocks are still extant, and several of his long-case and lantern clocks are illustrated in R.A. Lee's excellent book, *The Knibb Family Clockmakers*. For some strange reason Joseph does not seem to have made any table clocks until he moved to London.

He quickly made his mark in the metropolis. His skills were immediately recognized by his fellow craftsmen, and he was granted the freedom of the Clockmakers' Company. His style was always original. Lee draws attention in particular to his inventiveness in the matter of striking the hours and subdivisions of the hours, for which he used at least eight different methods.

Lee states that over two hundred clocks by Joseph still survive, and he may well have manufactured more than four hundred during his lifetime. He must have had a large workshop and a sizeable staff. No less than seven apprenticeships have been recorded during his working life in London (1670–97). There can be no doubt that he was the most successful and prosperous London clockmaker of his day. At first he operated at the 'Dyal' near Sergeant's Inn, Fleet Street, and towards the end of his career he moved to the 'Clock Dyal' Suffolk Street, near Charing Cross.

Knibb retired to Hanslope in Buckinghamshire in 1697, but contined to produce clocks, as a few of his are signed 'at Hanslope'. He died in 1711, and the family tradition of clock making was carried on by his brother John, who had taken over Joseph's Oxford business. John became very influential in Oxford civic affairs. After being elected to the Council in 1686 he in turn became Alderman, Bailiff and Mayor twice. A considerable number of John's clocks survive, all of which bear traces of his brother's influence.

One other token of an Oxford clockmaker is known (*W*119). It reads, MICHAEL BIRD HIS HALF PENY/OXFORD WATCHMAKER M.B. 1668. The cock prominently featured on the obverse is obviously a pun on the issuer's surname. It is rather strange that his wife's initial is not shown, as a poll tax of 1667 confirms the fact that he was married and had six children at the time that his half penny was issued. His wife Sarah, in fact, survived him.

Although Michael Bird obviously specialized in watches, it is known that he manufactured clocks too. No watches of his have survived, but a 30-hour clock exists bearing his signature. Bird was prospering in his business, for he was assessed at 8s od in the poll tax, quite a sizeable sum and was charged on four hearths. His prosperity is also indicated by the fact that his token was valued at a half penny rather than a farthing – one of only two such in the entire Oxford series.

He was the eldest son of an Oxford Freeman, and probably related to a John Bird who was mayor of the city in 1615. His house was situated on the east side of Corn market, as the poll tax and hearth tax records confirm. After being apprenticed in London to Thomas Taylor in 1648, he gained his Freedom in Oxford six years later and practised his trade from 1656 until 1689. In all he employed nine apprentices including three of his sons. It is interesting to note that in September 1665, he was appointed with others to check on 'foreigners' trading in the city. He supported Joseph Knibb's application to become a freeman two years later. In 1678 he was elected a city

5.2 Half penny token of Michael Bird, Watchmaker, of Oxford.

councillor and chosen to be mayor's chamberlain, a position which he held for ten years. Bird was a staunch Protestant as Dr Beeson points out, 'on the occasion of an anti-popery riot in April 1683 he was one of the chief rioters in an assault on under graduates and was arrested by the crowd'. He died in 1690.

There are three London seventeenth-century tokens which may well have been issued by clockmakers – those of Henry Burgin at Bishopsgate Without, M.S. in Budge Row and Will Brunsley at Lillys House, Strand Bridge. All show a clock dial and hands. However, this may only indicate their location beneath a well-known clock.

GOLDSMITHS

5.3 Early Goldsmiths' Arms.

5.4 Medieval goldsmith at work.

Dr Johnson's definition of a goldsmith reads, 'one who manufactures gold . . . a banker'. The banking side of the goldsmith's activities commenced in the seventeenth century and persisted until the end of the eighteenth. It is significant that even today several prominent bankers are members of the Goldsmiths' Company of London.

It had long been the custom for London merchants and businessmen to hold their assets in the Tower of London for safe keeping. Their trust in the Stuart monarchy, however, was not as strong as it had been in the Tudor. By 1640 they preferred to deposit their valuables with the goldsmiths. Individual goldsmiths had for some time acted as money lenders. It is known that in 1677 there were 44 London goldsmiths who acted as bankers by keeping 'running cash'. Sir Francis Child (1642–1713), frequently cited as the 'father of banking', was one of the first bankers to divorce banking from goldsmithery.

A number of trade tokens were issued by goldsmiths in the middle of the seventeenth century. Those farthings and half pence were essentially a poor man's currency, so it seems rather strange that wealthy goldsmiths should bother with them. Three London issuers were Henry Pinckney of Fleet Street, John Mayhew of the Hermitage, Wapping (1666) and Evodias Inman at Smithfield. Probably the most interesting is the Fleet Street farthing (*W*1089) which reads, H.P. AT 3 SQVIRRELLS/IN FLEET STREETE H.P. Henry Pinckney, like so many of his contemporaries, combined the professions of goldsmith and banker. He founded the banking house of Gosling close to St Dunstan's Church. He was apprenticed in 1629 to Francis Allen, made a freeman in 1637 and rose to prominence in the Goldsmiths' Company, becoming Fourth, Third and Second Warden in 1669, 1676 and 1677 respectively.

Samuel Pepys knew Pinckney well. He mentions him in his diary quite frequently, as on 1 December 1660, 'Mr Sheply and I went into London and calling upon Mr Pinckney the goldsmith, he took us to the tavern and gave us a pint of wine'. Evodias Inman was also a member of the Goldsmiths' Company. He was apprenticed to Walter Early in 1629, becoming a freeman in 1637. John Mayhew was not a member.

Few provincial goldsmiths issued tokens. These include Samuel Calle of Exeter, George Reve of Bath and William Robinson of Oxford, whose farthing issued in 1668 depicted the Goldsmiths' Arms. Robinson was apprenticed in 1659 for a period of eight years to Samuel Wilkins, father of Dr John Wilkins, one of the founders of the Royal Society. He finished his apprenticeship, however, with another goldsmith, Daniel Porter. George Reve's farthing, like that of Robinson, shows the arms of the company.

The unusual Exeter piece of Samuel Calle features a man smoking on the obverse and a covered cup on the reverse. Exeter was allowed to have an assay office in 1700 under the Plate Assay Act of that year, being one of five towns where mints had been 'lately erected for recoining the money of the Kingdom', namely Bristol, Chester, Exeter, Norwich and York. Goldsmithery was a flourishing trade in Exeter from the Middle Ages onwards, specialising in cups. Exeter-made communion cups of the sixteenth and seventeenth centuries are to be found in churches throughout the West Country. Thus it is no surprise to find a cup shown on Samuel Calle's token.

5·5 Farthing token of Will Robinson, Goldsmith, of Oxford.

Two Irish tokens are known, both pennies, of Dublin and Kelkenny respectively. The crude Dublin piece (*W*376) reads, IO. PARTINGTON GOVLDSME/KINGES HEAD SKINNOR ROW DVBLIN I^{D}. The Kelkenny penny is also undated. It was struck for William Keough. Williamson says that the issuer was sworn master of the Company of Hammermen at Kelkenny, a far cry from the worshipful Company of London. The population of the town had been so reduced on account of disturbances that the number of trade companies had been restricted. Thus the Hammermen included blacksmiths and cutlers as well as goldsmiths.

Strangely enough it is unlikely that the goldsmiths made their own dies or even struck the tokens themselves, although they would have been eminently well qualified to do so. They seem to have followed the customary practice of ordering them from London die sinkers, although the Irish pieces may have been struck locally.

SHOEMAKERS

In the early Middle Ages the cordwainers formed companies for mutual protection as did many other skilled craftsmen. One of the first was at Oxford during the reign of Henry I. The first ordinance of the London Cordwainers dates from 1272. The coat of arms bears a golden chevron and three goats' heads on an azure shield with the words CORIO ET ARTE (leather and skill). The company was granted its first charter by Henry VI in 1435. The present hall, the fifth on the site, was built by Adam in 1788. The London shoemakers who formerly clustered round the Royal Exchange drifted to St Martin le Grand on the other side of Cheapside, close to the bookstalls of Paternoster Row. The craft of patten making was carried on in the neighbourhood of St Margaret, Patten's Lane, Fenchurch Street. The patten makers became a corporate company along with the galoche makers under Charles II in 1670. Other London companies connected with shoes were the Skinners with their Hall at Dowgate Hill and the Leather Sellers whose Hall is at Bishopsgate.

The art of shoemaking reached its peak during the reign of Henry VIII in the work of three London cordwainers extraordinaires: Richard Castelor, Peachey and the 'Green King'. Castelor was nicknamed the 'Cock of Westminster' because he started work at four in the morning. His shop in Whitehall was famous throughout the capital. Peachey of Fleet Street, shoemaker to the king, employed forty men, not including apprentices. They all wore tawny coats as his livery whilst he wore a black gown trimmed with velvet. The Green King, so called from the colour which he and his sixty journeymen wore on great occasions, had his stall at St Martins le Grand's.

Towards the end of Elizabeth's reign shoe styles were beginning to change. The most startling innovation was the introduction of the heel, worn quite high for both men and women, which was probably derived from the sloping Venetian chopine, a platform-soled shoe. Changes in shoe style tended to accompany a change in monarch. So we find the footwear under James I substantial yet rather pinched and mean with a narrow oval toe and arch. The introduction of the heel was responsible for the disappearance of right and left shoes. Shoes became straight like socks and could be worn on either foot. Shoes fashioned for the right and left foot did not return until the beginning of the nineteenth century. Until about 1630 all boots and shoes had rounded toes, though later they were predominantly square. Men's and women's shoes were quite similar.

Boots were worn specifically for riding but by 1620 they were beginning to be used for walking also. Thigh-length 'bucket tops' were especially popular, attached to the breeches with tops that could be folded down. Huge military boots were a feature of Civil War uniform. Those of the cavalier Sir Lewis Dyre of Bedfordshire had a terrible spike projecting from the toe. Those of John Lilbourne the Leveller were so broad that he could not walk in them without looking ridiculous.

The restoration of Charles II in 1660 brought further changes in shoe styles. Paris became the centre of fashion for all English clothing and the Louis heel became an essential feature of men's shoes. The arrival of the buckle was yet another French invention. Samual Pepys, writing on 22 January 1660, states, 'this day I began to put buckles to my shoes'. The buckles were small and frequently set with stones. Women's shoes became more pointed with higher heels. Overshoes were increasingly worn to protect the often flimsy footwear of both men and women. Clogs or pattens were also worn for protection, making an awful clatter on the pavement.

Samuel Pepys complained about his wife's new pattens on 24 January 1660, 'called on my wife and took her to Mrs Pierces, she being exceedingly troubled with a new pair of pattens, and I vexed to go slow, it being late'.

The trade tokens illustrate the changes taking place in the shoemaking industry during the seventeenth century, and the various operations involved. Before shoes were made, leather had to be prepared by the tanner. The bullock's hide was placed into a lime pit so that the hair could be scraped off. Then it was put into a pit filled with the bark of an oak and a quantity of water. When the hide was sufficiently pliable it was taken out and dried in the sun. Few tanners' tokens are known, but at least three Irish tanners mentioned their occupation on their currency – Thomas Maire of Ballyboy, King's County, John Speare of Caledon, County Tyrone (*W*127) and Thomas Reynolds of Carlow. All three were valued at a penny. The second reads: JOHN SPEARE OF I.S/CALLEDON TANER. A dog is featured on the reverse.

Tokens were struck by two Buckinghamshire tanners – John Penn of Stony Stratford and Edward Winch of High Wycombe (*W*179). There is no indication on the tokens themselves that the issuers were tanners, but local records confirm this. Tanning was considered quite an honourable trade despite the smell. Winch was an alderman of the town and was elected mayor in 1669, just three years after the striking of the half penny.

When the hides had been tanned, usually in the country, they were sent to London and bought by leather dressers at Leadenhall Market, who treated them and then passed them on to leather sellers. One such tradesman was Edward Foster who described himself as LETHERSELER AT YE CORNER SHOP OF PANIER ALLEY. An appropriate illustration of a nag's head upon a gridiron can be seen on the obverse. Edward Foster dealt in hides and skins of all kinds, ready tanned and dressed for his customers, who would mostly be specialist shoemakers.

Campbell draws our attention to another leather worker who made his appearance towards the close of the seventeenth century. He observes, 'the leather cutter is a tradesman lately started up between the leather dresser and the shoemaker. This last till of late years, bought his leather in skins or half hides from the dresser and cut out his work himself, but the number of poor shoemakers, who are not able to lay out more money at once than the price of materials for a pair of shoes, have given rise to this branch. They cut out their leather in soals and upper-leathers, that is in bits that answer these uses in several sizes and sell them to the necessitous shoemaker'. Two London leather cutters' tokens are known – those of Edward Nutby at Hatton Street and Robert Wilmer in Little Britain. Is is significant that the reverse of Wilmer's token depicts the upper part of a shoe only.

I have come across one patten maker's token; again, as one would expect, in London (*W*2821). It reads, RICHARD HOVLDER IN/SHORDICH PATTIN MAKER HIS HALF PENY 1669. A press is shown on the obverse, reminding us that the issuer was a smith, who worked in metal. Campbell does not think much of the patten-maker's prospects, saying that 'it is but poor bread'.

More than fifty tokens were struck for shoemakers. A number of them give their occupation, including Thomas Lockhart of Derby, William Green of Nottingham, William Reade of Tuxford, Notts, John Farrah of Tooley Street, Southwark, John May of Guildford, Thomas Avery of Meriden, Warwickshire and John Tomson of Bingley, Yorks. A particularly interesting example is that of a female shoemaker, Sibbil Theame, who made shoes for the poor children at Christ's Hospital (*W*634). Her farthing reads, SIBBIL THEAME CHRIST/ASPETAL SHO MAKER S.T. The token of William Green, a Nottinghamshire craftsman, bears the chief tool of his trade – a cordwainer's knife. Thomas Hall of Leeds depicts a high-heeled shoe and a knife. The Louis heel, as we have seen, was in high fashion by 1667, when the token was issued. The shoe seen on John Tomson's token is similarly high-heeled. The Guildford piece of John May, however, is different in that it depicts a last. Incidentally, of the dated tokens bearing the actual word SHOOMAKER, all were halfpence struck between the years 1667 and 1669. A London shoemaker from Gray's Inn did not put his occupation in the legend, but instead, depicted a shoemaker fitting a lady's shoe on to a customer's foot. (*W*2205). Unusually it is a farthing and reads, THOMAS GALE NEERE/PEARPOOLE LANE END T.I.G.

Not surprisingly, a large number of tokens bear the Cordwainers' Arms of three goats' heads, derived from the Cordovan goat. The vast majority are dated and appear late in the series. The earliest is a pre-Restoration farthing of William Watts, King Street, Westminster dated 1650. All the others are post-Restoration. Three of these tokens displaying the Cordwainers' Arms were issued by women, *viz.* Ann Bloodworth of Derby, and Thomazin Duke and Mary Trafford of the Strand. I think there must be a link between these latter two, as the wording on the reverse is identical: IN THE STRAND NEERE YE EXCHANGE. John Kemp issued both a farthing (*W*9) and a halfpenny in the same year in two places. His farthing reads, JOHN KEMP IN PVTNEY/OR BATERSEY I.B.K. 1663. He may be a relative of the Will Kemp who issued a farthing IN PVTNEY OR AT PARSONS GREENE.

Stephen Hubbard of Kingston-on-Thames was prospering in his business according to hearth tax evidence; in 1675 he was assessed on five hearths and a few years later his assessment was increased to ten. Hubbard was a staunch Quaker. J. Besse in his *Sufferings of the Quakers* records, 'On May 12, 1670 this person was cruelly beaten with others by soldiers to keep them out of their meeting house and a distress was levied upon him with John Fielder and two others for attendance at meeting, goods worth £23 1s 10d being taken from the four of them'. In 1685 he was fined £20 per month for 'absence from the national worship'.

Not all cordwainers were Quakers; indeed several cordwainers were

5.6 Half penny token of Thomas Slauter, cordwainer, of Chesham, Bucks.

staunch members of the Established Church. John Bottrill, for instance, was church warden at Stony Stratford. Others became involved in the life of their community. John Hardy was a capital burgess of Stamford as well as being a constable in his own parish. Hardy issued a farthing on his own account in 1667 and also an earlier one jointly with another shoemaker (*W*243), which reads, JOHN HARDY ED DALE E.D./BOTH OF STAMFORD. Edward Dale was admitted to the freedom of his trade in 1658, fifteen years later than his partner. He also acted as parish constable in two parishes.

The only token bearing the word CORDWAINER is that of Paul Alferi of Wexford. This is an Irish penny dated 1665. He describes himself as CORDWINDER. The Southwark piece of Isaac Cammock is interesting as it displays a Cavalier's boot alongside the arms and crest (*W*275). The token reads, ISAAC CAMMOCK AT BLEWBOOT IN JACOB STREET/HIS HALF PENY 69. The square shape was obviously chosen to accommodate the lengthy legend.

Numerous other tokens depict shoes or boots, but we lack evidence that the issuer was connected with shoe manufacture. Nevertheless they are interesting in that they show the style of contemporary shoes, for example a half penny of Edward Legg of York features a typical bucket boot of the period. This device was, of course, intended as a pun on the issuer's name.

PEWTERERS

Pewter ware was found in every room in the house, not just the kitchen, at this time. It comprises basins and bowls, porringers and plates, flagons and ewers, tankards and mugs, pepperettes and pounce-pots, candlesticks and ink stands, and much more besides.

The company of the City of London issued ordinances in 1348, which established standard alloys of two distinct qualities. The first consisted of 'fine' pewter of pure tin with some brass. This fine metal was used for manufacturing flat items such as plates or dishes. Pewter of the second, slightly inferior quality contained 25% lead. It became known as lay metal and was used in making hollow ware, consisting of rounded pots, such as measures, ewers, tankards and flagons. The company was given the right to have a coat of arms – 'azure, a chevron or between three strakes argent; upon the chevron 3 roses gules, stalks, buds and leaves vert'. The strakes of tin symbolized the pewterers' craft.

The marking of pewter was first made obligatory for members of the London company as early as 1503 and for the entire kingdom in 1638. It had long been customary to mark gold and silver ware. The first mention of pewter marking occurs in the records of the London Company (1474): 'item, delivered a ponchon of iron with the broad arrowhead for the forfeit mark'.

The year 1550 witnessed the first reference to the celebrated touch plate, which consisted of a large pewter plate one eighth of an inch thick. After serving his apprenticeship and taking up his freedom, each livery man was required to strike on the touch plate an impression of his own trade-mark. An inventory of that year contains the following entry, 'a table of pewter with every man's mark there on'. Five London touch plates still survive. The earliest was purchased by the company in 1668 for eight shillings. The Hall had been burnt down in the Fire two years previously so the plate would probably not have been put to use until 1670, when it had been rebuilt and normal life resumed. The second touch plate was bought in 1674 and used a few years later.

Several of the livery men of the London Company of Pewterers, whose touch marks can still be seen on one or other of these plates, issued farthing or half penny tokens. These men include Samuel Artley of Little Britain (*W*1708), Robert Gisburne of Pall Mall (*W*2176), Stephen Mabberley of Broad Street and Henry Napton of Bishopsgate. It is also probable that the issuer of an Irish piece was the father of Sir John Fryers, the most celebrated of all seventeenth-century pewterers.

Samuel Artley's farthing reads, S.M.A. IN LITTLE BRITTAIN PEWTERER 1667. There is no legend on the reverse, which bears the arms of the company. The issuer was elected to the Livery on 19 December 1667, when the hall was about to be rebuilt. It is significant that his token was issued in the same year – he was certainly quick off the mark to advertise himself as a fully qualified pewterer.

Robert Gisburne of Pall Mall had his token struck in the same year. He was elected to the Livery just three weeks before Artley. He too must have acted very quickly to have had a token produced before the end of the year (*W*2176). It reads, ROBERT GISBERNE IN THE/HIS HALFEPENNY/OLD PELL MELL PEWTERER R.A.G. 1667. Unlike Artley, Gisburne rose to high office in the city company. He was elected steward in 1670, renter warden in 1683, upper warden in 1689 and finally master in 1691. His touch mark consisted of a rose beneath a crown, but unfortunately he put no device on his token – perhaps from lack of room.

The third elected livery man to have a token struck was Stephen Mabberly of Broad Street, whose farthing also appeared in 1667. The exact date of his election to the Livery is not known, but on the evidence of the tokens of his two fellow pewterers it may be surmised that he was elected in the same year. Mabberley was permitted to strike his touch mark, a dove above a snake, in 1671. His tokens bear the arms of the company and his address BROADSTREET EAND (End), together with the initials S.E.M. and the date 67.

Henry Napton of Bishopsgate, the last of the London pewterers definitely known to have been elected members of the Livery Company, issued his token three years later. His half penny, like Mabberley's, depicted the Pewterers' Arms. He was elected to the Livery in 1670, so it is no surprise to find that his token bears the same date. He had leave to strike his touch mark, a horseman crossing a river, with the initials H.M., in the same year. He practised his trade until he died in 1684.

An Irish pewterer, John Fryers of Clonmel in County Tipperary, issued a penny token (*W*178) in 1668, which reads, JOHN FRYERS 1668/OF CLONMEL PEVTERER ID. A ship is featured on the obverse. The issuer was probably the father of John Fryers, a London pewterer at the turn of the century. This man was elected to the Yeomanry on 18 June 1696, becoming a city alderman in 1709, and eventually knighted. He had leave to strike his touch plate on 30 March 1693.

We cannot be sure just how many pewterers issued tokens during the seventeenth century. More than a dozen, including three of the London Pewterers just mentioned, actually put the word PEWTERER on their token. These include Thomas Heath of Warwick, John Henty of Lewes, Thomas Hutten of Canterbury, Samuel Canner of Tewkesbury and Joseph Sherwin of Ashbourne in Derbyshire; also three Irish men – Ignatius Brown and Jonathon Butterton of Dublin and Francis Banks of Galway. Only one of their tokens carries the Pewterers' Arms – that of Thomas Hutten, the Kentish man. Incidentally, Hutten's token is interesting as being the only penny struck in the entire Kent series. Tankards appear on one of the Dublin pennies, that of Ignatius Brown, and on the Tewkesbury farthing. A fleur-de-lys has been designed on the Sussex piece and a pot of lilies on the Galway penny. These two emblems have particular associations with the craft of pewter making.

The Pewterers' Arms appear on several tokens which contain no other clue as to the issuer's occupation. We may infer that they worked in pewter. They include pieces of John Benson of Halifax, John Burgis of Bicester, Robert Bristow of Wapping Wall, John Furnis of King Street, Westminster, John Smith of Coventry, Richard Weber of Barnstaple and Mary Willis of Cranbrook, Kent. Mary Willis's token is particularly intriguing as one would not expect a woman to be a pewterer. She was married at the time to a clothier, whose initial is included on her token.

Another interesting token is that of John Baker of Hull (*W*132): JOHN BAKER/OF HULL 1665 I.B. The obverse device consists of an arm wielding a hammer. There is no direct clue as to Baker's trade on the token, although it clearly requires considerable physical exertion. Williamson informs us that he was a well-known pewterer, being elected Freeman of the Pewterers' Company of Hull on 5 June 1662, so he was an accredited pewterer for only three years before issuing his token.

A number of pieces depict tankards, pewter pots or dishes. One or two of them may well have been issued by pewterers. A good example is a farthing of Barnstaple issued by John Webber, depicting a tankard. Cotterell confirms that Webber was a pewterer and shows his mark to be a castle. He also states that his son John Webber Junior, circa 1680–1735, practised the same trade and used a similar mark. Curiously, Richard Weber of the same town, undoubtedly a member of the same family and also a pewterer, depicted a castle on his token – probably a family emblem. Another interesting farthing circulating in London carries the obverse legend YE PEWTER PLATTER and the initials T.M.W. The reverse informs us that the issuer worked in GRATIOUS STREET. The issuer may well have been a pewterer, on the other hand he may well have been an innkeeper at the sign of the Pewter Platter. This is one of the many riddles to be unravelled in the fascinating and vast series of London trade tokens.

Finally, Cotterell links the issuer of a Buckinghamshire farthing with a record he had come across of a pewterer of the same name of unknown provenance. He illustrates his mark of about 1730, a fleece. This token was issued by a Christopher Clifton of Stony Stratford: it is undated but early in style, and was probably struck in the 1650s. The pot of lilies boldly shown on the obverse was a favourite device of the pewterer. The fleur-de-lys was used on an official marking punch at Pewterers' Hall, London. A record of 1659 reads, 'paid for a marking iron of the fleur-de-lys to mark stone pots (lids) with . . . 10d'. A pot of lilies together with strakes of tin appeared on an earlier punch at Pewterers' Hall.

The Christopher Clifton who issued the farthing token was surely the father or grandfather of the one whose mark appears in Cotterell's book. The parish registers of Stony Stratford show a Christopher Clifton as church warden in 1653 and record his burial in 1686. He would be the token issuer, but there are references also to a son, Christopher, and to a grandson also of the same name. My guess is that it is the grandson's mark that we see in Cotterell. As the token issuer's father was also called Christopher and was a pewterer by trade, it seems likely that there were four Christopher Cliftons, in direct line, carrying on the family tradition of pewter making for over a century.

JOINERS AND GLAZIERS

The building trade is not well represented in the token series, probably because the workmen would have little capital to purchase tokens. A few were issued by glaziers and carpenters, such as *W*356, a halfpenny issued by a Suffolk glazier from Wickhambrook in 1669, with a rose and crown design. The legend is, JOHN RAYMENT IN WICKHA/BROOKE GLASYER 1669 HIS HALF PENNY. An Irish glazier issued a penny at Drogheda at about the same time (*W*235). This reads, HVGH FOWKES OF/DROGHEDA GLASER H.F. 1ᴰ. The Glaziers' Arms appear on the reverse.

The only token of the seventeenth century which actually advertises the craft of carpentry was issued by Will Craskees at Tothill Fields, London (*W*3151). This farthing reads, WILL CRASKEES JOYNER W.A.C./IN TVTHILL FEILDS W.A.C. Numerous other carpenters' tokens include two farthings of Beaconsfield in Buckinghamshire. These were issued by cousins, both having the same name Thomas Cocke; the first bears the initials T.I.C. and the second T.K.C. Records show that the male members of the Cocke family, who were very numerous in Beaconsfield, all seem to have been carpenters, although there is no clue on the tokens. One Thomas Cocke married a Jane, who died in 1717. Another carpenter of the same name married Katherine Rennell in 1665. He was born in 1623 and died in 1680. The initials on the tokens have identified both issuers. An example of the second farthing was recently found in a cottage in Aylesbury End, Beaconsfield, after a carpenter had been working on the beams. It seems most appropriate that a carpenter should discover a fellow carpenter's token even though it had been dropped three hundred years ago.

IRONMONGERS AND BRAZIERS

By the middle of the seventeenth century the brazier or ironmonger was coming into his own. Unlike the ironmonger of today he was no mere shopkeeper or salesman, but both craftsman and mechanic as Campbell reminds us, 'the articles that belong to him as a mechanic are the making of tea kettles of Brass and Copper and the other vessels and household utensils that are metals. These he makes a few of in his workshop and employs journey men. Some of these articles are beat out by the hammer, and others are cast'. He lists the stock to be found in ironmongers' shops: 'grates and stoves, pokers, fire shovels, tongs and fenders of polished iron, steel or brass, ranges for the kitchen, jacks, spits, coppers, kettles, fishpans, stewpans of all sorts and sizes, locks of all kinds, candlesticks, smoothing irons, box irons, nails, wood screws . . .'

Ironmongers issued tokens in places as far-flung as Exeter and Chester, but it is significant that the majority outside London appeared in the Midlands. The Ironmongers' Arms were actually depicted on a town piece of Stourbridge in Worcestershire, complementing the Clothworkers' Arms on the other face. Two Stourbridge ironmongers issued their own tokens – both halfpence and both bearing the Ironmongers' Arms – John Clare in 1666 and Andrew Muchall in 1669.

Neighbouring Staffordshire produced numerous ironmongers' pieces circulating in Stafford, Lichfield, Rowley Regis, Smethwick Wednesbury, Wolverhampton and Yoxall. Four of these towns are situated in the heart of what was to become the Black Country, and yet another Black Country ironmonger issued a token at nearby Dudley. The Ironmongers' Arms appear on almost all of these tokens, including those of Richard Russell of Rowley Regis and Thomas Parker of Smethwick. The Yoxall halfpenny was the latest to appear, in 1671, and the most unusual, being octagonal in shape. Occasionally tokens of ironmongers depict the actual wares sold; frying pans, for example, are featured on half pence of two London ironmongers – John Sylvester of Ludgate Street and William Hayes of Wood Street. Chafing dishes are shown on the token of Will Walker of Newgate Without.

There seems to have been little distinction between ironmonger and brazier in the seventeenth and eighteenth centuries. Half a dozen tokens specifically refer to the trade of brazier, most of which circulated in rural counties far from the Black Country. Benjamin Rudkin issued his halfpenny in 1669 at Walsingham, Norfolk. Other English braziers' tokens were spent in Bridgwater in Somerset, Lewes in Sussex, and Highworth in Wiltshire. Richard White of Lewes put a hammer on his two tokens as a symbol of his craft. Two Irish braziers had tokens struck: Edward Goble of Cork and John Seawell of Skinner Row, Dublin. The Cork piece bears the Armourers' Arms.

CUTLERS

A Nottingham half penny issued by Thomas Francis also features the Armourers' Arms, but Francis is described on the token as a cutler. Cutlers' tokens are scarce, but, as one would expect, no less than three appeared in Sheffield in the names of Robert Downes (*W*326), John Ramsker and James Taylor. There is no indication of trade on Downes's piece which simply states, ROBERT DOWNES 1670/IN SHEFFEILD HIS HALFPENY. A bunch of grapes is inscribed on the reverse as his trade mark. Williamson noted that the issuer held the officer of Master Cutler in 1697 and that members of the same family held similar high office in 1670 and 1700. John Ramsker's farthing depicts two crossed swords, a favourite device, and is dated 1655. The issuer had a shop in the Minories, London, where he sold cutlery manufactured in his Sheffield workshop.

A farthing of George Bishop of Oxford shows part of the Cutlers' Arms – an elephant's head and crossed swords. Bishop was apprenticed in 1650 to Charles Green, an Oxford cutler, for a period of eight years, gaining his freedom at the end of his apprenticeship. Anthony Wood records that in 1665 he paid two shillings for a razor bought from George Bishop. It is known from city records that he was a supporter of the Jacobite cause.

Finally, mention should be made of a tinman's half penny of Snow Hill, London (*W*2912), reading, JOHN WEST TINMAN AT THE/CROWNE ON SNOW HILL HIS HALF PENNY 1668. West's seems to be the only token struck for a tinman. His calling is described by Campbell, 'the tinman receives it in a sheet. It is his business by beating it on a polished anvil to give it smoothness or lustre – to form it into lamps, canisters, pans and saucepans. The tinmen are now generally lamplighters, from whence they receive the greatest part of their profit'. This early reference to tin cans is interesting.

LOCKSMITHS

Two Essex locksmiths issued tokens – Thomas Haven of Chelmsford (*W*59) and Edward Kitchener of Dunmow (*W*167). The former's token reads, THO HAVEN LOCKSMITH/IN CHELMSFORD 1669. The issuer's name is repeated in monogram on the reverse. The obverse device consists of three keys. Crossed keys, however, appear on Edward Kitchener's half penny. The legends are, EDWARD KEATCHENER/OF DUNMOW LOCKSMITH.

Campbell is full of admiration for the locksmith's skill. He writes, 'the Keys, wards, springs and plates he makes himself and employs the founder to cast his cases if in brass. The nicest branch of this art is tempering springs . . . After he has forged his springs he puts them into the fire till they receive a heat between the red and the white and plunges them into water'.

POTTERS

The craft of pottery has been practised since time immemorial, but remained uncomplicated until the seventeenth century, being largely dependent on local clay and a local market for the finished product.

Geraint writes, 'one of the main factors contributing to the rapid development of the pottery industry in the seventeenth century was the emergence of a class of pottery merchant – pot mongers or crate sellers'. Marketing became more skilful, transport was improved, warehouses were provided and competition became fiercer. The main area for the industry became centred on Burslem in Staffordshire and Ticknell in Derbyshire. The Ticknell pottery near Burton on Trent became one of the largest potteries in Britain by the end of the century, yet potters were to be found elsewhere,

5.7 Farthing token of George Bishop, Cutler, of Oxford.

especially in London. Three London potters issued tokens – Ann Tayler at her shop in Aldersgate Street (*W*57), John Hubbold in Cary Lane (*W*468), John Kempster in Leadenhall Street (*W*167), and George Caldwell in St John's Street.

Ann Tayler's half penny reads, ANN TAYLER A POTTERS SHOP IN/ ALDERSGATE STREET HER HALF PENY. The issuer may well have been a potmonger, a marketer rather than a producer. John Hubbold, however, describes himself as a potter, as does George Caldwell. The clue to the issuer's profession on John Kempster's token is a flower vase depicted on the obverse.

TURNERS AND COOPERS

A turner's token was issued in Richmond, Surrey, reading, MICHAEL CLAYLE OF/RICHMOND TVRNER 1669 HIS HALF PENY (*W*225). Turners and coopers alike made wash tubs, casks, barrels, and all kind of turned vessels. Campbell describes the craft as follows. 'He makes use of an engine called a lathe. His work is fixed upon a center and is turned by a string which either goes round the work if it turns upon two pivots or round a wheel fixed to the moving centre'.

Several coopers' tokens are known, including those of Thomas Best of Canterbury, and three of London – Thomas Hogsflesh of Great Tower Hill (*W*3198), John Gray of White Cross Street (W3451) and Daniel Arnold of Blackman Street, Southwark. The octagonal half penny of Tower Hill reads, THO HOGSFLESH COOPER IN THE STILL YARD/ON GREAT TOWER HILL HIS HALF PENY. Thomas Best's piece displays the Vintners' Arms, and is dated 1650. John Gray and Daniel Arnold describe themselves as 'wine coopers'. Gray's token reads, JOHN GRAY WINE COOPER/WHITE CROSS STREET HIS HALF PENY.

BELLMEN

Two large bells are depicted on the half penny token of William Atton, issued in 1663 by a Buckingham draper. The bells indicate a family link with the ancient craft of bell founding. The draper's grandfather, Bartholomew Atton, his uncle Robert and his father William were all well-known casters of bells at a foundry in West Street, Buckingham. Bartholomew made church bells for more than forty years, the majority being cast for village churches in North Buckinghamshire and the southern part of Northamptonshire. Fortunately it was the custom for bell founders to sign their products, so his bells are readily identifiable. William Atton's uncle, Robert Atton, put a rhyming couplet on a bell he cast for Kingsthorpe in Northamptonshire,

ROBERT ATTON MADE ME

THE TREBLE BELL FOR TO BE.

William's brother, Bartholomew, also carried on business as a draper at Brackley, Northamptonshire. He also depicted a bell on the obverse of his token.

Only one bell founder's token is known, that of Erasmus Bish, which circulated in Whitechapel, London (*W*3389). The token reads, ERASMVS BISH IN WHIT/CHAPELL BELLMAN. As one would expect, a church bell is shown on the obverse. The Whitechapel Foundry flourished in the seventeenth century, casting bells for churches throughout the Home Counties. Cocks estimated that more than a quarter of all the bells in Buckinghamshire were cast there. The foundry was established as early as 1420 in Houndsditch, but moved to Whitechapel in 1583. Soon afterwards bells were cast for Westminster Abbey. In 1738 the foundry moved to its present site in Whitechapel Road. Here many of the world's great bells have been cast, including Big Ben and America's original Liberty Bell.

CHAPTER 6

TOBACCONISTS AND PIPE-MAKERS

Tobacco reached Europe from South America in the middle of the sixteenth century. It was probably first brought to Portugal and France. A Fleming named Damien de Goes claimed to have grown tobacco in the royal garden at Lisbon in 1558. At about the same time a Frenchman, Andre Thevet, introduced Nicotiana Tabacum from Brazil, and a fellow-countryman, resident in Portugal, Jean Nicot, grew a plant of Nicotiana Rustica imported from Florida and forwarded the seeds to the King of France in 1560. It was considered first to be a medicinal herb 'very good for loosening and carrying off the superfluous humours of the brain', and was used in the form of snuff. William Harrison writing in 1573 observed: 'In these daies the taking in of the smoke of the Indian herb called "tobacco" by an instrument formed like a little ladell, whereby it passeth into the hed and stomach, is greatlie taken up and used in England, against Rewmes . . .'

Some monarchs regarded the habit with horror and attempted to suppress it – without success. In 1604, James I published an anonymous counterblast to tobacco in which he referred to it as 'this precious stink'. Rulers soon discovered that they could not stamp out the practice, and eventually encouraged it as an additional source of revenue. The Tobacco Pipe-Makers of Westminster were granted a charter by James I in 1619.

The pipe-making industry and tobacconist's trade were flourishing by the middle of the seventeenth century, as the following extract from a petition of 1643 shows, 'Before the late Act of Parliament for laying a duty on tobacco pipes near 1,000 poor men in London and Westminster lived by tobacco pipe making . . .' Near a school where I used to teach in Aylesbury, Bucks, the children were constantly finding seventeenth-century bowls and stems in substantial numbers. It is not surprising to discover that a considerable number of seventeenth-century trade tokens feature pipes and tobacco. There are numerous variations of type including the following: four pipes, three pipes, three pipes arranged in the form of a triangle, two pipes crossed and a roll of tobacco, one tobacco roll, three rolls, an ape smoking a pipe, a man smoking etc.

It is often not possible to deduce from the token itself whether it was issued by a tobacconist or pipe-maker. A few tokens actually include the word TOBACCONIST in the legend, including *W*3305: JOHN HARLING 1667 I.A.H./IN

6.1 Broadside depicting a gentleman of the mid-seventeenth century taking tobacco.

WAPPING TOBACCONIS HIS HALFE PENY, and *W*90: JOHN AVDLEY TOBACCONIST HIS HALF PENY/IN OWNDLE 1669.

I have only come across one which actually features the word PIPE-MAKER, that of Robert Whinicke of Warwick. Adrian Oswald, in Part Three of his excellent survey *Clay Pipes for the Archaeologist* (B.A.R. 14, 1975), includes forty-one issuers of seventeenth-century tokens in his lists of pipe-makers. The fact that some of them bore a device of crossed pipes was considered sufficient basis for their inclusion. Two Buckinghamshire tokens featuring crossed pipes were definitely issued by pipe-makers – those of Abraham Garraway of Chesham and Richard Robinson of Eton. Contemporary pipes bearing their initials have been found in the localities of Chesham and Eton respectively. Robinson's name appears in the Quarter Sessions Records (Midsummer 1689) as follows: 'Registration of the several houses here to mentioned . . . publick meeting houses for Religious Worship in accordance with the Act of William and Mary . . . the dwelling of Richard Robinson, pipe maker in Eton'. Robinson was obviously a Nonconformist. Two Yorkshire men appearing in Oswald's lists, Abraham Boyes and Will Moore of York, are also well-known pipe manufactureres. Boyes is recorded as sending export pipes to the West Indies and America.

The manufacture of pipes in the seventeenth century was not considered a highly skilled industry. Firstly the clay was prepared, sometimes by hand, sometimes by machine, then blanks were formed by hand in the shape of a pipe. The bore of the stems was threaded and the blanks were placed in a mould, the bowls were shaped by hand and then trimmed and burnished. The pipes were finally placed in a kiln. As the archaeologist's interest in clay pipes as recording evidence has grown in recent years, more pipes manufactured by token issuers may well be found.

However, not all the tradesmen whose tokens depict pipes actually made them, as several of the men featured in Oswald's lists appear in local records as practising other trades. At least two of the five Wiltshire token issuers were tobacconists rather than pipe manufacturers. We know that John Forman of Calne supplied the stewards of the town with tobacco at the Town Hall in 1685. John Smith of Marlborough, whose farthing token appeared in 1665, was described as a 'tobacco-cutter' when created a burgess of the town in 1679. His will confirms his trade; he left 'grubs, a kiver, 22 boxes, a dryer, an engine and tobacco worth £45-10-2'. The valuation is surprisingly large. A third Wiltshire token issuer mentioned by Oswald, William Webb of

6.2 Half penny token of Abraham Boyes, pipemaker of York.

Swindon, was almost certainly a tobacconist too. Richard Webb, a member of the same family, was licensed in 1637 to retail tobacco at Marlborough, Brinkworth, Chisledon, Stratton St Margaret and Tackenham Wick. It may be argued that these Wiltshire tobacconists actually made their own pipes, but there is no evidence to support this.

Bryan Lillywhite observes in his *London Signs* (1972) that the sign of the tobacco roll usually indicates a tobacconist:

'The smoakie black lung-puffed tobacconist
Whose joy doth in tobacco sole consist'.

A contemporary shop sign took the form of a pendant black roll imitating rolled tobacco. A character in Ben Jonson's satire, *Cynthia's Reads* (1660) says, 'I have my three sorts of tobacco in my pocket', probably referring to Trinidad, leaf and pudding tobacco. A number of tokens were issued of the sign of the tobacco roll, especially in London and Southwark. These include farthings of John Twyne at the 'Tobaco Rowle', Holborn, W.N. at the Tobacco R(oll) in St Martin's Lane, S.H. at the Tobacco Rowle in Paules Church Yard, R.S. at the Tobacko Role in Wapping (dated 1667), John Green at the Tobaco Role in Southwark and John Nelson at Ye (Roll of Tobacco) in Southwark (dated 1664). It is interesting to note that most of the London tokens bearing this sign and its accompanying legend do not give the full name of the issuer, having space only for the initials. A solitary token is known with the sign of two rolls of tobacco (*W*3096). It reads: AT TO TOBACO ROWLES/ IN THEAMES STREET M.M.G. Several are known, however, with the sign of three rolls, for example a Southwark farthing reading, JAMES TODD 3 TOBACO I.M.T./ ROLES IN SOVTHWARK (*W*97).

More than a hundred men and women issued tokens referring to the pastime of smoking between the years 1648 and 1672. The devices appearing on their tokens are varied and interesting:

Pipe and tobacco roll	1	Three rolls and sugar loaf	1
Pipe and cheeseknife	1	Hand holding chopper over tobacco leaf	2
Crossed pipes	20	Hand holding chopper over leaf, roll of tobacco and crossed pipes	1
Crossed pipes and tobacco	7	Man smoking	15
Two pipes	15	Man smoking between a tobacco roll and a pair of scales	1
Two pipes and tobacco roll	12		
Three pipes	15		
Three pipes in form of triangle	2		

Three pipes and four mugs of ale	1	Three rolls	4
Four pipes	1	Man smoking and making candles	1
Four pipes and tobacco roll	1	Man smoking and working at forge	1
Five pipes	1	Black boy smoking	17
Roll of tobacco	62	Black boy holding a mug and pipe	1
Roll and sugar loaf	4	Indian smoking	4
Roll between two loaves	1	Monkey smoking	2
Roll and hoop	1	Hand pouring into coffee cup – table with pipes	2
Roll and half moon	1	Hand holding cup; pipe and roll of tobacco	1
Roll and crown	1	Hand holding a coffee pot – coffee cups and pipes	1
Roll wound round drum	1		
Roll and cavalry men	1		
Two rolls	1		

Probably most of the seventy or so tokens bearing one or more rolls of tobacco were issued by tobacconists. In the middle of the seventeenth century, as indeed today, one could buy tobacco from a specialist tobacconist, at a grocer's shop or general stores. R. Campbell, writing in 1747, describes the trade in the following terms, 'By the Tobacconist I do not mean the Importers, him I speak of as a Merchant; but the Retailer who buys from the Importer and keeps open shop. The greatest Article he deals in is Cut-Tobacco for smoaking; in which he employs Labourers at twelve shillings a week, who cut it with an Engine for that Purpose, and prepare it for use. If they take any apprentices they are taught to cut, are employed in stripping the Leaf off the Stems and in spinning the Pig-Tail. The trade is reputable and profitable, and requires a large stock to set up with'.

Only six tokens in the entire series mention the word 'tobacconist' on the piece itself – four of them in the metropolis. These London tokens are those of John Perrot of St Anne's Lane, John Hartley of Moore Lane, John Harting of Wapping and Jerome Powell of Sheare Lane. The fifth was issued by John Audley of Oundle and the sixth by Charles Scory, whose locality is still unidentified. Displaying three pipes, his token simply reads: CHARLES SCORY TOBACO/NIST HIS HALFE PENEY. It is fascinating to note that only one of these six tokens depicts a roll of tobacco – that of John Perrot.

Scory's halfpenny shows three pipes as mentioned above, John Audley's a still, and Jerome Powell's a man smoking. The tokens of John Hartley and John Harting bear no illustrative device.

We have noted that a number of Wiltshire tobacconists are known from local records. They used crossed pipes as a symbol of their business. No less than seven Wiltshire issuers put this device on the tokens – Jacob Selbee of Bradford on Avon, John Forman of Calne, John Fry of Devizes, John Smith of Marlborough, Henry Restall and William Webb of Swindon and William Smith of Trowbridge. This number comprises 35 per cent of the tokens in the entire series bearing crossed pipes, a remarkable figure. It seems likely that a travelling agent took orders for the tokens and suggested the main illustrative design. A similar pattern emerges in north Buckinghamshire. No less than twenty-three tokens from seven places within an eight-mile radius of each other bear an identical device – a pair of scales.

The sign of the 'Tobaco Rowle' was adopted by many seventeenth-century tobacconists, yet it cannot be assumed that all tokens featuring this sign were issued by retailers of tobacco. Grocers, mercers, innkeepers and ironmongers are known also to have used this sign at their shops and on their

6.3 Half penny token of John Crawley and Mr Dimock, tobacconists of Winslow.

tokens. The grocers who put a roll of tobacco on their tokens include John King of Colchester, George Hide of Cripplegate, London and Will Chudley of Whitechapel. The word GROCER is stamped on all their coins. Two others added a sugar loaf – Robert Garrett of Cateaton Street, London and Hugh Blundell of Southwark – a favourite symbol of the grocery trade. John Farmer of Pirton in Hertfordshire issued two tokens. His earlier farthing, appearing in 1656, displayed a roll of tobacco on the obverse and the Grocers' Arms on the reverse. His later half penny of 1668 omitted the arms. Farmer's will of 1688 confirms that he was a grocer. Local records show that Henry Shaw of Darlington was a grocer, and his token shows a king's head crowned and a tobacco roll. The former is a loyalist device, extremely popular in Durham.

A Devonshire mercer, Francis Squire of Okehampton, advertised his trade by putting a roll of tobacco and a pipe on his token. The word MERCER actually appears on the token. Local records confirm other issuers of tokens depicting pipes and tobacco to be mercers, including George King of Leigh, Essex, George Benn of Puckeridge, Hertfordshire, and Thomas Allanson of Chorley, Lancashire.

A Shropshire ironmonger's token (Richard Bebb of Ludlow) depicts a man smoking, with the word IRONMONGER. George Boon has shown that a Welsh token issuer, Thomas Knight of Caernarvon, who used a roll of tobacco as his sign was also an ironmonger. It seems very strange that even a London cheesemonger should have a tobacco roll on the reverse of his token (John Hammond of Norton Folgate), but this peculiar combination of tobacco and cheese is repeated on a Yorkshire token issued in Leeds by Henry Ellis and Arthur Roome. A pipe and a cheese knife are featured on the token appearing in their joint names. It is possible that both trades were practised at the same address.

It is to be expected that inn and coffee house tokens should feature pipes and tobacco on occasions, as they were places of enjoyment and relaxation in which drinking and smoking were amongst the chief pleasures. Morat's Coffee House in Exchange Alley, London issued several tokens which mention the commodities sold at this coffee house – coffee, sherbet, tea, chocolate and tobacco. Several London coffee house keepers' tokens show a coffee table on which pipes can be seen, including Joseph Howard of New Street, Mary Stringer of Little Trinity Lane and Mansfield's coffee house in Shoe Lane.

The tapster of a celebrated Southwark inn, the George, which is now the only surviving galleried inn in London, issued a token depicting three pipes and four pots of ale. Boon records a token issued jointly by two innholders, J. Wheldon and W. M. Owen. Their token shows crossed pipes, a roll of tobacco and two ale pots. A Hertfordshire farthing of Bishop Stortford, illustrating a man smoking, is known to be an innkeeper's token from the issuer's will.

Few tokens depict the act of smoking, one exception being a farthing token of Thomas Jones of Exeter. At least two tokens show an ape smoking a pipe – John Ewing of St George's Church, Southwark and John Ede at Petworth, Sussex. John Ewing's token is octagonal. Other octagonal tokens featuring pipes are those of Frances Wall of Bicester, Oxon and one issued at High Timber Street, London. Two heart-shaped half penny tokens were issued in Oxfordshire in the same year 1668 – one by John Warry of Bicester and another by Edmond Rowbright of Chipping Norton. The latter shows a hand holding a chopper over a leaf of tobacco with two crossed pipes below. A Winslow halfpenny bears a similar device but without crossed pipes, and was issued by two tradesmen, John Crawley and Mr Dimock (Ill. 6.3). It is strange that the second man should use the prefix Mr rather than his Christian name, which also happened to be John. In contemporary documents the term Mr is used to denote respect.

Only four tobacconists' tokens valued at a full penny are known: two in Yorkshire (Ambrose Ambler at Leeds and Anthony Fawcet at Dent) and two in Wales (Thomas Knight at Caernarvon and Lawrence Cooke at Wrexham). All are dated, appearing late in the series.

6.4 Penny token of Lawrence Cooke, tobacconist of Wrexham.

CHAPTER 7

BOOKSELLERS AND STATIONERS

Before the seventeenth century the business of publishing and selling books and pamphlets was in the hands of comparatively few, chiefly in London. The early Stuart era witnessed a steady growth in the book trade in England, culminating in more rapid development in the 1650s and 1660s after a period of stagnation during the Civil War. Throughout the Commonwealth and Restoration a fairly rigid censorship had been imposed by both political extremes. Archbishop Laud had set a precedent in 1637 with his Star Chamber Decree, permitting only twenty printers and threatening the pillory and branding iron for all those who dared to criticize the church's authority in print. The Long Parliament of 1640 had encouraged printing at first, and for several years newsletters poured from the presses. Gradually, however, the Government changed its attitude as the Long Parliament itself came under attack. A mild censorship was imposed by an ordinance of 1643, which empowered a committee to appoint searchers from the Company of Stationers to root out presses engaged in producing 'scandalous and lying pamphlets'. The Company proved instrumental in helping to stifle the book trade by its determined attempt to keep it in the hands of a privileged few.

The benign influence of John Milton and others helped to lessen the effects of persecution during the years 1642–6. The Government was determined, however, to 'regulate the press', and passed an act in 1649 just as pernicious as the Star Chamber decree twelve years earlier. It forbade the printing or selling of scandalous or libellous books, ordained that all newsheets should be licensed before being printed and sold, and gave magistrates powers of search to discover 'malignant', meaning royalist, booksellers. Despite this act, the country continued to be flooded with pamphlets of every hue of political and religious opinion. H.R. Plomer observes that the greater part of published material during the Civil War consisted of political and theological pamphlets, mostly written by John Milton and James Howell. He points out that there was no dramatic literature and little poetry.

The range of literature improved on the conclusion of hostilities. The new polyglot Bible appeared, 1653 saw the publication of Isaac Walton's *Compleat Angler*, and two years later William Dugard printed the folio edition of Sir Philip Sidney's *Arcadia*. Strangely, there was less press censorship during Cromwell's rule than in the periods immediately preceding or succeeding.

The Restoration of Charles II in 1660, in the words of Plomer, 'brought the book trade once again under the heel of the oppressor'. A mass of anti-royalist literature marked Monk's victory. An official surveyor of the Press was appointed, one Sir Robert L'Estrange, who knew nothing about the printing or selling of books. Although fresh censorship was imposed, there was a ready market for books, pamphlets and prints of all kinds. The contemporary French writer, Sorbiere, commented in 1663, 'I am not to forget the vast number of booksellers' shops I have observed in London, for besides those who are set up here and there in the city, they have their particular quarters such as St Paul's Churchyard and Little Britain where there are twice as many as in the Rue St Jacques in Paris, and who have each of them two or three warehouses'. There were a surprising number of booksellers in the provinces too. It has been estimated that in 1640 about forty towns possessed their own bookshop. Sixty years later John Dunton put the figure at three hundred.

Quite a few booksellers and stationers, both in London, and the provinces, issued trade tokens during the period 1648–72. It is significant that of the dated tokens, the vast majority appeared after 1660. Only four predate the Restoration: those of Thomas Ewster of Cornhill (1657), Raphael Harford of Little Britain (1658), William Weeks of Plymouth (1659) and Thomas Butler, probably from London (1659). The London tokens provide about a third of all the known booksellers' and stationers' tokens issued.

The distribution of these token farthings and half pence confirms Sorbiere's observation that the London bookshops tended to be grouped in areas close to St Paul's – the Churchyard itself, Little Britain, Paternoster Row and London Bridge. John Mackay in his *Journey through England* (1724) noted traces of specialisation in the London trade, 'the booksellers of ancient books are in Little Britain and Paternoster Row, those for Divinity and Classics, on the north side of St Paul's Cathedral, law, history and plays about Temple Bar and the French booksellers in the Strand'.

William Place, whose farthing (*W*1237) was issued at Gray's Inn Gate, dealt in law books, as one might expect from his location, but also acted as district postmaster, for his shop lay on one of the principal posting routes out of London. His token advertises his postal business, WILLIAM PLACE AT/GRAYS INN GATE FOR POST LETTERS, and depicts a horseman, blowing a post horn. The halfpenny is undated, but its style indicates that it circulated in the mid-1660s. Place seems to have received his appointment as postmaster in 1661 as the *Mercurius Publicus* of that year states, 'all gentlemen and others are desir'd to take notice that the Post Office hath been abused by severall persons, who have falsely pretended themselves to be appointed to receive letters and have exacted a penny a letter and have also destroyed many letters to gaine the post to themselves. And to prevent the like abuses His Majesty's Post Master generall hath appointed the persons hereafter named to receive all letters in the respective places for the Post Office'. The list includes Mr Place, Stationer at Gray's Inn Gate. Williamson remarks on the man's undoubted energy and widespread business interests. He sold lozenges in his shop, not to mention an assortment of toothpaste 'to scour and cleanse the teeth, making them white as ivory, preserve them from the toothache, sweeten the breath and preserve the mouth and gum from the cankers, and to be a speedy remedy to any flux or looseness of the belly'.

William Place carried on his business from 1657 until about 1677. A

7.1 Penny token of Hugh Davies, Stationer, of Holyhead.

relative of his, John Place, also dealt in law books, both at Furnival's Inn Gate and Greyhound Yard, Holborn. Despite his activities as a bookseller, postmaster and purveyer of toothpaste, Place was invariably referred to as 'stationer'. It might be advisable to define the term. Campbell, writing in 1747, claimed that the word 'stationer' originally applied to booksellers who had their stations or stalls near the temples, but that it had evolved into referring to dealers in paper. Their wares included not only every variety of paper but pens, ink, sand and sand boxes, wafers, sealing wax, and copy books of account. Campbell is at pains to point out that many stationers combined their trade with bookselling, book binding and printing.

Other London booksellers referred to as stationers include Thomas Ewster of Cornhill, John Young of Fenchurch Street and Thomas Heath of Ludgate Hill. The first named issued his token early in the series (*W*718). It reads, THE SHIP AND STARR/IN CORNHILL 1657 T.I.E. An advertisement in the *Newes* of 14 July 1664 refers to his trade, 'Stol'n upon the first instant a flea-bitten nag about 14 hand high . . . whosoever shall give notice of him . . . to Mr. Thomas Ewster, a stationer at the Ship in Cornhill shall have 20s for his peyns'. Ewster published a collection of verse by Richard Lovelace together with a school text book, *The Plainest Directions for the True Writing of English* by Richard Hughes at his bookshop in Ivy Lane in 1649. John Young actually described himself as 'stationer' on his token. Thomas Heath, like Ewster, became involved in schoolbooks. He wrote a textbook on handwriting entitled, *Stenography or The Art of Short Writing made both plain and easy with Examples and Observations*, copies of which were sold in his stationer's shop on Ludgate Hill. Heath had previously been at Russell Street, Covent Garden, where he issued an edition of Sidney's *Arcadia* in 1651.

One of the most celebrated booksellers in London was Raphael Harford, whose farthing token (*W*1714) says, RAPHA HARFORD 58/IN LITTLE BRITAIN. A clasped book, probably a Bible, is featured on the obverse, and a heart, possibly a pun on the issuer's name, on the reverse. Harford took up his freedom in January 1627, his first premises being at the 'Guilt Bible' in Queen's Head Alley, Paternoster Row. He was there until the 1640s, publishing a series of sermons and political tracts. In 1651 he moved to the Bible and States Arms, Little Britain, where his token was issued. His son

Robert had a bookshop at the Angel, Cornhill, publishing a news sheet called *Mercurius Anglicus*, the first issue of which was printed on 20 November 1679.

Another well-known London bookseller was Robert Pawlett, whose shop in Chancery Lane bore the sign of a Bible. In fact his token reads, AT THE BIBLE 1666/IN CHANCERY LANE R.P. (*W*518). The issuer seems to have been referred to as Pawlett or Pawley. He published numerous political pamphlets in the 1660s. It would seem that he had Leicestershire connections, for a contemporary newspaper advertisement states, 'In Leicestershire between Thorp and Waltham was lost a sorrel gelding with a bald face . . . whoever shall bring tydings of him to Mr Pawley in Melton Mowbray in Leicestershire or to Mr Robert Pawley at the Bible in Chancery Lane, London, shall have 40s'. He died in 1683, leaving his business to his son George. An Edward Pawlett who issued a similar token at the 'Bible' in Grantham in 1666 may well have been a relative. The earliest provincial sale of books by auction took place at his premises on 4 August 1686.

As stated above, two of the most popular places in London for book lovers were St Paul's Churchyard and Covent Garden. William Shears started selling books at a stall at the great south door of St Paul's in 1631, when he also had premises in Little Britain and Westminster Hall. He was selling books at the Bible in St Paul's Churchyard, near the little north door this time, by 1655, but his principal store seems to have been at the Bible, Bedford Street, Covent Garden, where he traded from 1642 until his death twenty years later. His token (*W*745) appeared in 1658 with a royalist inscription FEARE GOD HONOR YE KING/IN COVENT GARDEN 58 W.S.

Some of his publications feature an engraving of his shop sign, a Bible, with his initials W.S. surrounded by the motto FEARE GOD HONOR THE KING, as on the token. Incidentally a Peterborough bookseller issued a token with an identical motto. Plomer reminds us that Shears published some of the best literature of the period, including Alexander Brome's *Cunning Lovers* (1654) and John Cleveland's *Poems* (1659). After his death his wife Margaret carried on the business for a few years.

John Harrison had a bookstall at the Holy Lamb at the East End of St Paul's Churchyard, the opposite side from the coffee house, which issued a token at the west end of the churchyard. Harrison published and sold *The Secrets of Angling* (1652) at his stall. His business was carried on by his son John, whose name appears on Robert Turner's *Microkosmus* in 1654. He apparently moved later to Whitecross Street, Cripplegate, for he issued a half penny there in 1665. An earlier farthing may also be attributed to him.

My final London token is rather an enigma. It appears in Williamson under 'uncertain tokens' (*W*12) and is described thus, THOMAS BUTLER A clasped book/PESTE HOVS 1659 T.B. The editor suggests PESTE should read POSTE, and I believe this token could well have been issued by Thomas Butler, bookseller, based at Lincoln's Inn Fields from 1656 until 59. Butler published a couple of books by William Blake.

Samuel Pepys reminds us that books could often be purchased at the new coffee houses which were springing up all over the metropolis. On 28 May 1663 he bought a book on the art of building at a coffee house in Exchange Alley. This was probably Morat's, which issued no less than four tokens during its short life from 1662 until the Fire. The diarist frequently called at the coffee house at the west end of St Paul's, after buying books from Mr Kirton, who lost his entire stock in the Fire. Many bookshops and libraries were devastated by the flames, charred paper being picked up within a fifty-mile radius. Yet printers and publishers were soon back in business, trying to make good their losses.

A growing number of booksellers were also becoming established in the provinces. Tokens provide evidence that bookshops were widespread in the 1650s and 1660s. Like their London counterparts, country booksellers considered publishing to be an essential part of their business. Campbell is critical of the performance of most booksellers here, speaking from the author's standpoint, 'the author has but a trifling sum for his trouble in compiling the copy of the ignorant part of the trade, who are sure to depreciate his performance with no other intention but to beat down his price. It is not one in ten that is judge of any more than a title page . . .'

Very few villages boasted a bookshop. Devon bookworms would travel to Exeter to the shops of Abisha Brocas and Michael Hide. Brocas sold books from 1655 until 1674 and Hide from 1663 until 1698. Both were publishers, the former circulating a broadside on the *Sun and Substance of Religion* by J. Tichell in 1655, and the latter Robert Vilvain's *Theosema Theologica* in 1663. Hide held book sales from time to time at the New Inn in Exeter, and issued catalogues. His stock was up for sale in 1698, twenty-eight years after his token appeared.

Another prominent West Country bookseller was George Treagle, who issued an early but undated token (*W*288) reading, GEORGE TREAGLE OF/ TAVNTON IN SOMMERSET G.F.T. Treagle published numerous pamphlets during the Civil War. There is no difficulty in deciding where his allegiance lay, when we note that he published in 1646, *Man's Wrath and God's Praise a thanksgiving sermon preached at Taunton 11 May for the gratias deliverance of that poor town from the strait siege*, by the vicar, George Norton. Incidentally the sermon was printed at the Marigold in Paul's Churchyard – it was still customary for most books and pamphlets to be printed in London. Taunton stood for Parliament in the Civil War, when its castle withstood a siege, under the command of the Cromwellian admiral, Robert Blake, whilst the rest of the town was occupied by royalist troops.

The Wiltshire town of Marlborough was also seized by the Cavaliers in 1642. Buildings were set on fire by the Royalists, using the local bookshops' stock in trade. John Hammond was doubly unfortunate as he suffered a further heavy loss in the Great Fire of Marlborough eleven years later. He wrote to a friend, 'I have but little saved, not above £8 worth of all my goods and books. The children are crying to go home and I tell them we have none to go to. What shall I do?' He was back in business by 1660, however, and issued a farthing token bearing the initials I.K.H. The K stands for his wife Katherine (*nee* Lawrence), whom he married in 1637. His cousin at Devizes also issued a farthing, but undated and with the device of three books, whereas the Marlborough farthing bore only one.

John Hammond of Devizes issued a token with the initials T.S.H., the S for his first wife Sarah, who died in 1670. A later John Hammond, probably his son, had bookshops in Bath and Devizes between the years 1695 and 1719.

Stephen Dagnall had a bookshop in Aylesbury, Buckinghamshire, and was a staunch supporter of the Baptist cause. His token, unusually, is of lead, reading STEPHEN DAGNALL/IN ALESBVRY 1655, and bears a book, undoubtedly a Bible. An elder of the Baptist Church, he was a man of great principle and very influential in the town, although his religious views did not endear him to all. Dagnall was one of the twelve Aylesbury Baptists sentenced to death in 1663 for refusing to conform to the Creed and meeting in 'conventicles', but who were eventually pardoned on a huge wave of public sympathy. His son, Matthias, continued his book business.

Not many bookseller's tokens appeared in the North or Midlands. John Brooks, a Coventry stationer, issued a token there in 1668. Three years later he published a pamphlet with the strange title, *A Funeral Handkerchief* by Rev. Thomas Allestree, rector of Astow. Edward Milward, a Lichfield bookseller and token issuer, sold John Brinley's *Discovery of the Imposture of Witches and Astrologers* in 1680.

In conclusion, this brief survey of booksellers' tokens would not be complete without mention of two Worcestershire pieces issued at Kidderminster and Worcester. The first reads, NEVIL SIMMONS BOOKSELR IN KIDDERMINSTER/EDWARD BVTLER MERCER 1663 THEIR HALFE PENY. Nevil Simmons, who shared his token and perhaps his premises with a mercer, also had bookshops in London. He conducted business at the Three Golden Cocks at the West End of St Paul's from 1665 until 1681. He is chiefly remembered for publishing and selling an agreed profession of faith by 'diverse ministers of Christ' in Worcestershire, which was signed by forty-three ministers and preachers, headed by the celebrated divine, Richard Baxter, 'teacher of the Church of Kidderminster'. John Jones issued his half penny at Worcester in 1666. He published books on a wide range of topics, nobably *The Carpenter's Rule Made Easy* by John Darby (1658) and *Kedarminster Stuff* about the local carpet industry (1681). Yet he also published religious pamphlets, one of the most interesting being *A Discourse in the cathedral church of Worcester on the Anniversary of His Majesty's Restoration* by Dr George Hicks of Worcester (1684). In 1697, his son John opened a bookshop in London – the Dolphin and Crown, St Paul's Churchyard.

Some booksellers, such as Matthias Dagnall of Aylesbury, bound their own books, but the majority used specialist bookbinders. Two bookbinders' tokens are known – those of Edward Rogers of Stratford-upon-Avon and William Courtney of Salisbury. We can be sure that the former would be kept busy binding innumerable volumes of Shakespeare's plays. His attractive token, which appeared in 1668, depicts the sign of the crosskeys under which he traded. Paul Morgan claims that Rogers was the first man in Stratford-upon-Avon to be plying some form of book trade. He married Maria Perkins on 20 November 1640 and a daughter, Maria, was baptised the following year. Morgan points out that a well-known branch of the Rogers family lived in the High Street, now known as Harvard Street. Edward Rogers served as a burgess on the Town Council from 1645 to 1653.

7.2 Half penny token of Edward Rogers, Bookbinder, of Stratford-upon-Avon.

CHAPTER 8

THE CLOTHING INDUSTRY

WOOLMEN AND CLOTHIERS

There were several factors underlying the success of the English cloth industry in the sixteenth and seventeenth centuries. Firstly, the pasture land was peculiarly suited to the rearing of sheep and wool was the principal clothing fabric. Secondly, Britain was enjoying a period of comparative peace, whereas her main competitors in the wool trade, Spain, Silesia and Eastern France, were involved in lengthy warfare. Thirdly, Britain's climate was suitable for sheep rearing and also for cloth manufacture, which required ample supplies of water and water power. The industry was gradually moving from the town to the country to escape restrictive guild regulations, so there was increasing scope for individual initiative. A continual influx of foreign immigrants was responsible for the introduction of new skills and processes of manufacture.

Let us look at some of the tokens which illustrate the various processes involved. First of all the wool had to be cleaned and sorted. Each fleece contains different grades or qualities of wool, thus the wool was carded or brushed in order to disentangle the locks and strengthen the strands. There are no known tokens of wool carders. In the worsted industry of East Anglia, however, the wool was combed instead of carded, the fibres being laid parallel with each other. The term 'worsted', derived from Worstead, a district in Norfolk, refers to a fabric made from yarn of combed long-staple wool. There are at least two wool combers' tokens – one issued, appropriately, in Norfolk (*W*89) and the other, rather surprisingly, in Southwark. The Norfolk farthing reads, ROBERT LEAK IN LINN/WOLL COMER R.M.L. The Southwark piece, also a farthing, was issued by Henry Miles in Kent Street and features a wool comb.

After the wool had been carded or combed it was ready for spinning. A spinning wheel or distaff and spindle was used to draw out and twist the fibres in order to form a continuous thread. The wool was converted into a thick, coarse thread known as 'roving' and spun into a fine, twisted thread called 'yarn' – hence the term 'to spin a yarn'. No tokens appear to have been issued by spinners, probably because they were too poor.

Weavers' tokens are extremely common, although few weavers describe

8.1 Half penny token of Elizabeth Rutt, Weaver, of Amersham.

themselves as such in the legend. These that do include Henry Austin of Ely in Cambridgeshire, Jeffery Budden of Wimborne, Dorset, Thomas Dan of Wye, Kent, George Smith of Mile End, London, William Alborrow of Wolverhampton, and William Syer of Ixworth, Suffolk. Only two of their tokens bear devices illustrating their craft; a shuttle appears on Henry Austin's farthing and a weaver's comb on the London piece. Shuttles appear on thirty or more other tokens in the English series. Quite a few were issued by women, such as Elizabeth Rutt of Amersham. Two men describe themselves on their tokens as worsted weavers – Nathaniel Howlett of Norwich (*W*154) and s.w., as yet unidentified, of Coventry. Williamson points out that Howlett's token is the only one to bear the Norwich city arms, and is one of only three which carry a merchant's mark. Howlett was sworn a Freeman of the city in 1660. The die sinker of the Coventry piece is obviously a little confused by the derivation of the word 'worsted', for he uses the wording WOOLSTED WEAVER on the token.

Many tokens bear the Weavers' Arms of three crosses on a chevron between three leopards' faces. One example is Thomas Balamey's half penny issued at Kidderminster, THOMAS BALAMEY IN T.M.B./KIDDERMINSTER 1667 HIS HALF PENY. Balamey was a well known 'clothier' in the town. In his will deposited in 1691, his personal estate was valued at £206, a not inconsiderable sum. His wife Margaret was the principal beneficiary.

The final processes in the manufacture of woollen cloth were fulling, shearing, dyeing and dressing. After the cloth had been woven it was fulled, that is, thickened and felted. Large shears were used by croppers or shearers to cut all long hairs off the cloth. Finally the cloth was dressed or finished to give it a fine smooth appearance, and then dyed.

A fascinating token was issued in Kendal by the Company of Shearmen in 1666 (*W*6). It reads, COMPANY OF SHEARMEN/IN KENDALL 1666. A pair of cropper's shears is featured on the obverse and a teasel brush on the reverse. The latter was used by the fuller to raise the nap of the fabric. It is interesting to note that there were twelve free guild companies in Kendal. The Mercers' Company of Kendal also issued a farthing in 1657. The full name of the Company which issued the later token was 'Shearmen – Dyers – Fullers and Websters'. Kendal was famed far and wide for its green cottons, which became known as Kendal green, referred to in Shakespeare's *Henry IV*. There are numerous records of Kendal green being used in the church. Thomas Sandes, Mayor of Kendal in 1647, dealt in this cloth. He had a token struck in 1656, which shows a teasel and wool hook on the obverse and a wool comb on the reverse.

A lone dresser's token is known, that of John Impiell of Ampthill in Bedfordshire. Yet there are several dyers' tokens known, including pieces from Derbyshire, Yorkshire, Berkshire and Devon. Almost all display the Dyers' Arms. Perhaps the most unusual is *W*98, which reads, IN COVENTRY SOVTHAM H.E.W./RUGBY LVTTERWORTH DYER 1666. Only the initials of the issuer appear due to lack of space. He obviously practised his craft far and wide!

Refugees from Spanish persecution in the Netherlands introduced into East Anglia the manufacture of the new draperies, which were marked under various headings – fustians, velours, bays and says. Two Colchester clothiers, William Moore and Jacob Vol, proudly proclaimed on their farthings that they were baymakers. The word bay refers to the reddish brown colour of the cloth.

This rapid survey of textile tokens has shown how complex the woollen industry was in the 1650s and 60s. Walker comments on the many varied forms of its organization. He claims that for the most part the producers were wage earners employed by middlemen known as master clothiers. A document of 1615 brought to our attention by Harrison and Royston gives a shrewd contemporary analysis of the clothing industry. It describes in considerable detail four types of clothier:

1. The rich clothier that buyeth his wool of the grower . . . and in the winter time hath it spun by his own spinsters and woven by his own weavers and fulled by his own tuckers and all at the lowest rate for wages.
2. The meaner clothier that seldom or never travels into the wool country to buy his wool, but borrows the most part of it at the market, and sets many poor on work and sells his cloth upon the bare thread as in Devonshire and Yorkshire and others dress it and sell it in London for ready money.
3. Clothiers that have not stock enough to bestow some in wool and some in yarn; they buy but little or no wool but do weekly buy their yarn in the markets and presently make it into cloth and sell it for ready money, and so buy yarn again, which is weekly brought into the markets by a great number of people that will not spin to the clothier for small wages, but have stock enough to set themselves on work, and do weekly buy their wool in the market by very small parcels and weekly return it in yarn.
4. Poor clothiers of the new drapery.

I am convinced that representatives of all four types issued tokens. Many clothiers describe themselves as such on their coinage, including fourteen in Oxfordshire, eight of which are from Witney. Various devices on the Witney farthings include fleece, shuttle, clothworkers arms and woolpack. Mention of a woolpack reminds me that a Derby woolpacker, Richard Knowles, had a half penny struck in 1671.

Finally, mention should be made of tokens issued by merchants of the Staple. An unidentified and undated farthing (*W*92), featuring a fleece, simply reads, THE FARTHING OF A MERCHANT/OF THE STAPLE OF ENGLAND. Four London merchants issued tokens at the Wool Staple in Westminster – William Bayle, William Frost, John Newman and Robert Williams.

HATTERS AND CAPPERS

Today hats are usually only worn on formal occasions, but in the seventeenth century hats were commonly worn by all classes. Both tall and short broad-brimmed hats, normally crowned with an ostrich feather, were in vogue in the middle of the century. The Puritans, however, disliked all form of ostentation and made sure that their headgear was sombre and featherless.

Trade tokens issued by makers of hats and caps in the seventeenth century are not nearly as common as one would expect; only about fifty are known. Almost all include a hat in their obverse design. Their scarcity is explained by the small number of specialist hatters in business. Hats were chiefly manufactured and sold by tailors, drapers, milliners and haberdashers. It is significant that there was no hatters' guild in London; hatters belonged either to the Merchant Tailors' Company or to the Haberdashers' Company.

Campbell, writing in the *London Tradesman*, describes their manufacture, 'Hats are made of the fur of hares, coneys and beavers, and some are made of wool. The materials are made into the shape of hats by paste. They are wrought originally white and afterwards dyed black. It is a very ingenious business, but a very dirty one . . .'

Of the hatters tokens issued, Yorkshire can claim the most with at least seven, no less than three of which appeared at Hull. All three are of great interest. Edward Hodgson describes himself on his half penny as MARCH^T^. A triangular design consists of six hats arranged in a 3-2-1 formation. William Robertson's farthing (*W*152) reads, WILLIAM ROBERTSON/HIGH STREET IN HVLL W.R. A hat and a rabbit are featured. Conjuring is not just a modern practice! A half penny in the name of William Robinson also shows a rabbit, but a hatter's iron has replaced the hat. It is likely that William Robertson and William Robinson were one and the same.

Another Yorkshire hatter's token (*W*222) reads, JOHN HENDERSON OF NEW/ MALTON HIS HALF PENY. A feathered hat is featured on the obverse and the Haberdashers' Arms consisting of a lion on a diagonal bar on the reverse. Haberdashers normally dealt in small accessories such as thread, ribbons, tapes and buttons. They supplied both master tailors and ordinary housewives with these items. Henderson, the Malton haberdasher, obviously included hats in his stock. Contemporary writers, as we shall see shortly, refer to 'haberdashers of hats'.

Several hatters issued tokens in other extremely rural counties – Buckinghamshire, Devonshire and Somerset. John Smallbones, a Fenny Stratford hatter, issued two tokens in 1656. The initials J.E.S., which appear on both, stand for John Smallbones and his wife Elisabeth, who died just two years later in 1658. John may well have been related to the Winslow hatter, Thomas Smallbones, who issued an undated farthing. The latter depicts a stylish broad-brimmed hat of the period. Thomas was a pillar of the established Church, acting as churchwarden in 1670. The third bell in the parish church at Winslow is inscribed THOMAS SMALLBONES C.W. 1670. There are several references to him as a haberdasher of hats in the Quarter Session Records, as standing surety for the appearance of certain Winslow citizens appearing before the Court. His status as churchwarden would obviously help in this respect.

The other Winslow issuer, William Giles, was a prominent Puritan, and a member of the Baptist meeting house at Winslow. He issued two early undated farthings and a half penny considerably later in 1666. They all depict a short, broad-brimmed hat with hat band but, as one would expect, without a feather. He and his wife Mary had a hatter's stall on the market. He was quite prosperous, owning several houses overlooking the market, including his own. Although he was a Nonconformist and faced gaol on a number of occasions, like his elder Benjamin Keach, he was obviously held in high regard by the community as he is frequently referred to as 'Mr Giles' in the records. A reference dated 5 October 1682 reads: 'Thomas Smallbones of Winslow (not the hatter – but probably related!) labourer, who pleaded guilty to stealing a turkey hen value 6d and a duck value 4d from Mr William Giles of Winslow is ordered to be whipped in the gaol until his body be bloody and then discharged paying his fees'. The part that Giles played in the Baptist Church life of Winslow is related in Chapter 14.

At least three traders specialized in hats made of felt. They described themselves as felt makers – Nathaniel Forde of Shaftsbury, Edward Owen of Coventry and Luke Burrow of Rugby. Edward Owen obviously considered himself to be well-known in the city where he conducted his business, for his token (*W*82) simply reads, IN COVENTRY 1667 E.O./FELTMAKER and features a hat decorated with feathers. Thirteen years later he would have been even better known, for he was elected Mayor.

The trade of capping was beginning to decline during the reign of Charles II due to the new male fashion of wearing hats. Before this, they had been in common use, and an Elizabethan Act required that 'all above the age of six years shall wear upon the sabbath and holy days one cap of wool, knit, thickened and dressed in England upon forfeiture of 3 and 4d'. This proved a fillip to the capping industry at Bewdley in Worcestershire and Monmouth in the early years of the seventeenth century.

Two Bewdley cappers issued tokens, Thomas Farloe and Walter Palmer (*W*11). The former issued all three of his half pennies as late as 1670. Two of them were heart-shaped. We know that Farloe was a Nonconformist, for the parish register of February 1671 refers to the re-baptism of his son Thomas, who had been baptized six years previously by a minister 'not ordained by a bishop'. Walter Palmer's token bears the simple inscription WALTER PALMER OF/BEWDLEY CAPPER 1656 W.A.P. and naturally depicts one of the issuer's caps. Cotton claims that Palmer was one of the most eminent cappers in Bewdley and had a shop in the High Street. Interestingly, it is recorded that an order of the common council of London in 1665 required all caps to be brought to Blackwell Hall except those made in Monmouth and Bewdley, implying that their standards alone did not need to be checked for quality in London. Undoubtedly large numbers of caps were made by Farloe, Palmer and others would cross Bewdley Bridge on their way to Gloucester, Bristol and London. However, hats gradually grew more popular, and a contemporary writer observes, 'cap making in Bewdley is grown so low that the great part of the ancient cap-makers in that town are wholly decayed and the rest are at this present day in a very low state'. In 1747 Campbell observed that woollen caps were obsolete and that cap makers were employed only in making velvet caps and women's hoods.

MERCERS AND DRAPERS

8.2 Mercer's farthing of Aylesbury, Bucks.

Mercers and drapers took the lion's share of the retail clothing trade in the seventeenth century, so it is not surprising to find that large number of tokens were issued by them. It is often difficult to distinguish between mercers and woollen drapers. In a study of Buckinghamshire tokens, Peter Preston Morley and I discovered that quite a number of Buckinghamshire issuers who displayed the Mercers' Arms on their tokens were variously described as mercers and drapers in local records. Thomas Hall issued an attractive heartshaped half penny (*W*49), reading, THOMAS HALL HIS HALF PENY/ MERCER OF CHESHAM, and describes himself as a mercer and shows a roll of cloth on the obverse, but the Grocers' Arms are depicted. An Ivinghoe shopkeeper who states himself to be a mercer on his farthing is described in his will as a grocer. Robert Honnor of Stony Stratford, like Thomas Hall of Chesham, shows the Grocers' Arms, but is really a mercer and linen draper. John Gaynes of Olney gives no other clue to his trade than a pair of scales on his two tokens, but is described in numerous records as mercer, draper and even baker.

Of the twenty-seven tokens issued by Buckinghamshire mercers and drapers, 9 bear the word MERCER, 2 bear the word DRAPER, 10 bear the Mercers' Arms; 3 bear the Drapers' Arms, and 2 bear the Grocers' Arms.

In the Welsh series George Boon discovered that no less than fifty-four mercers circulated tokens. More than half actually described themselves as such on their tokens. A typical example is the halfpenny of Abraham Heely of Carmarthen (*W*17), which reads, ABRAHAM HEELY OF/CARMARTHEN MERCER HIS HALF PENY. A double-headed eagle is shown as his trademark. No less than twenty-three Welsh mercers put the Mercers' Arms (a crowned virgin issuing from a bank of clouds) on their tokens. Boon suggests that the preponderance of mercers' tokens in the Welsh series is due to the fact that the term 'mercer' is very close to the Irish 'merchant'. He quotes from a definition of 1696, 'in the city the mercer deals only in silks and stuffs; in the Country Towns he trades in all sorts of Linen, Woollen, Silk and Grocery Wares'. He gives in full detail the inventory of a Caernarvon mercer Griffith Wynn, whose token (*W*28) reads, GRIFFITH WYNN I^{D}/OF CARNARVON 69. The castle is depicted on the reverse. Wynn's inventory is not just of cloth, but also haberdashery, grocery, ironmongery, tobacco, spirits and even stationery. Boon also points out that three mercers who issued tokens in the north of the principality – Ellis Jones of

Caernarvon, Henry Hughes of Conway and William Reynolds of Pwllheli – appear in local records as liable for duty on consignments of coal.

A Haverfordwest shopkeeper whose token reads, THOMAS BOWEN MERCER/ IN HAVERFORD WEST T.B. displays the Drapers' Arms rather than that of his own company. The only Welsh token to bear the Drapers' Arms is that of Mallett Bateman of Narbeth, who is described as a draper in his will. Incidentally the only woman mercer to issue a token in the Welsh series is Jane Sparke of Haverfordwest.

Campbell makes a distinction between the mercer and the woollen draper. He observes, 'the mercer is the twin brother of the woollen draper. They are as like one another as two eggs – only the woollen draper deals chiefly with the men and is the graver animal of the two – the mercer trafficks most with the ladies and has a small dash of effiminacy in his constitution'. Drapers provided the taylor with broad cloths and linings. Campbell notes, 'they not only serve the taylor here in London by retail but the country shops wholesale'. Incidentally he is scathing about the length of a draper's apprenticeship, claiming that the business could be learned in a few months rather than seven years. He has more to say about the mercer's trade, 'he deals in silks and velvet brocades and an innumerable train of expensive trifles. He must be a very polite man, dress neatly and affect a court air. Our mercer must have a good deal of the Frenchman in his manner as well as a large parcel of French goods in his shop. Nothing that is mere English goes down with our modern ladies'.

The Mercers' Company of London, whose arms are featured on about three hundred mercers' tokens, was first of the great livery companies in order of preference. It received its first charter in 1394. The first mercers were pedlars and chapmen, but soon became prosperous clothiers dealing in fine fabrics such as damask, satin and silk. As they dealt also in hats and trimmings, their trade tended to impinge upon that of the haberdashers.

Some mercers had their own coat of arms. William Clemens of Salisbury issued an undated farthing which reads, WILLIAM CLEMENS/OF SARVM MERCER W.E.C. His shield bears three six-point stars. The mercers' connection with silk is clear from a corporation record of 1674, 'William Clemens Mercer acting as surety for a loan to William Coope, Silk Weaver'. Many mercers took an active part in local politics; William Clemens was no exception, serving on the corporation and being elected mayor in 1684.

8.3 Farthing token of Edward Cope of Aylesbury, showing the Drapers' Arms.

Drapers' tokens are considerably fewer, nevertheless more than a hundred are known which bear the Drapers' Arms, such as the farthing of Edward Cope of Aylesbury (*W*11). This token reads, EDWARD COPE/OF ALEISBVRY E.D.C. Cope's wife Dorothy died in 1674. This token is extremely common. More than seventy-three exist, most in splendid condition. The Drapers' Arms consist of three clouds with sunbeams issuing, crowned with imperial crowns. This combination of cloud and triple crown has nothing to do with rugby, but is an allusion to the assumption of the Virgin Mary, Queen of Heaven.

The Drapers' Company was one of the five great companies connected with cloth. The word Draper is derived from the French 'drap', meaning cloth. The first royal charter was granted in 1364.

A Norwich draper, William Playford, issued an undated token (*W*182), reading, WILL PLAYFORD W.A.P./OF NORWICH W.A.P. He was admitted Freeman in 1645, lived in Pockthorpe and was overseer there in 1667. A Court Book of 1665 contains an interesting reference to the putting up of market stalls. 'It is ordered and agreed that ffrancis Sheppard and Will'm Playford shall have the liberty of pitchinge and buildinge of boothes in and aboute the Castle dikes and hills w^th^in the county of this Citty . . . and they are to paye for the same to the Chamberlyn of this citty thirty shillings . . .'

A few tokens specifically describe their issuers as linen drapers. Thomas Bryan, who issued a farthing in 1658 and a half penny nine years later, uses the term on both pieces (*W* Uncertain 31 and 30). His farthing reads, THOMAS BRIAN 1658 T.H.B./LININ DRAPER T.H.B. and his half penny THOMAS BRYAN LINNEN DRAPER/HIS HALFE PENNY 1667. There is no indication of where these pieces were issued. Linen drapers specialized in retailing linen cloth for curtains and covers. C.M. Rowe points out that linen underclothing was just coming into use at this time.

LACE BUYERS

The craft of lacemaking has been practised in Buckinghamshire and neighbouring counties for more than three hundred years. Tradition has it that it originated with Henry VIII's first wife, who owned several manors within the country including Steeple Claydon. There can certainly be no doubt that a good number of the Flemish weavers and lacemakers who sought refuge in England during the 1570s and 1580s settled at Olney, Newport Pagnell and Stony Stratford. The word bone-lace is mentioned as early as 1577, the term being derived from the bobbins fashioned out of bone. They were later made of wood. The term pillow lace was later used.

There was little enough profit made by the village women who actually wove the lace. It was the middlemen, known as lace-buyers, who stood to gain most from the industry. It was their job to go round the villages recruiting workers and providing fashionable patterns as well as the linen or silk they required. Linen was chiefly used, although lace makers in Amersham preferred black silk. The finished work was then collected by the buyers and either sold to lacemen in the markets or to established mercers and drapers in the towns.

The lace trade in Buckinghamshire was becoming increasingly active by the middle of the seventeenth century. It is not surprising that we find it well represented in contemporary tokens. Interestingly, no token actually advertises the craft in its legend, although several depict a strip of lace. As one would expect, no token issued by a lacemaker is known, yet no less than twelve lace-buyers issued tokens in the county of Buckinghamshire.

Eight out of the twelve conducted their business in the north of the county. Eleven of the twelve are referred to either in their wills or in other contemporary records as lace-buyers, but one, Moses Freeman of Olney, uses the term 'bone lace merchant'. No less than six are known to have been Nonconformists: John Rennals of Buckingham, William Breden of Newport Pagnell and Thomas Taylor of High Wycombe were Baptists; William Ashby of Northall and James Brierly of Olney were Quakers. Two were pillars of the Established Church: Francis Ingeby of High Wycombe and Peter Reynolds of Buckingham both served as churchwardens in their respective parishes.

It is proposed now to give a thumbnail sketch of each of the twelve lace merchants. The Amersham laceman, William Statham, issued his farthing in 1653. It is an interesting piece, bearing only the issuer's name, the date of issue and the initials W.B.S. Not much is known about Statham; he must have been married twice for his wife's initial B on the token does not correspond with his wife Mary, to whom he left his possessions in his will of 1686. She was brought before the Quarter Sessions in October 1683 on a charge of being absent from church.

The two Buckingham lace-buyers bearing the same family name, although spelt differently, pose something of an enigma. Thomas Wright reminds us that Reynolds was an old Huguenot name. John Rennals had two tokens struck, both half pence, in the same year 1668. The obverse bears his name and the date. A strip of lace is shown, surrounded by the initials I.E.R. representing the issuer John and his second wife Elitia. Rennals married his first wife, Elizabeth Goodman, at Wroughton in 1653, but she died a year later, probably in childbirth. Arnold Baines claims that he was a Baptist and one of the Signatories of the Orthodox Confession, outlined in a later chapter. Peter Reynolds, on the other hand, was no Baptist, but was churchwarden at Buckingham. His token was issued ten years before those of his namesake. His farthing also depicts a strip of lace and bears the initials P.F.R., as he married Frances Woodcoke in 1637. His burial took place on 27 December 1671.

Two lace-buyers circulated tokens in Newport Pagnell. Both were farthings; William Breden's was undated and John Burgis's dated 1668. Both depict a pair of scales. It is unusual for a farthing to appear as late as 1668. William Breden was born in 1636 and married Elizabeth Barnes when he was twenty. His wife's initial appears on the token. Her burial was recorded in 1672. Breden was a practising Baptist and was presented as a non-church attender in 1662. Little is known of John Burgis. His will dated 1682 refers to his wife Sarah, whose initial appears on the token. He was elected a petty constable and tithing man in 1677.

One of the two Quaker lace-buyers was William Ashby of Northall, a small village near Ivinghoe. He issued his half penny in 1668. The initials W.A.A. are inscribed on the piece. The second A stands for his wife Avis, whom he married at Edlesborough in 1635. The second Quaker was James Brierly of Olney, whose token like all Olney pieces features a pair of scales. It is a farthing dated 1658. Thomas Wright draws attention to a deed preserved at the Cowper Museum at Olney dated 24 February 1650, conveying property from Richard Babbington of Turvey to James Brierly, lace-buyer of Olney. The Quaker issuer died in 1669. His home was unofficially used as a Quaker meeting house in the 1660s and his garden as a burial ground. His son was able to make the family home the official meeting house of the Society of Friends in 1689.

The other Olney laceman's farthing was issued by Moses Freeman in 1668. It depicts the inevitable scales. The initial E stands for his wife Elizabeth, who outlived him by thirty-four years. Moses died in 1673, just seven years after his token had been struck. He must have been a comparatively young man, as he fathered a son in 1670. In his will he is referred to as a bone lace merchant. The only lace-buyer's token struck for Stony Stratford is an undated half penny of Thomas Forfeit, which bears a puzzling griffin on the obverse. Forfeit evidently hailed from Bradwell two miles outside the town. He married Ann Gray on 2 July 1654, and was in trouble with the authorities in 1681, being summoned before the magistrates for 'not keeping the Assize in bread and beer'. His will was published on 6 April 1684, in which he bequeathed to his wife Ann 'all that house, messuage and tenement . . . being on the west side of Stony Stratford, facing on the market hill Mr William Hartley's house on the west, and the house of Richard Collins on the east and a parcel of ground called the . . . toridge on the south' – a delightfully precise description of the site in question!

Finally, four tokens were struck for three Wycombe lace-buyers. Thomas Bates issued two farthings in 1661, the second sharing the original reverse die. Francis Ingeby issued his farthing in 1666. Only his initials F.I. appear on the token, yet he married Dorothea Weedon at Hughendon in 1666, so his token must have appeared shortly before his wedding. His father Joseph married a Frances Wheeler in 1638; it is interesting to note that her name was transmuted to her son. Ingeby acted as churchwarden in 1675 and 1677. His name appears as a juror in the Quarter Sessions records of October 1691, but I have not yet traced the date of his death. His wife Dorothea died in 1719.

Thomas Taylor, our final lace-buyer, was a prominent Baptist. His father had been an alderman of the town from 1599 until 1628, being elected mayor in 1600. The token issuer himself was elected burgess in 1657, when it was safe for Baptists to enter public life. Obviously he had to surrender his position at the Restoration. His token bears the initials T.E.T., representing Thomas and Elizabeth Taylor. He married Elizabeth Harding in 1654. The exact date of his death has not yet been ascertained. His token features a roll of lace and is extremely rare; in fact only one example is known and that is contained in the collection of the Buckinghamshire County Museum.

Lacemaking was considered a particularly appropriate occupation for the poor. Sir William Borlase's workhouse at Marlow employed twenty-four 'women children' in the making of bone lace. Lacemakers at work are depicted on a halfpenny token issued by the Overseers of the Poor at St Neot's in Huntingdonshire (*W*53), which reads, THE OVERSEERS OF THEIR HALFEPENY/THE TOWNE OF ST NEOTS. There is a second reverse die with a different reading. Two female lacemakers are sitting on chairs facing each other, with a lacemaker's pillow between them. Daines and Thompson observe that the women are sitting in front of a cylindrical pillow, which would be made of hessian or canvas stuffed firmly with straw and supported on the lace maker's lap. It is very strange to find two women apparently working on the same pillow. Daines and Thompson suggest that the device illustrates the teaching of lacemaking to the children of the poor. A hoard of about a dozen of these tokens came to light in a timber-framed cottage in Eynesbury near St Neots in June 1983.

SKINNERS

A number of skinners issued tokens, including Matthew Grace of Epping, William Tonge of Oxford, Henry Armistead and William Mancklins of York, Edward Falconer, Edward Fripp and Richard Minifie of Salisbury and two Irishmen, Richard Harris of Loughreagh in County Galway and Roger Halley of Dublin. William Tonge's farthing (*W*174) appeared in 1657. It reads, WILLIAM TONGE W.I.T./SKINER IN OXON 1657. E. Thurlow Leeds discovered a considerable amount of interesting detail of the issuer's background. He became a Freeman on 2 July 1621, and was apprenticed to Simon Hasell, skinner. He was a town councillor from 1645 to 53 and elected chamberlain in 1661. He lived in a house leased from Christ Church. In his will, proved by Tonge's widow Jane in December 1664, he left £20 to his eldest son William, but 'if my son William Tonge proves troublesome to his moather and will not submit to this my will . . . he shall have onely five shillings as the other fower children'. Incidentally, this son William also issued a token, but he was a cordwainer by trade. He is described in his apprenticeship indenture as the son of William Tongue, furrier.

Furriers and skinners were virtually synonymous. Campbell makes the slight distinction that 'the furrier deals in all manner of skins dressed with the fur on and sells hair and beaver wool to hatters'. He points out the furs were chiefly supplied from North America and Russia. C.M. Rowe writes, 'the furriers during the token issuing period formed an interesting link between the old and the new world. The wealth of the trade can be judged by the formation of the original Hudson Bay Company in 1670'.

Both the York tokens appeared in the same year, 1666. Henry Armistead's token (W380) reads, HENERY ARMISTEAD OF THE/CITTY OF YORKE SKINNER HIS HALF PENY 1666, whilst the legend on William Mancklin's half penny (*W*418) is: WILLIAM MANCKLINS 66/ARTIZAN SKINER OF YORKE HIS HALFE PENNY. The designation ARTIZAN SKINER is interesting. The reverse legend of a Dublin issuer reads ARTIZAN AND SKINNER IN SKINNER ROWE. Both the York pieces depict the Arms of the Skinners' Company. The company dates from the fourteenth century, and controlled the fur trade until the eighteenth century. At the annual ceremony of Cocks and Caps a hat is tried on by everyone until it fits the man due to be elected Master.

One of the Salisbury skinners, Edward Falconer, issued no less than four farthings. *W*177, the earliest, reads, EDWARD FAVLCONER/IN NEW SARUM 1656 E.M.F. Again the Skinners' Arms are shown. Three varieties were struck in 1657, 1658 and 1659 respectively. Although he was a burgess in 1656, the year in which his first farthing appeared, he had to wait thirty years before being elected Mayor. Although Edward Fripp's token displays the Skinners' Arms, a minute in the records of the Salisbury City Council refers to the admission of Edward Fripp, milliner. Richard Minifie, the third skinner to issue a token in Salisbury, was also described as a milliner on his admission to citizenship. His token (*W*208) reads, RICHARD MINIFIE/IN SALSBVRY R.M. Rowe tells us that Minifie's pomander box is displayed at the city museum. A pomander box was filled with sweet herbs to counteract evil smells and the plague. Another Salisbury tradesman, Charles Phelps, issued a token bearing the Skinners' Arms, but he is described as a CONFECTIONER. Rowe suggests that Phelps may have prepared mixtures used by furriers for cleaning, dressing or softening skins, rather than selling sweets.

GLOVERS

By the seventeenth century kidgloves were worn commonly by both sexes, and are illustrated on a number of tokens, including those of John Farre of Wimborne, Richard Pennell and Thomas Nutt (jointly) of Tewkesbury, Clement Darks of Winchcomb, Robert Norris of Thames Street, London, Laurence King of Oxford, and Thomas Juxson of Brecon. Glovers' tokens are not common. *W*208 is a particularly interesting Gloucestershire half penny which reads, CLE DARKS HALF PENY 1672 WINCHCOMB/REMEMBER THE POOR. The issuer probably took a particular interest in charity.

Tokens issued by two tradesmen are quite unusual. The Tewkesbury piece (*W*199) reads, RICH PENNELL & THO NVTT THEIR HALFE PENY 1668/GLOVERS IN TEWKESBURY T.N. R.P. The Arms of the Leathersellers' Company are displayed. This Company was linked to the Glovers of London in 1502, but severed its links in 1639. The Leathersellers, of course, had many tradesmen in its ranks, including cordwainers, and breeches' makers. Campbell observed, 'the glover dealt in a species of leather different from that of the shoemaker. The skins he uses are not tanned but allum'd. He makes gloves of sheep, kid and doe skins, and makes breeches of shamy (a species of sheep skin)'. (He was referring, of course, to the chamois.) Giles Houlder of Hereford and Joseph Hanson of Oxford also put the Arms of the Leathersellers' Company on their half pence. The Hereford half penny, issued in 1668, was heart-shaped. The Glovers' Arms, however, are shown on a Leominster half penny (*W*61) reading, JOHN NAISH GLOVER/IN LEOMINSTER 1669 HIS HALFE PENY/I.M.N. The original ordinances of the company, (1349) ordered that gloves and belts of false material were to be burnt in the High Street of Chepe.

8.4 Octagonal half penny of Thomas Juxson, Glover, of Brecon.

A Welsh glover issued a striking octagonal half penny at Brecon in 1669. It reads, THOMAS IVXSON GLOVER/IN BRECKNOCK 1669 HIS HALF PENY.

MILLINERS

Most modern dictionaries suggest that the milliner is a person who makes or sells women's hats. Campbell, writing in the early eighteenth century, gives the trade far greater scope. He claims that they provide women with linen apparel of every kind from a commode cover to a smock. He observes, 'the milliner furnishes them with holland, Cambrick, lawn and lace of all sorts and makes these materials into smocks, aprons, tippits, handkerchiefs, neckaties, ruffles, caps, dressed heads with as many etceteras as would reach from Charing Cross to the Exchange'. The seventeenth-century milliner similarly sold a wide range of linen ware, being akin to a linen draper. Campbell reminds us that the word 'milliner' is derived from the Italian city, Milan, noted for its decorative materials. He continues with tongue in cheek, 'they furnish everything to the ladies that can contribute to set off their beauty, increase their vanity or render them ridiculous. The milliner must be a neat needle woman in all its branches and a perfect connoisseur of dress and fashion. She imports new whims from Paris by Post and puts the ladies heads in as many different shapes in one month as there are different appearances of the moon'.

Campbell asserts that this is not a male trade and refers to needlewomen and seamstresses. It is interesting to note, however, that the majority of milliners' tokens were issued by men. Just two female milliners' tokens are known – both of Londoners, a 1668 half penny of Sarah Willcockes of Fore Street, off Cripplegate, and a half penny of Ann Kanes of St James Market dated a year earlier.

Many different trade signs appear on milliners' tokens. Sarah Willcockes, for instance, exhibited seven stars. Other signs include a unicorn, a goat browsing, a sunflower, a hand holding a dagger – none of which seem particularly suited to millinery. Much more appropriate is the sign of the looking glass used on three farthings of John Bishop of Oxford. *W*121 reads, JOHN BISHOP AT YE GVILT (*Looking Glass*)/OF OXON 1657 I.B. A variety appeared six years later. He issued a third farthing in 1669 which actually mentions a looking glass in the legend. Leeds provides some information regarding the issuer. He was appointed constable of the northeast ward in 1654, paid tax on three hearths in All Saints' parish in 1665, and served as chamberlain from 1666 until 1671. Leeds notes that although he illustrated a mirror on his first two tokens, it was not until shortly before his third token was struck that he obtained a licence as a 'Myllyner' to hang out the sign of the looking glass at his house. In 1671 Bishop was elected a bailiff and retained that office until 1687.

Another London milliner, Nicolas Fitzjeffery, issued a farthing in 1656 from his Fleet Street premises and an undated half penny (*W*2974) later on when he moved to a shop in the Strand. His half penny reads NICHOLAS FITZIEOFFRY/IN YE STRAND MILLINER HIS HALFE PENY. An Abingdon milliner used four devices to make his token distinctive – an open pair of scissors and a pair of pince-nez spectacles on the obverse and a fish hook and a double-sided comb on the reverse. One wonders why a fish hook should be included. Most milliners' tokens include the actual name of the trade in the legend.

It is not often that the word 'shop' appeared on a token. A London milliner's farthing (*W*1798) reads, GEORGE PRIST 1663 A SEMSTRS SHOP/IN LONG AKER G.D.P. He obviously had seamstresses working for him. Campbell thought them to be very susceptible to flattery and consequently vulnerable. He claims that most seamstresses finish up as streetwalkers! By curious coincidence another Long Acre clothiers' token (*W*1797) uses the word shop in its legend, ISACK POSTE YE WOSTED I.E.P/SHOP IN LONG AKER I.E.P.

COAT MAKERS AND GIRDLERS

One or two specialist coat makers issued tokens in London. James Gripp circulated a half penny in Coleman Street (*W*710), IAMES GRIPP LIVEING I.G./IN COLEMAN STREET 1666 A COATMAKER I.E.G. Joseph Brocke describes himself as a coat seller on his half penny issued at Ratcliffe Cross (*W*2325) JOSEPH BROCKE COATE I.B./SELER NEAR RATCLIF CROS HIS HALFE PENNY. A man's coat is featured between the initials on the obverse of both half pence. It is interesting to note that James Gripp left out his wife's initial on the obverse in order to show the coat. Her initial is inserted on the reverse.

Some craftsmen specialized in making belts for clothing. Campbell comments, 'the girdler is a tradesman employed in making belts and other accoutrements for the army etc, but is of very little importance at present'. York was an important military base in the seventeenth century. This may account for the fact that two girdlers' tokens were struck in the city, both half pennies. The earlier (*W*439) reads, JOHN WALLER IN YORKE GIRDLER/1669 and the later (*W*398), WILL GARNETT HIS HALF PENY/GIRDLER OF YORK 1670. Waller's piece shows a carnation on the reverse, probably a family emblem, whilst Garnett depicts a bull's head on the obverse and the Girdlers' Arms on the reverse.

PIECE BROKERS AND SACK SELLERS

Three London piece brokers issued tokens. Two of them described themselves merely as brokers – Edward Geery in St Clement's Churchyard (*W*2457) and Peter Alsop in St Martin's Lane (*W*2633). Edward Geery's token reads, EDWARY GEERY IN ST CLEMENTS E.L.G./CHVRCHYARD BROKER 1667 HIS HALFE PENNY. Peter Alsop's half penny was undated. The third token was issued by James Cole in Grays Inn Lane (*W*1244). He uses the full term, 'piece broker', to decribe his trade, IAMES COLE IN GRAISE HIS HALFE PENY/INNE LANE PEICE BROKER I.K.C. 'Piecing' was the term used for patching or making up a garment by adding pieces. The word is derived from an old Gallic word 'pece'.

Campbell is very scathing about the piece-broker's business. He writes, 'the piece broker is a shopkeeper very much suspected of corrupting the taylor's honesty. He buys from the honest taylor shreds and remnants of all materials that go through his hands and sells them again to such as want them for mending. I do not find that they take apprentices or are regularly bred. They are generally decayed taylors or some cunning men who have crept into the secrets of the trade'.

John Hill issued two interesting tokens at Melton in Suffolk – an undated farthing and a half penny dated 1668 (*W*42 and 41). Both depict a sailing vessel on the obverse. The farthing reads, JOHN HILL IN MELTON/AT THE SACKE SHOP I.E.H. The later half penny reads, JOHN HILL IN MILTON/IN SVFFOLKE 1668 HIS HALF PENY. Sacks were the female counterpart of slops, consisting of a full, loose jacket or a loose dress.

THE SLOP SHOP

When we talk about someone being sloppily dressed, we mean that he is wearing sailors' clothing. Slop shops were to be found all over seventeenth-century London. Campbell writes, 'the slop shop sells all kinds of shirts, jackets, trouzers, and other wearing apparel belonging to sailors' ready made'.

A slopseller's token (*W*2362) is known for Ratcliff Highway in London reading, MARY RVSSELL 1669 HER HALF PENY/SLOPSELLER IN RATCLIF. A piece of loose clothing is featured on the reverse.

BODICE AND STAYMAKERS

One of the more specialized clothing trades in the seventeenth and eighteenth centuries was the making of bodices, corsets and stays. Campbell wryly remarks, 'The staymaker is employed in making jumps and bodices for the ladies. He ought to be a very polite tradesman as he approaches the ladies so nearly. He is obliged to inviolable secrecy in many instances where he is obliged to mend a crooked shape . . . Her shape she owes to steel and whale bone . . . I am surprised that ladies have not found a way to employ women staymakers rather than trust our sex with what should be kept as inviolable as free masonry. The work is too hard for women'. Staymakers' tokens are extremely scarce. *W*83 was struck in Essex and reads MOSES LOVE SLAY/MAKER OF COGGSHALL M.L. A shuttle appears on the obverse.

Several bodice makers' tokens are known, including those of James Leach and the unidentified W.S., both of London, and Richard Fowler of Henley on Thames. The latter issued his half penny in 1668 with a corset on the reverse, and also circulated tokens at Faringdon in Berkshire – two farthings bearing the Grocers' Arms and two heart-shaped half pence, one dated 1669 and the other undated. These half pence illustrate the issuer's trade, showing a pair of stays. Milne draws our attention to the will of a Richard Fowler, bodice maker of Caversham, dated 1677, who left property to relatives at Bedwyn in Wiltshire. He suggests that Fowler may have retired from Henley to Caversham. He was certainly making bodices in 1662 and 1665, for he paid tax on three hearths during those years.

The two London bodice makers' tokens were issued in the Barbican and Holywell Street off the Strand. *W*118 reads, JAMES LEECH BODIS MAKEER/IN BARBICAN. The reverse design illustrates Cupid holding a dart. The second London token (*W*1495), reads, AT THE BODY MAKER W.S./IN HOLYWELL STRET. The reverse depicts a pair of stays or a bodice. Campbell is at pains to point out that bodices were reinforced with pack thread rather than whale bone.

8.5 Heart-shaped half penny of Richard Fowler, staymaker of Faringdon, Berks.

UPHOLSTERERS

A Wiltshire upholsterer issued a farthing (*W*220), reading, WILL SACKLER 1666/VPHOLSTER IN SARVM W.M.S. The reverse shows the arms of the Upholsterers' Company: three pavilion tents, with a chevron supporting three roses. Its members were sometimes called upholders, sometimes upholsters as on the token. Melling tells us that in 1474 a petition was granted by the Lord Mayor and Aldermen to give the Upholders the right of search and control over feather beds, pillows, mattresses and cushions. Members originally dealt in frippery – we would say 'jumble'. Some were even admitted to the Skinners Company as dealers in secondhand furs. The word Upholster in the seventeenth and eighteenth centuries came to mean a general furniture dealer. This is confirmed by Campbell's observations in 1747, 'I have just finished my house and must now think of furnishing it with fashionable furniture. The upholder is chief agent in this case. This tradesman's genius must be universal in every branch of furniture, though his proper craft is to fit up beds, window curtains, hangings and to cover chairs that have stuffed bottoms. He employs journeymen in his own proper calling, cabinet makers, glass grinders, looking-glass frame carvers, the woollen draper, the mercer, the linen draper, several species of smiths and a vast many other tradesmen'.

An upholsterer's half penny was issued in Oxfordshire by Philip Wisdome (*W*72). There is no indication of his trade, however, in the lengend, PHILLIPP WISDOME HIS HALF PENY 1670/OF CHIPING NORTON P.K.W. Milne provides evidence that he was an upholsterer from court records, and also identifies the initial of his wife Katherine, who died at the ripe old age of eighty in 1715, just six years after her husband's decease.

ROPE AND THREAD MAKERS

Although Bridport had a virtual monopoly of the rope-making industry by the beginning of the seventeenth century, craftsmen did operate in other coastal areas where the climate was suitable for the growth of hemp and flax. They produced not only rope but twine, string, thread, nets, sails and tarpaulin. A Boston rope maker issued a token in 1666 (*W*30) reading,

THOMAS NICHOLSON ROPE/MAKER OF BOSTON 1666 T.M.N. A coil of rope is featured on the obverse. Campbell describes the rope maker's craft as follows, 'the rope maker is the first person to be employed after the ship is launched. Rope yarn is spun in a long walk. The spinner fastens one end of the threads to two spindles of a wheel. The hemp is turned round the middle and he retires backward from the wheel, spinning both his threads as he goes till he reaches the farther end of the walk. The wheel is turned by another hand. When the thread are all spun they are twisted together and smeared over with tar'.

An Olney ropemaker, Robert Aspray, issued two tokens in 1662. There is no indication of his trade on the tokens, as the device he uses is a pair of scales, which appears on all the Olney pieces irrespective of the issuer's craft. The initials R.M.A. stand for the issuer and his wife Mary. Manton and Hollis claim that these initials, together with the date 1687, were still to be seen on a house in Olney in 1933. The churchwardens' accounts contain numerous references to Robert Aspray, including the following:

1663–7	To Robert Aspray in part for Belropes	18	4
	To Robert Aspray for belropes when he destrained	10	8
1675–7	Pd to Robert Aspray for nails used about the bells and seals . .	4	6

Two thread makers issued tokens in Southwark (*W*8 and *W*248). The first reads, CALEB BIGG THREAD/MAKER IN SOVTHWERK C.E.B. A raven appears on the obverse, perhaps a family emblem. The second token reads, JAMES BVRLY THREAD/MAKER HORSLY DOWN I.D.B. A hank of thread is appropriately featured on the obverse.

CHAPTER 9

MINES AND MILLS

COAL MINES

The seventeenth century witnessed an acceleration in coal mining activity. Although coal or coke was not yet used in the smelting of iron, it was increasingly used in many manufacturing processes, and had become the regular domestic fuel of London. John Nef compiled the following table, which illustrates an astonishing development in the coal mining industry from 1550 to 1660.

	1550	1680
Durham and Northumberland	65,000	1,225,000
Scotland	40,000	475,000
Wales	20,000	200,000
Midlands	65,000	850,000
Cumberland	6,000	100,000
Somerset	10,000	100,000
Forest of Dean	3,000	25,000
Devon and Ireland	1,000	7,000

Coal was fast becoming one of the greatest sources of national wealth. The origins of the present National Union of Mineworkers can be traced to the harsh conditions of damp, dangerous, unlit, unventilated mines, which fostered a spirit of comradeship in the mid-seventeenth century. In 1662, two thousand miners from the Durham and Northumberland coalfield petitioned Charles II to improve their conditions of work, with particular regard to ventilation, albeit unsuccessfully. The sailors of the Tyne coal barges added their voices to the protest.

This enormous surge forward in the coal industry during the middle of the seventeenth century is not reflected in the number of trade tokens issued by colliery owners. Only three are known – a half penny at Broughton coal pits in Cumberland (*W1*), a half penny at High Peak Coal Mines in Derbyshire, and a third half penny at Middleton Coal Pit in Yorkshire. The Cumberland token is an interesting octagonal shape, reading, JOHN LAMPLVGH/ BROVGHTON COAL PITTS HIS HALF PENY. A castle is depicted on the obverse. Unfortunately no records relating to Broughton in the seventeenth century have been traced, but the token can be dated by its style to 1665–70.

9.1 Half penny token of the High Peak coalmine, Derbyshire.

The Derbyshire token (*W*105) reads, HIGH PEAKE COLE MINES/IN DARDYSHEIRE. The arms of the ancient family of Shallcross of Shallcross are featured on the obverse. Papworth describes the Shallcross armorial thus: 'Gules, a saltire between four anulets or, Shalcross, Shalcross Co. Derby'. He mentions that six descents are given in the visitation of 1611, that the last male heir of the family died in 1733 and that the youngest female heiress died unmarried in 1776.

George Williamson, relying on the notes of Llewellyn Jewitt, a local man of Derby, suggested that the token was probably issued by a Richard Shallcross, a member of an ancient family. He noted that his father John Shallcross was Sheriff of Derby in 1638 and that his son John filled the same office in 1668. The coal fields, especially in the North and Midlands, had been predominantly ecclesiastical property but after the Henrician dissolution of the Monasteries, they had passed into the hands of landowning families. The Shallcross crest, occupying the field of the reverse of the token, is a martlet carrying a cross in its beak.

My attention has been drawn to a couple of volumes of Shallcross Pedigrees edited by Rev. W.H. Shawcross, alias Shallcross, published in 1846 and 1908. Included in these pedigrees is an entry for Richard Shallcross, who was baptised at Taxall on 1 February 1632. He was called to the Bar in 1660 and was Surveyor of the North Duchy of Lancaster and Bailiff of the High Peak. He became a Justice of the Peace in 1675 and was buried at Taxall on 21 March 1676, his will being proved in the same year. He was a very wealthy man, and left large amounts of money to his daughters, and all his silver plate to his kinswoman Mrs Elizabeth Down. His will also mentions that he assigned his office of Surveyor of the North Duchy of Lancaster for the benefit of his son until he reached the age of majority. He similarly assigned his office of Bailiff of the High Peak. Unfortunately there are no references to the source of the family's wealth in the volumes and none in particular to the High Peak coalmines. There is no doubt in my mind, however, that the colliery was owned by this Richard Shallcross during the 1660s and 70s. The style of the undated token indicates a date between 1664 and 72.

The third colliery half penny token (*W*235) reads, FRANCIS CONYERS OF MIDLTON IN YORKESHIRE HIS HALF PENY 1669/FOR THE USE OF YE COLE PITS. A falcon appears on the reverse, probably a family emblem. It is interesting that this token bears the name of the county, as does the Derbyshire half penny.

This is unusual as the small flan of a token does not lend itself to lengthy legends. Thus we see county pride being exhibited by both issuers.

Very little seems to be known about the Middleton mines in the seventeenth century. John Batty's *History of Rothwell* observes, 'Middleton from all evidence, is the oldest worked coal field in the parish. As the registers give the occupation of 'colier' in 1639, it may be naturally inferred that the Leghe family, the ancient proprietors of the Middleton estate, were the first to open up the pits. It was not until the latter part of the seventeenth century that the Brandlings became connected with it. Ralph Brandling of Felling, Co. Durham (born 1662) acquired the estate through marriage with Anne, daughter and heiress of John Leghe of Middleton'.

Batty does not mention Francis Conyers, the issuer of the token. A recent publication of the Middleton Historical Society states that a Francis Conyers was living in William Gascoign's old house, and that he had a share in the Middleton mines. The coal pits at Middleton were quite expensive and it is conceivable that the ownership was shared. It is likely that Conyers owned several – hence the issue of his own tokens. The Historical Society's pamphlet also refers to a small ravine in the area, known locally as Conyer's Spring.

A few London coal dealers had tokens struck. Two are dated 1666, a third 1668, whilst a number are undated. A typical one (*W*1336) reads, NATHANIELL ROBINS AT THE SEA COALE SELLER 1666/HAY MARKET IN PICKADILLA HIS HALFE PENNY 1666. The description 'sea coale seller' indicates that the coal derived from the Tyneside coalfield. Another sea coal seller issued a farthing token in Green's Rent. His name unfortunately does not appear on the piece, which bears his initials W.A. and that of his wife N. These initials have yet to be identified.

WOODMONGERS

Wood was still the chief domestic fuel in town and country in the seventeenth century. In rural areas they could collect their own firewood; in London and Southwark the woodmongers did a useful trade. Campbell asserts that woodmongers cannot really claim to be tradesmen as they do not take apprentices. He writes, 'their business is to deal in fuel, for the use of Bakers and private families'.

Several London woodmongers issued tokens, including Robert Chapman of Bridewell Dock, Robert Austin of Broken Wharf, Thames Street, Dan Burry of Cousin Lane, Richard Fisher of Millbank, Westminster and two from Whitefriars: John Clay and Govin Govldegay. The majority of their tokens bear the Woodmongers' Arms. Rob Austin's token bears a bundle of wood between two stars (*W*437). It reads, ROB AVSTIN WOODM/AT BROKEN WHORFE. Richard Fisher's depicts a crooked billet, whilst that of John Clay shows a horse and cart, the woodseller's means of transport.

Two woodmongers issued tokens in Westminster, John Hudson and William Longe. The former put his address on his token – Brewer's Yard, in King Street. The latter gives no indication of his location in Westminster (*W*255), WILLIAM LONGE WOOD/MVNGER WESTMINSTER W.I.L. 1659. He also issued a token in Southwark (*W*61) reading, WILLIAM LONGE/MOVNGER SOVTHWARKE W.I.L.

PAPER MANUFACTURE

Paper making was introduced into this country from the continent in the late fifteenth century. Several European countries, including Spain, Italy, France, Germany and Holland, had been manufacturing paper for some considerable time. One cannot be certain of the exact date and site of the first English paper mill. A.H. Shorter puts in a well-argued claim for Sele Mill near Hertford, which was operating in the 1490s under John Tate. He reminds us that Tate's paper was used for a book published in 1495. Sele Mill was situated on the Beane, a tributary of the Lea. The earliest Kent paper mill was at Dartford, being established in 1588 and continuing production until 1721. Spilman, the most celebrated miller there, obtained patents for the sole manufacture of white writing paper. He also possessed a monopoly of the collection of rags within the kingdom. Shortage of rags was a constant source of anxiety for paper millers. Linen rags were required for the manufacture of high quality paper, whilst coarse rags were used in brown paper.

Shorter outlines the main processes of manufacture in a water-driven mill, using for illustration a composite drawing of a German mill dated 1662, 'the rotted rags were sorted and washed and allowed to ferment – then placed in water-laden troughs called mortars and were smashed into pulp by iron-tipped wooden steam hammers. They were lifted and dropped by means of the camels fitted to the main shaft which was worked by water power developed by an undershot wheel. The stuff resulting from this beating process was placed with water in a vat and kept luke-warm. It was agitated by means of a pole which became a mechanical paddle called a hog by the end of the century. From the pulp the vat-man formed a sheet of paper by inserting a wire-meshed mould of the required size and giving it a series of shakes, so drawing off the water and causing the fibres of the pulp to intertwine and form a matter layer on the surface of the mould. As each sheet of paper was formed, it was taken off the wooden felt to form a pile. When complete (6 quires or 144 sheets) it was put in the screw lever press and as much water as possible squeezed out. After being air-dried on lines covered with horse-hair to prevent staining, the sheets were pressed, dried and finished'.

An inventory of 1703 lists the equipment of a typical 1 vat paper mill – 2 presses, 1 furnace, 1 large cistern, 3 chests, 48 tables, 1 cog wheel, 1 great water wheel, 15 hammer mortars, 4 4-hammer mortars, 1 pit mortar, felts, basins, strainers.

During the first half of the seventeenth century the number of paper mills increased dramatically, especially in Buckinghamshire. No less than twelve are listed by Shorter, including one at Wooburn. Only three are listed for Kent, but all three produced high quality white paper. Wooburn Mill (Bucks) is particularly interesting as it issued a half penny token, the only one known to be struck for a paper mill. The token reads, JONATHAN KINGHAM IN / WOBVRN MIL HIS HALF PENY. A water wheel of four spokes is depicted on the obverse whilst the reverse displays a mill rind. The miller's initials J.K. are placed each side of the rind. The style of the token indicates that it was struck in the middle or late 1660s. Wooburn Mill originated as a fulling mill, but had been converted to corn milling and paper making. Wooburn produced both corn and paper simultaneously during the period that its half penny

9.2 Half penny token of Jonathan Kingham, Paper miller, of Wooburn, Bucks.

circulated. The Wycombe parish rate books for 1670 contain two entries, 'John Kingham for Treadway' and 'Him for the mill', indicating that he was responsible for both sections of the mill complex. L.J. Ashford observes that several mills in the Wycombe area had a similar shared function. The mills from Wycombe to Loudwater concentrated on the manufacture of white paper, whilst those on the lower stretch of the river, such as Wooburn, made boards. The Wye valley of Buckinghamshire was particularly suitable for producing pulp from rag, as the river did not contain impurities which would discolour the paper.

Jonathan Kingham, the issuer of the token, was a Quaker. A meeting took place on 6 March 1679 at Thomas Ellwood's house in Beaconsfield. There present were informed that, 'Mary Kingham, one of ye daughters of Jonathan Kingham, late of Woburn, deceased, hath walked disorderly and entertained a man of ye world, being herself before engaged to another man'. The meeting decided to ask Jeremiah Stevens 'to visit ye said Mary, inquire into ye matter, reprove, exhort and admonish her, as he should find cause and give an account of ye business at ye next meeting'. Unfortunately his report has not been traced.

It has been estimated that there were approximately 116 paper mills in the British Isles by 1690, including 17 in Buckinghamshire and 14 in Kent. These two counties head the list because of the purity of the rivers Wye, Darent and Len respectively. Kentish mills were particularly fortunate in their water supply. William Gill, miller at Turkey Mill, Maidstone, commented in 1719 that he had brought into use some fine, clear water from two or three springs which had arisen in a field adjoining the mill and that this had enabled him to make his paper 'fine and white'. The eighteenth century witnessed a number of minor technical changes in the paper industry, but paper continued to be handmade.

CHAPTER 10

TOWN PIECES FOR YE POOR

A considerable number of municipal authorities viewed with interest and not a little dismay the proliferation of private traders' tokens in the 1650s and 60s. The system of tokens appealed, but not the fact that the profits disappeared into private hands. Town councils, mindful of the ever-increasing number of unemployed, handicapped, and homeless people and their families, who were becoming an intolerable burden on the poor rate, realized that if they employed a token system, the profits would, to some extent, offset this. It is significant that a large number of farthings and half penny tokens issued by town councils and officials refer to the plight of the poor. Four Dorset tokens, for instance, appearing at Blandford, Sherborne, Weymouth and Wimborne in the same year, 1669, all state specifically that they are 'for the use of ye poore'. A Lincolnshire token proclaims itself to be THE POORE OF SPALDINGS HALF PENNY 1667. At Grantham in the same county an entry in the town records for 20 December 1667 reads, 'whereas Mr Alderman this day acquainted the court that several corporations have set forth brass half pence with the town's arms on them for the benefit of the poor of the said towns and that it might be very advantageous to the corporation to do likewise . . . where upon the same court orders that the present Chamberlain do send to London for brass half pence with the chequer on the one side and Grantham and the year of Our Lord on the other side. And to be written about the rim "To be exchanged by the Overseers of the Poor"'. An octagonal half penny of Lichfield (*W*27) bears the rhyme, TO SUPPLY THE POORES NEED/IS CHARITY INDEED.

Stuart society was extremely concerned about the growing problems of urban and rural poverty. The main cause was the increase in unemployment consequent upon the break-up of the old manorial system and its replacement by enclosure. The wars at the end of the sixteenth century had had a dislocating effect on the national economy. An old nursery rhyme relates, 'the beggars are coming to town'. Meanwhile the traditional sources of relief for indigence had disappeared; Henry VIII had dissolved the monasteries and Somerset had seized the charitable funds of the guilds. Under Henry VIII, Edward VI and Mary, attempts had been made to remedy this state of affairs and especially to deal with vagabondage, but to little effect. It was left to Elizabeth's government, and to William Cecil in particular, to tackle the problems of unemployment and poverty.

The celebrated Elizabethan Poor Law of 1601 confirmed the principle that the state was responsible for the relief of the poor, a role which it had taken over from the medieval church. For the first time an attempt was made to distinguish between men who were honestly unemployed, the 'deserving poor' and men who were vagrants by choice, 'the sturdy beggar'. Different classes of poor were to receive treatment appropriate to their particular needs. The aged and sick, for instance, were to be relieved either in their own houses or provided with almshouses or hospital treatment. Pauper children were to be boarded out and later apprenticed to a trade. Vagrants were to be sent to prison or a house of correction, and the genuine unemployed were to be given employment in 'work houses'.

The Poor Law gave the Justices of the Peace powers to impose a compulsory poor rate. An important new parish official appeared on the scene known as 'overseer of the poor'. He was responsible with the clergy for the collection of the poor rate and for the provision and supervision of the work done by the able-bodied poor. It was customary for the two church wardens and four other persons nominated by the local bench of magistrates to serve as overseers in each parish. The statute of 1601 commanded the overseers to have a 'convenient stock of flax, hemp, wool, thread, and other stuff to set the poor to work'.

Tokens were issued by overseers of the poor in no less than twelve towns. Most of them are half pence, appearing late in the series, chiefly in the eastern counties of Bedfordshire, Lincolnshire, Huntingdonshire and Northamptonshire. A Peterborough octagonal half penny of 1666 reads, THE OVERSEERS HALF PENY OF PETERBROUGH 1666 (in five lines). The arms of the town are featured on the reverse (*W*104). The minutes of the town book for 11 February 1668 give the reasons for issue, 'It is ordered that the Town Baleifs of Peterburgh doe lay out of ye towne money in his hands the sum of ten pounds for ye stampg and coynage of the publique half penny with ye towne armes and the impressement thereof to and fore the putting out of poor and fatherless children as apprentices or other charitable uses'.

Undoubtedly the profits from this particular issue were to help the overseers in their task of providing for needy orphans. The corporation's officers were evidently becoming worried about the tokens that were being used by tradesmen for their own advantage and thus to the disadvantage of the poor, as on 4 May 1670 the town book records, 'And there upon they gave and ordered that no farthings or ½ pence of any person or persons shall pass current longer than the Whitsuntide next'. Significantly, no tradesmen's tokens were struck at Peterborough bearing a date later than 1669. Six days later it is ordered 'that Mr Mortimore doe forthwith pay into ye hands of Mr Gibbon ye sum of twenty pounds who is desired with all speed to send ye some to London to be layd out in a stamp of Towne half pence wh. does have ye inscription of Peterburgh half pence to be changed by ye Towne Bayliffe'.

This new issue was also octagonal and thus easily distinguishable from the private tradesmen's tokens being recalled, which were all round. The word 'bailiff' was simply an alternative title for mayor. Perhaps it was thought that the new tokens would carry more weight if issued in the name of the chief citizen rather than by mere overseers.

A charming heart-shaped token issued at Biggleswade in Bedfordshire depicts a crippled woman leaning on a crutch on the obverse and a spinning

10.1 Overseer's token of Peterborough.

wheel on the reverse (*W*21). It reads, A BIGILSWORTH HALF PENY/CHANGD BY THE OVERSEERS. The cripple is a reminder that poor relief included provision for the disabled. A cripple is also featured on Andover town farthings. An early one (*W*11) reads, REMEMBER THE POORE/ANDEVER 1658. A cripple is shown on both faces, as also on a later farthing of 1666. The spinning wheel on the reverse of the Biggleswade half penny symbolizes the work that was provided for the able-bodied poor. A number of overseers' tokens are of unusual shape; a Louth halfpenny of 1671 was in the shape of a lozenge. Poor womenfolk are featured on a couple of overseers' tokens of Huntingdonshire. A St Neots half penny depicts two women making lace. At neighbouring St Ives two washerwomen are shown at their tub on a farthing and a half penny both dated 1669, with the words POOR WOMEN. The King's Cliffe half penny of neighbouring Northamptonshire announces on its reverse that it may be CHAINGED BY YE OVERSEERS.

Sometimes town tokens were issued in the name of an entire corporation, more frequently under a single named official such as the mayor, bailiff or chamberlain. Corporation tokens were issued at Blandford, Henley on Thames, Romsey, Rye and Southampton (*W*184). The Blandford farthing (*W*9) reads, THE BURROUGH OF BLANDFORD THEIRE CORPORATION/FARTHING FOR THE VSE OF Y^{E} POORE 1669. The parish register dated 1673 states, 'the corporation farthings was returned in to the value of £2 18s and placed in the council house'. A royal proclamation had ordered the recall of all tokens in 1672. The £2 18s worth of farthings recalled at Blandford is equivalent to 2,784 farthings. The Romsey corporation piece reads, SET FORTH BY THE CORPORATION OF YE TOWNE OF ROMSEY/$\frac{1}{2}$ TOKENS FOR Y^{E} BENEFIT OF Y^{E} POOR^{E} 1669. The word 'token' rarely appears on a token! These tokens state specifically that they are intended for use by the poor, not just to raise funds for them. I feel sure that some would be given out as alms by the overseers to needy people. The main purpose of most town tokens was to provide an essential service for their poorer residents, both as charity and small change. A Tamworth chamberlain's piece confirms this by stating on the reverse, FOR CHANGE AND CHARITY.

The corporation records of Bewdley in Worcestershire refer to their bridge wardens' half pence as being 'found convenient for more ready change of money and useful in point of trade and commerce especially to the poorer sort of the same borough'. Although the bridge wardens were originally appointed to administer traffic and tolls, by the seventeenth century they had assumed the role of town chamberlain, being responsible for all accounts.

Probably the massive issues of Bristol town pieces were chiefly intended to

10.2 Overseer's token of King's Cliffe, Northants.

facilitate trade and shopping for all classes of society, yet it would be the poor who would benefit most. George Boon reminds us, 'established folk still bought commodities in quantity. A system of 20,000 tokens might have been obtained for that sum'.

A farthing and a half penny were issued at Wotton under Edge in Gloucestershire, both in 1669. The wording on the former is, THIS FARTHING WILL BE OWNED In Wotton vnder edge/BY THE MAIOR AND ALDERMEN 1669. A woolpack appears on the reverse as a symbol of local trade. The half penny is similar, but the mayor's name, William Brown, is added. The fact that these pieces were always redeemable at the Town Hall would have been a comfort to the poorer citizens. In Somerset the chief municipal officer was dubbed portreeve. Tokens were issued by the portreeves of Chard, Langport, and Yeovil. The Chard farthing (*W*82) reads, THE BVRROUGH OF CHARD MADE/BY Y^{E} PORTRIFF FOR Y^{E} POORE C.B. 1669. John Mitchell, the portreeve of Langport, had his initials put on his town token. In other towns the first officer was termed bailiff. Bailiff's tokens appeared at Peterborough, as we have seen, and Ilchester.

The treasurer of a council was usually termed chamberlain. We have already noted a chamberlain's token of Tamworth. Others circulated at Bridgnorth, Nottingham and Northampton. Preston Morley and Pegg draw attention to the minutes of the Common Council of Nottingham for 21 October 1669, 'it is this day ordered that Master Ralph Edge and Master John Parker shall provide halfe pence, stampt with the Armes of the Corporacion, to the value of 15 1'. Ralph Edge was town clerk. The chamberlains in 1669, when their token appeared, were Arthur Richards and Henry Twells.

Tokens were issued by feoffees (sidesmen of a parish church) at Moreton Hampstead in Devon (*W*208) and at Oundle. They may well have had oversight of the poor as part of their duties. The Devon piece reads, YE 8 MEN & FEEFEES OF MORTON 1670/ FOR Y^{e} BENEFIT OF Y^{e} POOR. The parish church depicted on the reverse is a reminder that the church still had a part to play in poor law administration. A talbot is featured on the obverse of the Oundle token. Wells suggests that its inclusion is a reminder that the Talbot Inn, erected in 1626, was used as a meeting place by the feoffees and overseers. The feoffees' accounts for 1672 contain an entry, 'paid at the Talbott on the account day 07 06'.

10.3 Chamberlain's token of Northampton.

10.4 Feofees' token of Oundle, Northants.

Several important varieties of town tokens for the poor were issued at Hereford and Taunton. The Hereford farthings and half pence appeared in 1662 and 1663, in the name of Henry Jones, sword bearer. The Taunton farthings were issued by the constables of the town. Constables had a distinctive role to play in the administration of poor law – ensuring that thieves and vagabonds were sent back to their place of birth, and not permitted to be a burden on the poor rate of any other town. G.M. Trevelyan affirms that constables were neither trained nor professional, 'the magistrates could only afford the part time service of a farmer constable who spent his day in agriculture and left the plough to lead the hue and cry as far as the parish bounds'.

CHAPTER 11

MEDICAL CARE

APOTHECARIES

Visits to a qualified doctor or physician in the seventeenth century were the prerogative of the rich. The vast majority of ordinary folk consulted the apothecary, who was the mainstay of medical practice. Campbell, writing in 1747, claimed the apothecary to be superior to the chemist. He comments, 'at first he must know that rhubarb is not Jesuit's bark, that oil is not salt, and that vinegar is not spirit. He must be able to call all the army of poisons by their proper heathenish names, and to pound them, boil them, and mix them into their proper companies such as pills, bolus's syrup and emulsions. He must understand the mysterious character of an unintelligible doctor's scrawl . . . this is a mere apothecary, a creature that requires very little brains; he wants only a strong memory to retain a number of cramp words such as he is daily conversant with'.

He continues, 'there is no branch of business in which a man requires less money to set him up than this very profitable trade. Ten or twenty pounds judiciously applied will buy gallipots and counters and as many drugs to fill them as might poison the whole island. His profits are inconceivable; 500 per cent is the least he receives. The greatest part of his outlay is in viols, small boxes and cut paper, and these are often worth ten times what they contain. But the army of apothecaries are no sooner equipped with a shop than they commence Doctor. They prescribe in all common cases, and only call in the doctor to be present at the death of the game which they have run down, or to justify by his recipes their enormous bills'.

The apothecaries were originally affiliated to the Society of Grocers on account of their common dealing in medicinal herbs. They gained increased prestige when they broke away from the grocers in 1617 and formed their own company. The Charter of James I referred to 'empericks and unskillfull and ignorant men who compound many unwholesome, hurtful, deceitful, corrupt and dangerous medicines . . . to the abuse and scandal of the learned physicians and of the Apothecaries of our City of London, being educated and expert . . . but also to the great peril and daily hazard of the lives of our subjects'.

The grocers were understandably annoyed at being referred to as 'unskillfull and ignorant men' and petitioned the king to revoke the charter. James supported the apothecaries, stating categorically that grocers were not competent judges of the practice of medicine. This remark so annoyed the influential London grocers that for seven years no Lord Mayor ever invited the apothecaries to hear the Christmas sermon at St Paul's.

The first home of the Society of Apothecaries was Cobham House, Blackfriars, where physics was taught to the members. The present hall, situated in cobbled Blackfriars Lane, was rebuilt after the Great Fire in 1666. Another development was the Physics Garden, constructed at Paradise Row, Chelsea at about the same time. Hans Sloane was one of many student apothecaries who observed the growth of unusual plants at the Chelsea garden. A greenhouse was erected there in 1680. Henry Hyde, second Earl of Clarendon, often took refuge there to escape the company of his royal brother-in-law, James II. Many cedars of lebanon in our gardens today originated there. It is no accident that the greatest annual display of flowering plants in the British Isles today bears the name of the Chelsea Flower Show.

Undoubtedly, the Society of Apothecaries of London had its heyday in the seventeenth century. Its members included Gideon Delaine, apothecary to Ann of Denmark, John Parkinson, apothecary to James I, Robert Tabor who cured Charles II of malaria, and James Peturier, Demonstrator of Botany of the Chelsea Physic Garden with a practice at Aldergate and apothecary to St Bartholomew and the Charterhouse, whose volumes of dried plants are still preserved in the Natural History Museum, and David Malthus, apothecary to Queen Anne.

Quite a few London apothecaries issued trade tokens in the 1650s and 60s, including William Adkinson of St Paul's Churchyard, James Grover of Temple Bar, Abraham Hudson of Chancery Lane, Calixt Rust of the Strand and Philip Wetherall of Great Queen Street. James Grover advertised his trade on his farthing (*W*3041), which reads, IAM GOVER APOTHECAR/AT TEMPLE BARR 1657 I.K.G. There is no device illustrating his profession; a gate is featured, symbolic of the Temple Bar at the gates of the city. Calixt Rust on the other hand, like most London apothecaries, illustrates part of the Arms of his company (*W*3006). His farthing depicts a rhinoceros, the Apothecaries' crest, on the obverse and a pot of lilies on the reverse. The legends are as follows: CALIXT RUST IN/THE STRAND 1665. The crest consists of 'a rhynoseros proper, supported by too unicorns'. The Clerk to the Society has pointed out that James I, who gave the society its charter, was the first king to introduce the unicorn into the Royal Coat of Arms – and the society adopted it. Although the unicorn is a legendary animal, it is said to be related to the rhinoceros. The ground horn of the rhinoceros is also reputed to have medicinal qualities. The actual motto on the crest OPIFERQUE PER ORBEM DICOR is written on just two pieces – those of William Drage of Hitchin in Hertfordshire and Nicholas Staight of Tewkesbury.

Over a hundred apothecaries' tokens were struck for use in the provinces, the vast majority of which bear the arms of the society: 'In a shield Apollo, the inventor of physique proper with his head radiant, holding in his left hand a bow and in his right hand an arrow'. A few provincial issuers, such as Edward Davies of Ludlow, Samual Farmer of Chipping Norton, Robert Fitzhugh of Shipston on Stour and John Rogers of Thetford in Lincolnshire, are all known to have been members of the London Society of Apothecaries. Two apothecaries' tokens of Worcestershire bear the arms of the London Society – the half penny of Robert Fitzhugh of Shipston and the half penny of Edward Perkins of Pershore.

A number of apothecaries' tokens bear a mortar and pestle, including a farthing of William Dent of Durham (1666) and a half penny of Richard Pearce at Limerick. Another Irish issuer, Robert Meller of Dublin, issued a token bearing a mortar and two pestles. However, all tokens containing a mortar and pestle in their design were not necessarily issued by apothecaries, as the device was also used by grocers or mercers, among others.

A pot of lilies appears on a number of apothecaries' tokens, including two of Henry Bollard of Dublin (*W*278) and one of Thomas Piggott of Warrington in Lancashire. Professor Trease suggests that lilies have a pharmaceutical significance.

The old link between apothecaries and grocers is preserved on Isaac Colman's token, issued at Colchester in 1667. The Apothecaries' Arms appear on the obverse, together with the designation GROCER. A token issued by Richard Barber of Gainsborough, Lincolnshire, bears the Apothecaries' Arms and the term MERCER.

An interesting Lancashire token is the penny of Andrew Bury of Manchester, which is dated 1671, extremely late in the series. The arms of the London Society appear on the obverse and those of the City of London on the reverse. It is interesting to speculate about the exact nature of the link between this Lancashire chemist and the City of London; perhaps he was apprenticed there or made a Freeman. Trease points out that the issuer was related by marriage to Peter Heywood, who took the lantern from Guy Fawkes as he attempted to blow up the Houses of Parliament.

One or two apothecaries' tokens were issued by women. A Devonshire token (*W*247) reads, MARGRET EATON/IN PLIMOVTH 1665 M.E. She was probably the widow of the apothecary Christopher Eaton whose professional services are referred to in the account of the siege of Plymouth (1642–46).

A Lancashire apothecary, John Pemberton, was given a bishop's licence to practise medicine in 1663. His token (*W*65) reads, JOHN PEMBERTON/IN LIVERPOOLE 1666 HIS HALF PENY. Pemberton built the first house to be erected in Moore Street. He is described in the Moore rental as a 'base, ill-contrived fellow', so obviously acquired a bad reputation, although he was a bailiff of Liverpool in 1660.

Apothecaries issued tokens in almost every English county, and at least one is known in Wales, Basil Wood at Ruthin, Denbigh in 1665. Ten Irish tokens are known, including six at Dublin. Surprisingly no less than nineteen tokens were issued in Nottinghamshire, thirteen in the county town alone. One prosperous Nottinghamshire apothecary, Samuel Smith, had no less than four separate issues distributed.

A father and son, practising the trade of apothecary, issued tokens at Chesterfield in Derbyshire. The father's piece, a farthing (*W*48) reads, RICHARD WOOD/OF CHESTERFEILD R.W. Three men playing field sports are shown with their dog. The son's half penny (*W*47) reads, EDWARD WOOD APOTHECARY/IN CHESTERFEILD HIS HALFE PENNY and bears the Apothecaries' Arms. Richard Wood was active in local politics, being mayor twice, in 1649 and 1657. His son was not as active, but did become a warden of the Chesterfield Company of Grocers. Both Richard and Edward were men of means and combined money lending with their pharmaceutical activities.

Edward lent quite large amounts, including the sum of £300 in 1653. His father owned a smelting mill, Ditchfield Bridge Mills, valued at over a thousand pounds.

In a paper published in 1757, Samuel Pegg, a Sheffield antiquary, gives a detailed description of the token press and dies used in the manufacture of both the Wood tokens (*see* Introduction).

SURGEONS

Physicians were ranked the most highly of medical men in the seventeenth century. They had to be licensed by the Royal College of Physicians, yet a rudimentary knowledge of Greek ideas about medicine was sufficient to gain a licence, especially in the provinces. Doctors in London were expected to be more learned. Many physicians prescribed remedies without even visiting their patients. Others, nicknamed 'water doctors', used their patients' urine to diagnose disease. The application of red-hot poultices and continual blood-letting were favoured by doctors if not by their patients. An official list of drugs prescribed in 1618 included bone marrow, sweat, blood, and shavings from the skull of a condemned criminal. There were a mere handful of physicians who actually practised medicine in a skilled and scientific manner. An outstanding example is the Puritan, Thomas Sydenham, who discovered and named scarlet fever.

Surgeons were ranked considerably lower than physicians. Many were barbers by profession, who practised bone-setting and blood-letting in their spare time. The Barber-Surgeons were granted a charter in Henry VIII's reign which gave them the right to dissect the bodies of four criminals per year. On account of this severe restriction many of the more able surgeons went abroad, including William Harvey who went to Padua, and later was to discover the secrets of the circulation of blood round the body.

In the middle of the seventeenth century, however, surgeons were able to perform only the simplest of operations such as bone-setting, amputations, blood-letting, and extracting 'stones'. The practice of blood-letting is commemorated on the present-day barber's pole, a rare surviving trade sign, symbolizing the baton used in vivisection, two bandages and the barber-surgeon's blood-letting dish.

Only one barber-surgeon's token is known, that of Henry Carter at Manningtree in Essex, which shows the Barber-Surgeon's Arms (*W*234).

RODENT OFFICERS

A Salisbury rat catcher had two farthings struck (*W*184 and *W*189). The first reads, GEORGE GODFERY/IN SARVM 1659 G.G. The legend on the reverse of the second differs slightly; RAT KILR IN SARVM G.G. A large rat is featured on both obverses. Rats were known to be the prime cause of the 'plague', as it was realized that the disease was transmitted through the bites of the fleas they carried. C.M. Rowe points out that in the ledger records of the Salisbury corporation Godfrey was admitted a free citizen of the borough on 18 September 1639, being described as a pinner. A skilled pinner would be in great demand as a rat catcher, as he would be adept in making traps. Godfrey is recorded as one of the eighty-six burgesses who voted for the return of two Members of Parliament in 1656.

TRUSSMAKER

Sufferers from a hernia or rupture in the seventeenth century would send for the trussmaker, who would fit a 'truss' or pad to hold the offending hernia in place, with the aid of a heavy strap. A naked boy holding such a truss is featured on the obverse of a penny token issued by a London trussmaker (*W*3145), CORNELIVS GLOVER TRVSSMAKER/IN 3 NVN ALY NEAR YE OLD POST HOVS. A postman on horseback, blowing his horn, is depicted on the reverse as a reminder of the location of his business premises.

SPECTACLE MAKERS

In the seventeenth century opticians made the actual spectacles themselves. Campbell observes, 'he grinds his convex glasses in a brass concave sphere, of a diameter large in proportion to the glass intended, and his concave glasses upon a convex sphere of the same metal. His plane glasses he grinds upon a just plane, in the same manner as the common glass grinder. He grinds them all with sand and polishes them with emery and putty. The cases are made by different workmen and he adjusts the glasses to them . . .' There is no reference in Campbell's notes to scientifically devised eye tests. Any tests that were carried out would have been very crude.

The wearing of glasses was still fairly uncommon in England even by the seventeenth century, and few spectacle-makers' tokens are known. John Heaward proudly advertises his profession on his token, issued at St Katherine's by the Tower, JOHN HEAWARD IN S/KATRNS SPECTELE MAKER I.M.H., depicting a crude pair of spectacles.

A similar design appears on a London halfpenny issued at Temple Bar, but the issuer does not name his craft (*W*3064), JOHN RADFORD AT YE GOVLDEN/ WITHOUT TEMPLE BARR 68 HIS HALFE PENNY I.L.R.

HOSPITALS AND SCHOOLS

Several new hospitals were established under the Tudors, one of the most notable being Christ's Hospital in Newgate Street, a hospital for orphans founded by Edward VI ten days prior to his death. The old Greyfriars Monastery in Newgate Street constituted the original buildings. Within a short time nearly four hundred children had been housed there, most of them boys. The word 'hospital' should be understood in its mediaeval sense of 'charitable home or school'. Samuel Pepys records on 2 April 1662, 'Mr Moore and I walked to the Spittle, an hour or two before my Lord Mayor and the blue-boys come, which at last they did, and a fine sight of charity it is indeed'. The diarist uses the cockney nickname for the hospital, and refers to the distinctive uniform of long blue coats and yellow stockings. Tradition avers that the yellow socks were to prevent the rats from gnawing at the boys' ankles.

11.1 Half penny token of John Bannister at Christ's Hospital, Newgate Street, London.

The blue-coat boys were a well-known sight in London, hired out for weddings and funerals. Pepys used to go to Christ's Hospital on Sundays on occasion, as on 17 June 1666, when he writes, 'To Christ Church and there heard a silly sermon, but sat where we saw one of the prettiest little boys with the prettiest mouth that ever I saw in my life'. Three months later the hospital buildings were razed to the ground in the Great Fire.

Two fascinating tokens were issued at Christ's Hospital – a farthing (*W* 633) and a halfpenny, both undated. The farthing reads, JOHN BANNISTER AT THE/MATRONS SELLER IN THE HOSPITAL. The legend on the half penny is identical, but adds, HIS HALFE PENNY. A cripple is depicted on the obverse, as handicapped children were looked after at the hospital. The device was intended to underline the charitable nature of the institute and encourage people to be generous. The reference to the Matron's cellar is interesting and is reminiscent of the legend on the Newgate Prison halfpenny, BELONGING TO YE CELLOR ON THE MASTERS SIDE. The word 'cellar' was the normal expression in the seventeenth century for a wine store or a stock of bottled wine. John Banister was probably a porter whose duties included providing wine for the table. Williamson draws our attention to a burial record of a Mrs Banister of Lad Lane and her daughter on 28 April 1653, and also of old Mr Banister in Lad Lane the following year. He is probably a close relative of the issuer. Even more sigificant is a record dated 11 February 1669, 'Died Henry Banister, porter of Christ's Hospital'.

Sibbile Theame, a shoemaker who issued a token at the hospital, was mentioned in chapter 5. Just as modern hospitals contain shops and services, so did their seventeenth-century counterparts. Pepys recalls visiting Bartholomew Fair with some friends on 31 August 1661. Later they went into Christ's Hospital to buy some 'fairings', 'and I did give every one of them a bauble, which was the little globe of glass with things hanging in them, which pleased the ladies very well'.

The rebuilding of Christ's Hospital after the Fire was undertaken by Hooke and Oliver, under the close supervision of Christopher Wren. The Hospital's main function by then was as a boarding school for orphaned or destitute boys. Wren commenced designs for the 'writing school', which were completed by Hawkesmoor. Girls were no longer admitted but had their own hospital, which opened at Hertford in 1704. Christ's Hospital School for Girls is still flourishing, and proud of its heritage. The Boys' School remained in London until 1902, when a new school was built at Horsham in Sussex. Its close links with the past are much in evidence on St Matthew's Day (21 September) when several boys from the school attend a service at St Sepulchre's, Holborn, with the Lord Mayor and Alderman, followed by tea at the Mansion House.

CHAPTER 12

TRAVEL

If one travelled by road in the seventeenth or early eighteenth centuries one took one's life in one's hands. Most roads, even main thoroughfares, were little more than muddy bridle paths, being completely unsuited to wheeled traffic. There was little attempt to repair old roads or construct new ones, due to the lack of effective administration of road maintenance at local and national level. Each parish traversed by a highway was legally bound to maintain the section within the parish bounds. Farmers and villagers had to provide six days' unpaid labour per year, a 'surveyor' being elected from one of their number. Such a haphazard system contributed to the neglect of the roads, and the setting up of turnpike trusts in the 1660s was the first major step in road improvement for more than a thousand years.

In Stuart times most people stayed at home by choice. Holidays were spent on the village green or in the tavern – not on the road to the coast! Those whose occupation entailed travelling, circuit judges for instance, normally rode on horseback. Apart from farmers, not many country people could afford a horse, but in the towns the more prosperous merchants and businessmen were beginning to prefer travel by coach. Large broad-wheeled wagons rumbled along the bumpy tracks in place of the droves of packhorses, carrying passengers as well as goods. There were a few private coaches for the wealthy, but they were little more than boxes on wheels. Public stage coaches started to appear in 1640, with outside passengers sitting in a basket between the rear wheels. Country housewives, becoming more ambitious in their shopping requirements, increasingly relied on the service of carriers (*see* below), who brought their shopping from town twice a week. Contemporary trade tokens provide graphic illustration of many of these features of road travel.

TURNPIKE AND TOLLMEN

Tolls had been levied on bridges since the early Middle Ages. Although the roads were in a dreadful condition, bridges were held in considerable esteem. Manorial lords were encouraged not only to build good bridges but to keep them in a satisfactory state of repair, and so it was customary to charge a toll

12.1 Half penny token of William Flower, Tollman at Stilton, Hants.

on all users of these manorial bridges. As early as the thirteenth century the king required each manorial lord to perform three duties: to answer the call to arms, to maintain their castles and to care for the bridges of the realm. The system of turnpike trusts was based on the medieval custom of pontage which permitted a manorial lord to levy a toll on the users of his bridge.

Turnstiles appear on several London tokens, including a half penny of John Scott at Clerkenwell Green (1667) and undated farthings of Edward Forman at High Holborn and Robert Mills at Postern Gate, Cripplegate. The actual word 'tollman' appears on several tokens, notably those issued at Stilton in Huntingdonshire (*W*68), Doncaster Bridge (*W*73), and Nottingham Bridge. The Stilton halfpenny reads, WILLIAM FLOWER TOLEMAN W.F./OF STILTONE 1666 HIS HALFE PENNY. The Doncaster tollman, William Hall, issued his piece in 1669 reading, WILL HALL TOLEMAN OF/DONCASTER BRIDG YORKSHIR HIS HALF PENNY 1669. The operator of the toll is depicted with his staff. In 1675, just eight years after the token was struck, the corporation disputed the legality of the toll on the grounds that the inhabitants of Sprotborough and Bentley had been responsible for the maintenance of the bridge. The toll does not appear to have been a turnpike levy though an act was obtained in 1663 to erect turnpike gates.

Neither William Hall at Doncaster Bridge nor Steven Garner on Nottingham Bridge actually stood at the toll gate; they merely received the toll and administered the funds. Garner was an apothecary by profession, and issued tokens both as tollman and apothecary. He displayed the town arms on his toll pieces, and a rhinoceros, the symbol of an apothecary, on his trade halfpence. His brother Sam was also an apothecary, and issued a token. Steven Garner was a Nonconformist, an elder of the High Pavement Chapel, Notthingham and a lay member of the town's Puritan Church Association, which decided to disband in 1660. The bridge was replaced in the 1870s by the present Trent Bridge, which spans the river just a mile south of the city centre. Garner's token cannot be associated with the turnpike system, as it was not introduced into Nottinghamshire until the 1720s.

It has been suggested that the Batchworth Bridge token of Rickmansworth in Hertfordshire may well have been a tollman's half penny. It reads: JOHN WEADEN 1667 HIS HALFE PENY/AT BATCHWORT BRIDG. The old wooden bridge over the Colne was destroyed in 1833, and replaced with a more modern single-arched cast iron structure. Three wooden arches and a railing to prevent carts from falling into the river appear on the token.

The bridge wardens of Bewdley in Worcestershire issued an octagonal half penny in 1668, which is referred to in the town records of that year, 'where as the eight-square peeces of brass . . . upon experience are found convenient for the more ready change of money and usefull in point of trade and commerce, especially to the poorer sort of the same borough . . . now for the encouragment of such as shall take them it is ordered that the Bridge wardens shall give in exchange for every foure and twenty of such peeces one shilling in current silver . . .'. The bridge wardens, also known as chapel wardens as there was a small chapel on the bridge, became responsible for all the town's finances and their accounts make interesting reading, especially during the Civil War period. Those for 1642 and 43 reflect increasing fear of Roundhead intrusion,

1642	Pd	for candells when ye soldiers did watch	0	0	6
	Pd	for a drum by Mr. Bayliff's appointment	0	11	6
1643	Pd	to Will Hill for ye soldiers	0	2	0
	Pd	Walter Taye for hanging the gates	0	1	2
	Pd	beere at ye setting of ye gates	0	0	6
	Pd	for mending ye gunpowder barrell	0	0	3
	Pd	for 12lb and halfe of powder	0	16	8
	Pd	for a hinge to the bridge house gate	0	0	6
	Pd	for a chain to the bridge house dore	0	0	9

These accounts were signed by John Wilkes, chapel warden. The beer money for the hanging of the gates was to no avail however, for a trick played by Tinker Fox in 1644, pretending to lead a Royalist detachment, allowed the Cromwellians to cross the bridge by night and capture the Royalist garrison. Bewdley Bridge was badly damaged by the Scots fleeing from the Battle of Worcester in 1651. As no major repairs were undertaken until the Restoration, the tokens may well have been struck with these repairs in mind. Unfortunately the records in the account cease in 1663. The old bridge managed to hold out until the great flood of 1795, and Telford himself planned the new one.

The most fascinating of the turnpike tokens is that of Edward Lawrence of Wadesmill in Hertfordshire (*W*197). Wadesmill lies a couple of miles to the north of Ware. The reading on the token is: EDWARD LAWRENCE AT Y^E^ (Illustration of Turnstile)/AT WARDSMILL 1669 HIS HALF PENY. A turnpike was divided between many trusts, each responsible for a section of the road, controlling it by a turnstile or toll bar. The trust surveyors could still call upon the inhabitants of a village to provide up to six days' labour, but eventually they employed professional roadmen. The establishment of turnpike trusts undoubtedly led to better roads with fewer potholes and serious attempts to clear the mire in winter.

There are many references in the Sessions Books to the toll at Wadesmill and to Edward Lawrence himself. The earliest reference that I can find to the toll is an order of 3 April 1665, giving power to 'farm' the toll to some responsible person for one year. In April 1666 a Commission was formed to manage the toll. The first reference to the token issuer himself occurs in August 1664 when a Richard King of Layton, husband man, was summoned to appear before the magistrates for assaulting him. The first reference to him as tollman in 1671 is not complimentary: 'That Edward Lawrence of Wadesmill, gentleman, receiver of tolls for horses, carts and carriages passing through the turnpike received and converted to his own use divers sums of money from people who did not pass through'. It is significant that although he is being accused of dishonest practice he is referred to as a gentleman, so was obviously a man of some importance in the community.

On 7 April 1673 Lawrence was appointed one of the surveyors of the highway. Seven years later he was appointed treasurer to the surveyors. This was an unusual post created to deal with unusual circumstances, 'whereas complaint has been made in court that the highways in Standon, Braughing and Westmill are much out of repair, it is ordered that the surveyors of the highways of those parishes shall cause the highways to be speedily repaired by days' works and teams. And whereas the court is informed that there wants timber and other necessaryes and a great deal of workmanshipp for the effectual repair of these highways, the Toll Act is still in force providing that all persons chargeable towards the repair of the highways shall pay 6d in the pound, according to the true value of their state. It is therefore ordained that the respective surveyors for the parishes a foresaid – in Standon and Westmill 6d in the pound and in Braughing 3d only as their wages are not so bad. The court appoints Edward Lawrence as treasurer to receive the moneys'.

Lawrence has obviously been forgiven for his earlier misdemeanors at the Wadesmill turnpike. He lived at Hertford, not at Wadesmill, and by 1681 he had obviously relinquished his duties there, for we read that justices were appointed to manage and farm the toll. It is interesting to note that the turnpike house at Wadesmill was sold in 1681 for £20-19-6 to help repair the highway. This sum would have been entered in Lawrence's books as treasurer to the surveyors.

POST MASTERS

Post boys galloping along the dusty roads were a familiar sight in seventeenth-century England. A number of tokens issued by Thomas Wilmot at Guildford show a post boy on foot, carrying a postbag and a staff for protection. The high-crowned hat he is wearing seems to have been part of their uniform. One cannot be sure of Thomas Wilmot's position; he may possibly have been one of the new post masters established after the Act of Parliament of 1657 which instituted the official Post Office. Before this, the postal system had been very haphazard. Henry I employed letter carriers, and Edward I established stages where the carriers' horses could be stabled. Henry IV is credited with initiating the postbag system, which was continued for almost four hundred years until replaced in the late eighteenth century by Palmer's mail coaches.

The medieval post boys were messengers of the Crown and had the right to take short cuts across private land. Ordinarily people who wished to send letters had to rely on servants, friends or the local carrier. Henry VIII reorganized the 'King's Messengers' under Sir Brian Tuke, the first 'Master of the Posts'. He used a system of relays with stages or taverns every ten or fifteen miles. Local constables were responsible for the provision of horses at each post. Henry also instituted a first-class and second-class mail, reminiscent of recent postal legislation. Important mail went by 'standing post', with fresh messengers stationed at each post to take the mail on to the next stage.

During Elizabeth's reign it became customary for the Royal Messengers to take unofficial letters although priority was still given to royal mail. There were five main post routes, all starting from London: the Dover road to link with Europe, two western roads to Plymouth and Bristol (as the main naval base and the principal port outside London respectively), the Great North Road to Edinburgh and the north-west road to Chester, linking with Holyhead and Ireland. Later a sixth road was added – the east road to the Fen country, ending at Yarmouth. Thomas Witherings, appointed Master of the Post by Charles I, tried to speed up the postal system. Previously letters had taken several days to reach their destination; in 1598 it was normal for a letter to take three days from London to Exeter. Many of Witherings' postmen travelled on foot, as the stages were invariably within a day's walk of each other. A book printed in London is called *A Strange Foot Post*, and the title page shows a sketch of a postman wearing a high hat and a longstaff, reminiscent of the postman on Thomas Wilmot's token.

After the official establishment of the Post Office in 1657, postmarks began to be used. They were termed 'Bishop's marks' after the new postmaster-general, Colonel Henry Bishop. A number of London and provincial postmasters issued tokens. At least eight are known; Thomas Baker of Chester, Samuel Northcott of Plymouth (1653), Thomas Kingsford of Sandwich, William Place of Grays Inn Gate, Henry Cleaver of Hounslow, W.L. of Love Lane, Thomas Hatton of the Antelope, West Smithfield and A.L. of Norwich (1661). Almost all clearly state their connection with the Post Office. It is significant that their post offices were situated on five of the six post roads. The Sandwich piece (*W*500) reads, THOMAS KINGSFORD HIS HALF PENY/OF SANDWHICH POST MASTER. It is recorded that a common post for carriage of letters was set up in Sandwich in 1569. In 1661, just about the time when Thomas Kingsford circulated his token, the Mayor petitioned the Duke of York for a continuance of the privilege of a foot post to carry money and goods to and from Sandwich, Deal and London, according to ancient custom, not withstanding the Act of Parliament for creating the Post Office.

Thomas Baker and Samuel Northcott were particularly busy men as their offices were situated at terminal posts. Thomas Baker was elected a Sheriff of Chester in 1676; Northcott was Mayor of Plymouth five years after issuing his token. In the course of his mayoral duties he was asked to circulate a Parliamentary proclamation in the parish church. He refused from 'scruples of piety' and was imprisoned in London.

Seventeenth-century postmasters were frequently criticized by their superiors, anxious to preserve the good name of the Post Office. Their chief defects seem to have been their use of poor horses and careless post boys, and keeping the mail at their stage for too lengthy a period. The post mistress at Faringdon was told, 'I am credibly informed that your horse tired at Lechlade last week and was there supplied by one out of a cart. This is scandalous.' All the postmasters on the Dover road, including the token issuer at Sandwich were taken to task for the lateness of post travelling from Canterbury to London.

The post masters were expected to exercise a great care in sealing their mail bags. The London office stamped letters with the date and put them into the appropriate bag for each post town. These were then put into a large sealed bag. As each post master on the road received the mail, he took out his own bag and then sent the rest forward. A 'by bag' was also carried by the post boy into which were put letters from one post town to another on the road. Sometimes a dishonest postmaster made a false statement concerning the number of letters in the 'by bag' and pocketed the profits. Colonel Whitley, Postmaster-general from 1672 to 77, accused the post master of Chester of 'concealing the number and putting ye money in your own purse'. It is quite likely that the post master criticized was Thomas Baker.

Undoubtedly some of the hundred and fifty post masters of the 1650s and 60s combined their duties with other trades. Some were probably innkeepers. Henry Cleave, for example, issued a halfpenny at Hounslow displaying a still, equipment for making spirits. William Place, who issued the only London postmaster's token (*W*1237) at Gray's Inn Gate, depicting a postboy on horseback blowing his horn, was a man of many parts. As one might expect from his position close to Gray's Inn, he was a bookseller and stationer first and foremost (*see* Chapter Seven). A document of 1652 lists the twenty-one letter receivers of the City of London. The list includes Richard Best, stationer in Gray's Inn Gate. London had to wait until 1680 before a service was provided for the collection and delivery of local letters within the metropolis.

Two London postmasters, Thomas Hatton of West Smithfield and W.L. of Love Lane, definitely combined the job with innkeeping. Hatton's token (*W*2861) reads, ANTILOP WEST SMITHFEILD THO HATTON/BIBIS VINVM SALVTA HIS HALFE PENY 1664. The *Intelligencer* of 16 November 1663, issued just a few months before the token, contains an advertisement, 'Upon the 11 instant there was printed and published a convenient way for Travellers to pass with a Messenger between London and Holyhead weekly and to all other Towns and Places upon Chester Rode and to have change of horses every day according to the purport of the said Printed Paper and such as are desirous to travel that way if they repayre to the Antilope in West Smithfield and the Post Houses at St Albans, Brickhill, Daventry, Coventry, Lichfield, Stone, Namptwich or Chester; or at severall other stages erected for that purpose, they may be furnish'd and have good Diet and Lodging provided for them'.

The Latin tag on the postmaster's piece may be translated: You are drinking wine. Cheers!

The Love Lane farthing (*W*1841) reads, KINGS HEAD POST/HOVSE LOVE LANE 57 W.I.L. The obverse shows the tavern sign – the crowned head of James I, with globe and sceptre.

An announcement of the Postmaster-general, published in the *Mercuius Publicus* of July 1661 and the King's *Intelligencer* of the same period, states, 'it is likewise notified that the office for the Kentish Daily Post is now kept at the Round House in Love Lane Near Billingsgate for the conveniency of trading into that county. And all letters into Kent delivered at the King's General Post Office shall be sent thither daily'. Thus the Love Lane Post Office was the collecting office for the Sandwich Road.

CARRIERS, WAGONNERS AND COACHMEN

Carriers' tokens are numerous, appearing in many counties from Yorkshire to Wiltshire, and have many different devices. A Halifax piece of Robert Watmough shows a packhorse. Interestingly his reverse reads CARRIER FOR HALLYFAX. A Cambridgeshire farthing from the village of Haddenham

12.2 Half penny token of Thomas Bearly, a carrier, of Harringworth, Northants.

depicts the carrier, John Morfield, walking, although the pack saddle was the trademark of many carriers. A Northamptonshire carrier put one on the reverse of his token half penny (*W*32), THO BEARLY HARINWORTH HIS HALF PENY T.A.B./THE PACK SADLE A CARRIER. He probably had the sign ouside his door. Thomas Barrett, from the small village of Dunstew in Oxfordshire, put a basket pannier on his tokens, an undated farthing and a half penny of 1669. It is no coincidence that most carriers' pieces were struck for villagers, who were unable to visit their market town as frequently as they would have liked or who were physically incapable of carrying their goods themselves. A large proportion of villagers in the seventeenth century did not possess transport of any sort. Carriers would carry almost anything their customers requested, from eggs to live geese, firewood to furniture.

There is only one chapman's token in the entire series, that of George Brown of Wendover in Buckinghamshire. An undated half penny, it illustrates the Haberdashers' Arms. Chapmen were travelling salesmen, specializing in haberdashery.

Coaches were becoming popular by the middle of the century despite the poor condition of the roads, and there were coach hire businesses resembling modern car hire firms. Typical coaches of the period had crude suspension of leather braces, wooden frames covered with leather and studded with nails, dome-shaped roofs, no windows, and leather curtains instead of doors. Only one token actually uses the word COACHMAN; a half penny of Highgate, Middlesex, in the name of John Hilton. The device of a coach and horses appearing on tokens of William Osborne of Ashbourne, Thomas Taylor of West Smithfield, and John Luffrum of Egham, Surrey indicates that they were tavern keepers at the sign of the Coach and Horses or that they hired out coaches to would-be travellers.

A similar piece was issued at Aldgate, London (*W*66), JOHN GAME AT THE COACH/AND HORSES IN ALLGATE. Samuel Pepys records on 1 May 1663, 'And after a glass of wine, we all took horse and I (upon a horse hired of Mr. Game) saw him out of London at the end of Bishop-gate Street and so I turned and rode with some trouble through the fields, and the Holborne towards Hide

12.3 Engraving of a coach and four by D. Loggan, 1675.

12.4 Halfpenny token of a London coachman, John Game, at the Coach and Horses, Aldgate.

Park . . . By and by, about seven or eight a clock homeward; and changing my horse again, I rode home, coaches going in great crowd to the further end of the town almost. In my way to Leadenhall-street there was morris dancing which I have not seen a great while. So set my horse at Games's, paying 5s for him and so home . . .'

Few wagonners seem to have had tokens struck. A particularly attractive half penny appeared in 1669 in the Oxfordshire market town of Burford (*W*49). It reads, LEONARD MILLS AT/BVRFORD WAGONNER L.M. 1669. A stout cart is clearly visible. Mills' business was quite prosperous, for J.G. Milne has shown from local records that he paid tax on five hearths in 1662 and again in 1665. He was elected bailiff in 1660. He lived in Sheep Street, paying an annual rent of nine shillings.

FARRIERS AND SADDLERS

Wagonners and carriers alike required the services of the farrier or blacksmith. Strangely enough, few blacksmiths' tokens are known. A Kent farrier, Andrew Clifford, issued a half penny at Dymchurch, which bears an anvil instead of the more usual horseshoe. Horseshoes appear on tokens of Robert Horseley (Brinsley, Notts.), Thomas Goddard of Newark and Thomas Adderley of Castle Dermot in Ireland (*W*155). This Irish penny also shows a hammer and pincers on its reverse.

Campbell describes the farrier as a compound of the smith and the doctor, 'He is supposed to be acquainted with all the diseases incident to that useful

12.5 Engraving of a stage wagon by D. Loggan, 1675.

12.6 Half penny token of Leonard Mills, waggonner of Burford.

animal and possessed of the method of cure and administers to the horse without consulting the Faculty of Physicians or understanding one word of their dispensary . . . he affects mystery in his profession as much as the graduate of the college, and to do him justice is just as certain of success as they are'.

Several saddlers issued tokens. The saddler was considered by Campbell to be one of the most ingenious of all craftsmen, as like the shoemaker he used leather, awl and thread, and like the tailor he sewed caparisons and horse cloths. A Gloucester saddler issued a farthing depicting a pack saddle, probably used by a carrier or farmer (*W*84). The piece reads, RICHARD CHANDLER/SADLER IN GLOCESTER R.C. The Saddlers' Arms appear on a Holbeach token. Saddled horses are featured on tokens of William Hurst of Mansfield and William Wilcocks of Mount Mellick, Ireland.

FERRYMEN AND TILT BOATS

From the Middle Ages until well into the eighteenth century the Thames was the main highway in London. Contemporary prints show large numbers of vessels including tilt boats and tiny rowboats. Tilt boats were used for carrying passengers or dry goods from Billingsgate down river to Greenwich and Gravesend. Small rowing boats were necessary to ferry passengers across the river, and some had their own watermen.

Several boatmen's tokens are known. Richard Jennings issued a half penny at Hackney Ferry in 1668 (*W*59), reading, RICHARD IENNINGS AT/HACKNY FERRY 1668 HIS HALF PENY R.M.I. A man rowing a boat is depicted on the obverse. A similar token circulated in Fulham (*W*53), MATTHEW

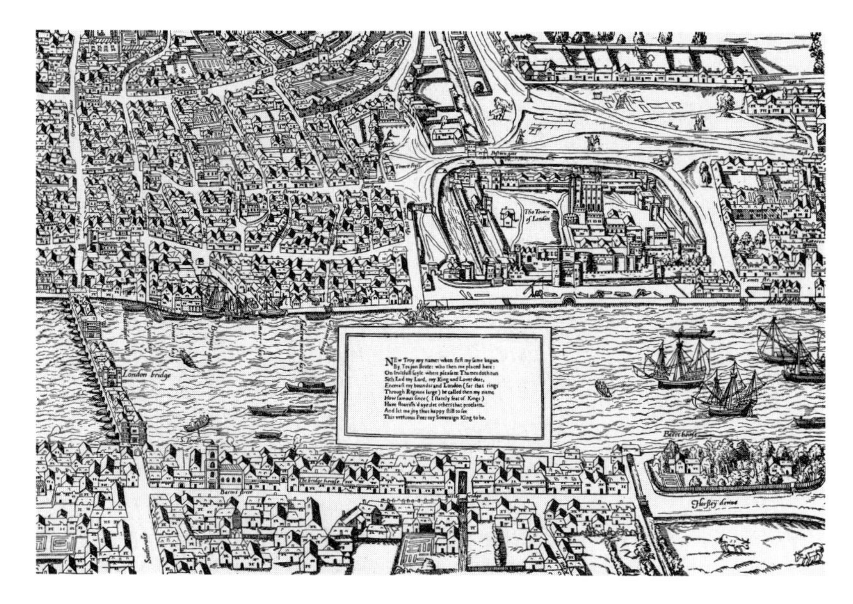

12.7 Contemporary print showing tilt boats on the Thames.

HARWELL IN/FVLLVM NERE THE FERY M.M.H. This farthing also shows a man in a rowing boat. William Hobbs issued a half penny in Lower Shadwell depicting crossed oars. He may well have been a boatman at Shadwell Dock.

A fascinating token was struck at Paul's Wharf stairs (*W*2196), reading, AT Y^E NEXT BOAT BY PAVLS/WHARFE AT PETERS HILL FOOT M.M.B. A ferry boat with boatman and two passengers is shown on the obverse; above, the words NEXT BOAT are repeated.

London boatmen vied with each other at Paul's Wharf to take people across the river to the Bear Garden and theatres on the Bankside. The Lord Mayor and Court of Aldermen clearly set out the fares in a declaration of 7 September 1671, 'over the water directly in the next sculler between London Bridge and Limehouse or London Bridge and Foxhall 2d'. The 'Next Boat' half pence would have been used to pay the fare from Paul's Wharf to Bankside or Vauxhall.

An Irish boatman's token reads, RICH BODKIN OF TOOME/FOR FERRY FORGE AND FISH (*W*710). Like so many Irish pieces it was valued at a penny. Richard Bodkin, like so many of his contemporaries, needed at least three occupations in order to eke out a living.

A tilt boat is shown on John Michell's penny issued at Somers Quay, Lower Thames Street, London (*W*2917). This fascinating octagonal token reads, IOHN MICHELL LIVING AT LITLE SOMERS KEY NEAR BILLINGSGATE/A PENNY. The boat shown contains both boatmen and passengers. Tilt boats carried passengers or goods, having a tilt or awning spread over them, being of canvas lashed over ash hoops. They were fairly large, as indicated by the Milton Parish Register which states 'on May 1592 a tilt boat of Gravesend having on board about 40 people was overrun by a brig opposite Greenwich. The Court being there, the Queen saw it and was much upset'. The hulls were clinker built with a low free board and in design derived from the Thames Wherry. Nine oars per side seem to have been the normal complement.

12.8 Octagonal token of John Michell of Somers Quay, London, showing a tilt boat.

Two farthing tokens were circulated by the Yeomen of the Waterside (*W*205 and 206). It is not quite clear who these 'yeomen' were, but they probably ran a private boat company. The tokens read, THE 4 YEOMEN OF THE/WATERSIDE TOKENS and YEWMEN OF THE WATER/SID AT BILLINGSGATE. A scallop shell is featured on both reverses; a ferry boat appears on the obverse of the first, and a lobster on the second. It is interesting to note from the first piece that the yeomen numbered just four, and that it bears the word TOKENS.

Several boatmen issued tokens along the Surrey stretches of the Thames, including Richard Broughton at Putney (*W*204) and John Randell at Richmond (*W*233). Richard Broughton's token reads, RICHARD BROVGHTON/OF PVTNEY 1668 HIS HALF PENY R.E.R. The Waterman's Arms are featured. It is recorded that General Lambert, Lord of the Manor, granted a small piece of land near the waterside to the Company of Free Watermen of Putney for the purpose of erecting a shed and conducting a ferry.

The Waterman's Arms are also featured on the halfpenny of John Randell of Richmond, JOHN RANDELL 1668/IN RICHMOND HIS HALFE PENNY I.S.R. Randell was assessed for six hearths in 1662. He married Sarah Batman in the same year and died on 12 March 1706, nearly forty years after issuing the token. He is described in the burial register as John Randall Watterman.

12.9 Farthing token of the Yeomen of the Waterside, Billingsgate.

MARINERS

Two York sea captains had half pennies struck in the same year, 1667. One wonders why their tokens were struck and for whom. Were they issued as change for passengers? What sea voyages did they undertake? *W*391 reads JAMES CAVTON MARRINER/IN YORKE 1667 HIS HALFE PENNY I.M.C. and *W*441 DENNIS WATERHOVSE/MARRINER IN YORKE 1667. An anchor appears on the obverse of Cavton's token, and three sailors inspecting a globe on the other.

Campbell is at pains to point out that mariners are not mere sailors. He writes, 'to make a common practical Sailor requires no more than a natural inclination to the sea and a sturdy healthy inclination but to make a mariner and one fit to manage a ship requires a good deal of sagacity'. He outlines the qualities desired in an expert seaman, including a knowledge of mathematics, languages and astronomy, and skill in drawing, and bemoans the fact that most seamen are ill-bred and boisterous – even suggesting that would-be officers should take dancing lessons.

CHAPTER 13

SPORT AND ENTERTAINMENT

TENNIS COURT TOKENS

The modern game of lawn tennis is a Victorian creation. There were several claimants to be the originator of the game, all English, notably Major Gem and Captain Pereira, both stalwart members and officials of the Edgbaston Cricket Club, Birmingham and Major Wingfield, who patented his version in 1873 to which he gave the curious name 'Sphairistike'. Wingfield stated that he had evolved the game after years of research into indoor racket and ball games in ancient Greece and Elizabethan England. The first Wimbledon tournament took place four years later in 1877.

There is little doubt that the new outdoor game owned much to the indoor game of rackets which had been so popular in Tudor and Stuart times. Although the ball had changed from compressed rags within a woollen cover to rubber with a hand-sewn white cover of flannel, the tennis rackets, being pear-shaped, closely resembled those used in the earlier game. The laborious scoring of fifteen aces used in rackets was replaced, however, by the quicker and more efficient system still in use today.

The Tudor game, played inside an enclosed stone courtyard, is still practised today as 'court', 'real' or 'royal' tennis. These royal titles owe their origin to the fact that many of the leading monarchs in Europe were not merely patrons of the game, but active participants. Henry VIII was a keen player, as one would expect, and a contemporary print depicts James, Duke of York, playing tennis in 1641 at the age of eight. It is thought that the court shown was situated in Whitehall. A French print shows Charles IX wielding a racket at the age of two.

Some of the earliest tennis courts in Britain were to be found in Oxford, a town much beloved by royal princes. It is known that tennis was played in the city as early as 1508, and there were two courts at Smith Gate in 1530. Skill in tennis was considered an important attribute in a student. A freshman at Magdalene in 1604 is described as:

'Having this experience and withall
Achieved some cunning at the tennis ball'.

Another freshman, John Earle of Merton, wrote to a friend in 1628, 'the two marks of his seniority is the bare velvet of his gown and his proficiency at

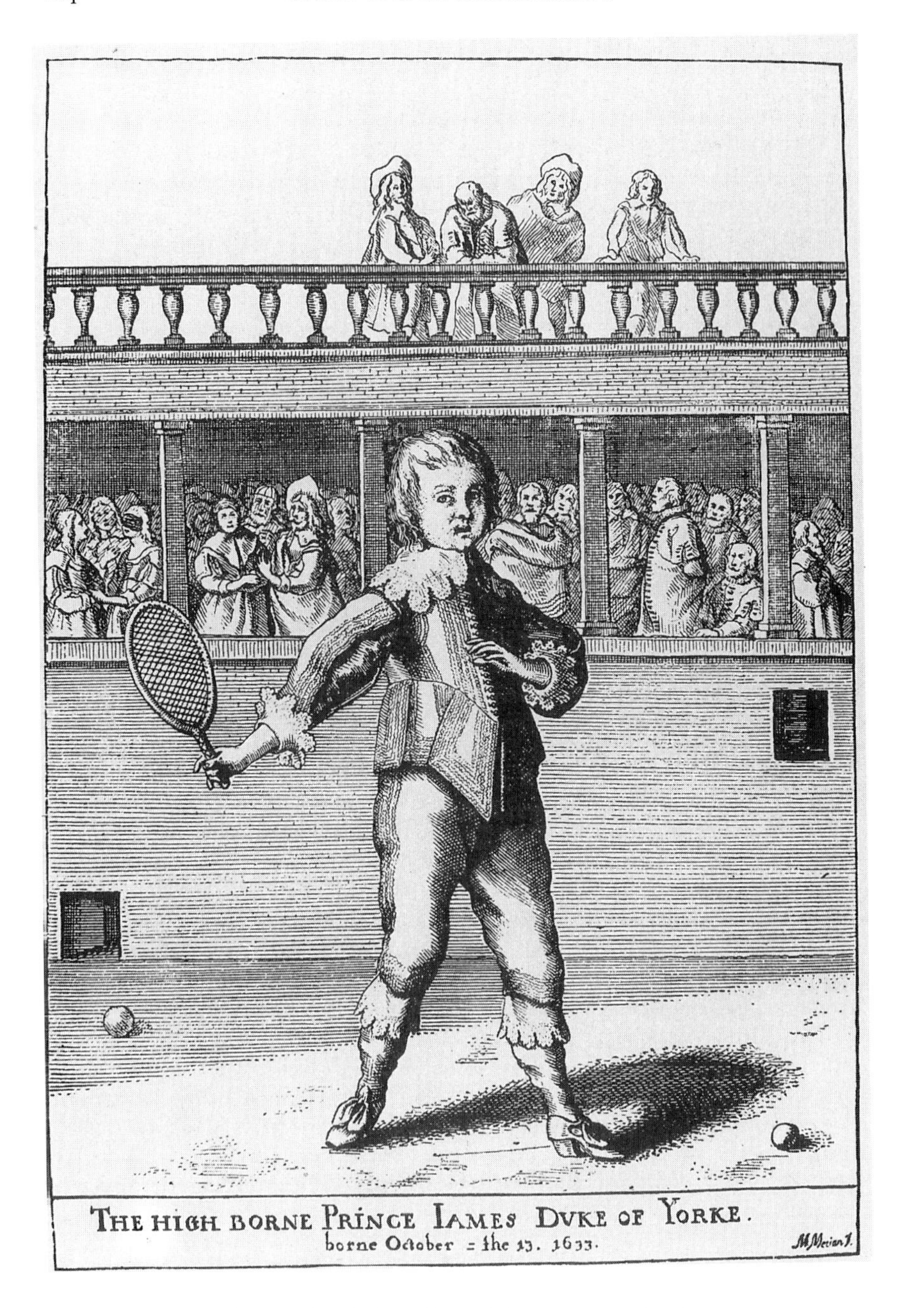

13.1 Prince James, Duke of York, later James II, playing tennis when a young boy.

tennis. When he can play a set, he is a freshman no more'.

Most of the early racket courts have disappeared, but three ancient courts still survive. The only one in use is in Merton Street, and is let by Merton College to the Oxford University Tennis Club. The second was acquired by Oriel College in 1876, and has been incorporated into a lecture room. Many

13.2 A contemporary print of a tennis match in Stuart England.

celebrated people are reputed to have played on it, including Charles I during his sojourn at the time of the Civil War. The ashlar walls of the court can still be seen in Blue Boar Lane.

Three scarce seventeenth-century tokens commemorate these old courts and the exciting matches played on them. They were issued by three 'keepers of rackett courts' – Thomas Butler, Thomas Burnham and Thomas Wood. The earliest is undoubtedly that of Thomas Wood, dated 1652. The style of the piece indicates that it was struck by David Ramage. On the obverse is a racket and the name THOMAS WOOD. The reverse reads VINTNER IN OXON and bears the date 1652 and the initials T.M.W., for the issuer and his wife Mary. Both sides of his business are advertised – the selling of wine and the management of a tennis court. Wood started in business in 1647 as tavern keeper of the Salutation, in St Martin's parish. Four years later in 1651, he leased a house from Katherine Edwards at 104–105 High Street. He took the sign of the Salutation with him and continued trading as a vintner there, but at the same time took over the management of the adjoining racket court. This was the court mentioned above as now being part of the lecture rooms of Oriel College. Wood was a man of many parts for a contemporary diarist refers to him as a 'dancing master'.

His farthing token was issued just a year after he had started in business and may well have been used for small change both by thirsty customers at the Salutation and by athletic students hiring the court for an hour or two. It is quite likely that tennis players used the tokens to buy ale after the game. Thomas Wood died in 1663, being buried at the Church of St Mary the Virgin on 26 November of that year. His wife continued to reside at 104 High Street, but the tennis court was taken over by Thomas Burnham, the issuer of the second token. The legend on the obverse of this piece reads THOMAS BVRNHAM AT and the design shows a racket. On the reverse is YE TENIS COVRT IN OXON with T.I.B. in the centre (*W*126).

13.3 Farthing of Thomas Wood.

It is unfortunate that this token is undated, because we cannot be sure whether it was issued at the Oriel Street court or at another court in St Aldate's parish, which he took over in 1670. The style of the token indicates that it was issued between the years 1664 and 72, so it may well have been issued for the second court.

E. Thurlow Leeds has succeeded in tracing Thomas Burnham's career. He took up his Freedom on 7 September 1650, but the entry of his admission gives no indication of his trade. He became a servant employed by the family of Thomas Wood, occupying the house of 'a Mrs Wood in her backside'. He was married by this time to Joanne Potter, whose initial appears on his token, and two sons were born in this house. On his master's death in 1663, he became keeper of the racket court belonging to Oriel College. The poll tax book of 1677 contains the entry, 'Thomas Burnham gent, Joane his wife, Mary, Anne, and Thomas, children, £1-1-0. Burnham's move to another court is an interesting one. Christ Church's records show that he leased the Unicorn inn in Blue Boar Lane from the College on 10 June 1677. The property is described as 'an inn with a backside and stables there to belonging and a fair Rackett court'. Thomas Burnham did not, however, use the premises as an inn, but spent his money on improving the tennis court by covering it.

Burnham also interested himself in civic affairs. He became a chamberlain between 1659 and 1665, and later was elected town bailiff. His funeral in 1676 was attended by many students of Merton College, and he was buried in the parish church of St Aldate's 'neare the doore entering the chancel'.

The racket court in Blue Boar Lane, valued at £550, a huge sum in the seventeenth century, was left to his wife Joane. She carried on the business for some years. A tax return of September 1679 describes her as 'Joane Burnham tenis court keeper'. Incidentally, tennis was played on this court until 1835.

The third tennis court token issued at Oxford appeared under the name of yet another Thomas. The obverse legend states: THOMAS BVTLER AT YE, and the design is of a racket and ball. On the reverse are the words RACKIT & BALL IN OXON and the initials T.M.B.

Thomas Butler served an apprenticeship with the previous issuer, Thomas Burnham, from 1660 to 1668. When his apprenticeship was completed in 1668, he was admitted a Freeman of Oxford. In 1670 he set up on his own at a racket court near Smith Gate in the parish of St Peter in the East. His move

13.4 Farthing of Thomas Burnham.

13.5 Farthing of Thomas Butler.

coincided with the move of Thomas Burnham to Boar Lane. Although the court was leased in the name of Susanna French, it was administered by Thomas Butler until at least 1680. It is almost certain that his token was issued at the Smith Gate court.

Undoubtedly the joint efforts of Thomas Wood, Thomas Burnham and Thomas Butler contributed much to the fitness of students in mid-seventeenth century Oxford. One can imagine the eagerness with which they rushed from lectures to spend their tokens, hiring a court for an hour or two's play. Today the rush is to play badminton or squash.

COCKFIGHTING

The brutal sport of cockfighting is still practised in the twentieth century, but behind closed doors and with heavy penalties for those caught, yet in the seventeenth century it was still an extremely popular pastime, along with bear and bull baiting. Not everyone approved. Samuel Pepys, by no means the most sensitive of men, was disgusted, albeit fascinated, on his first visit to a cock pit: 'Being directed by sight of bills upon the wall I did go to Shoe Lane to see a cocke-fighting at a new pit there, a sport I was never at in my life. I soon had enough of it, and yet I would not but have seen it once, it being strange to observe the nature of those poor creatures, how they will fight till they drop down dead upon the table and strike after they are ready to give up the ghost – not offering to run away when they are wounded or weary past doing further'. When reading Cotton's description of cockfighting as a sport 'full of delight and pleasure' in the *Compleat Gamester*, Pepys added in the margin 'and of barbarity'.

A farthing token was issued at COCK PITT COURT in Shoe Lane by Samuel Clever. It is unlikely that the issuer was the proprietor of the cockpit, but more probably a tradesman in the neighbourhood. The token is undated, but would have appeared round about 1663, the year of Pepys' visit, when the diarist infers that the pit was newly opened.

A SPA TOKEN

'Spas' become popular in the seventeenth century, the name being derived from Spa, a Belgian resort famed for its mineral waters. An early spa was established in St George's Fields on the site of a spring. An advertisement of 1733 refers to 'a very fine chalybeate spring of the nature of Piedmont Water but superior. The water could be had fresh daily at the gardens and at a cork cutter's under Exeter Change in the Strand'. A music hall and a cockpit were established at the 'Restoration' Gardens, named after the healing powers of the water. A token was issued by Will Hagley (*W*357), reading, WILL HAGLEY AT YE REST HIS HALFE PENY/ORATION ST GEORGES FEILDES W.M.H. This may well have been used as small change for customers buying the spa water.

CHAPTER 14

RELIGION AND POLITICS

Religion was an integral part of everyday life in the seventeenth century. Church-going was the norm and the Bible was interpreted literally by both parish priest and dissenting pastor as the accepted code of conduct. A Bible was in every home – often the only book. As yet there was little conflict between the biblical scholar and the scientist; the religious conflict in Britain, as in the rest of Europe, was one of interpretation and authority. This conflict came to a head in the middle of the seventeenth century with the development of Puritanism outside the established Church, and the formation and multiplication of numerous sects.

Henry VIII had not envisaged the establishment of a Protestant church in England on Lutheran or Calvinistic lines when he broke with the Papacy. His contribution to a Protestant revolution was his suppression of the monasteries and the redistribution of their wealth for his own political ends. Self-interest on the part of the new landowners ensured the demise of monastic influence. In the boy-king Edward VI's reign they actively encouraged the spread of Lutheran doctrines. Elizabeth saw the need for a return to High Church ritual and dogma but it was catholicism without the Pope. She revelled in her position as the head of the Church of England but her religious settlement was comprehensive and broad-based, allowing puritan elements to exist within the Anglican Church.

The Stuart king's repeated call of 'No Bishop no King' angered the Puritans within the church. Charles I was a High Anglican with no sympathy at all for Puritanism. His insistence on the divine right to rule led to civil war and open Nonconformity on the part of many of his subjects.

Cromwell was the natural leader of the Puritan faction, drawing together Baptists, Independents, Quakers, Anabaptists, Fifth Monarchy Men and Presbyterians in a common purpose. The Civil War was not so much a religious conflict as a war of ideas in church and state. There were many shades of opinion on both sides; many Royalists who actively supported the Anglican Church were opposed to Laud. It is significant that the Royalists were strongest in the regions of the country where recent economic and social changes had been least felt, namely the shires and towns furthest from London. It is equally significant that the Puritans who preached enterprise and hard work were strongest in the business houses of the capital, the seaports and the new manufacturing towns.

Oliver Cromwell was a supporter of religious tolerance. That is why there was no persecution during the Protectorate, although the Church of England was outlawed. Many of the tokens circulating before the Restoration were issued by Puritans. It is often forgotten that large numbers of people changed their religious and political views between the beheading of Charles I in 1648 and the Restoration of Charles II in 1660. Samuel Pepys himself did. He was reared in 'Puritan' Huntingdonshire, and his mentor Edward Montague had seen active service with Cromwell's Eastern Association. As a schoolboy of fifteen he enjoyed the spectacle of the execution at Whitehall, yet just twelve years later he helped to engineer the return of the monarchy.

The year 1660 witnessed a three-fold Restoration – a political restoration of King and Parliament, a religious restoration of Bishop and Prayer Book and a social restoration of upper class gentry. The Church of England was now firmly established, and the Presbyterians survived. All other Dissenters were proscribed. Although Charles II was no serious churchman, the Church rapidly became as High Anglican as it had been under Laud. Hyde was completely uncompromising. Sheldon who was appointed Archbishop of Canterbury in 1663 hated Puritanism in all its forms. The Clarendon Code made second-class citizens of all Nonconformists, filling the prisons and forcing many into poverty. It is interesting to reflect that all the tokens struck between 1660 and 1672, circulated during this period of bitter persecution, when Dissenters were forbidden even to meet in each other's houses. Another decade was to elapse before religious toleration was finally accepted as an essential part of the English freedom and democracy of the Bloodless Revolution of 1688.

EARLY QUAKERS

The birth of the Society of Friends coincides almost exactly with the issue of the first tokens. The period of their issue (1648–72) again coincides with the 'suffrances' of Quakers at the hands of a society which considered them to be not merely unorthodox but positively dangerous. Friends laid great stress on the ethic of hard work, so it is not surprising that many of them were successful enough in their business to issue tokens. Unlike the early Methodists of the following century, who tended to be recruited almost entirely from the working class, Quakers came from all walks of life, as indeed their tokens tell us.

Their leader and founder, George Fox (1624–91) was the son of a Leicestershire weaver. He had been brought up in the Anglican Church, but became convinced that everyone could experience God's love and goodness at first hand. He felt the priesthood to be superfluous as God's grace was freely available to all, and advocated a priesthood of all believers. He formed a very close-knit and disciplined society with the restraints imposed by creed and clergy replaced by an even more rigid code of conduct, which controlled every action. Friends believed the Bible to be the inspired word of God. They sought God's help through silent prayer and worship, rejected violence in all its forms and adopted pacifism, both in their everyday dealings with their fellow men and also in the realm of international affairs. They believed implicitly that all men are equal in the eyes of God, rejecting all social conventions which drew distinctions between classes of people. They refused to doff their hats and insisted on addressing their social superiors as 'thee' and 'thou' even in court.

It is not surprising that this attitude greatly displeased those in authority in both Church and State after the Restoration in 1660. The Quakers refused to obey laws restricting their freedom to worship as they pleased and requiring them to pay tithes and perform military service. It has been estimated that no less than 15,000 Friends suffered legal penalties of one kind or another between 1660 and 1689. It is known that 450 died in prison, yet their sufferings only served to strengthen their resolve. By the end of the century there were 50,000 Quakers in the British Isles and a similar number in the West Indies.

The Quaker movement was particularly strong in Buckinghamshire and the adjoining counties. William Penn, Isaac Pennington and Thomas Ellwood all worshipped in Buckinghamshire farmhouses and barns. They now lie at rest in the peaceful graveyard close by the simple meeting house at Jordans. Several Buckinghamshire Quakers issued tokens, including William Ashby of Northall, James Brierly of Olney, Thomas Burgess of Stony Stratford, Edward Cooper and John Thornton of Newport Pagnell, Jonathan Kingham of Wooburn and Nicholas Steele of North Crawley. Joseph Besse's fascinating book, *A Collection of the Sufferings of the People called Quakers*, 1753, contains a number of references to those men, all of whom suffered fines or imprisonment during this period.

In 1664 Brierly, Steele and eighteen other Quakers were taken out of a meeting at Newport Pagnell and committed to Aylesbury Gaol for three months for defying the Conventicle Act. They were in fact detained considerably longer owing to the 'contrivance of the Gaoler and Clerk of the Peace who revived old indictments laid against them for absenting themselves from Church. Their usage in Prison was cruel, being kept in a dark room, exposed to the weather, so that they could not lie dry in their beds, when they had any, for they were obliged for some time to lodge upon straw and some of them, being poor tradesmen, were denied the use of a place to work in order to provide for themselves the necessaries of life' (*Besse*).

James Brierly, the Olney lace buyer, was heavily fined for meeting in the street in 1670. Friends were not permitted to use their meeting house at Sherington and consequently held their meetings wherever they could. Brierly was caught and made the scapegoat. His token (*W*109), struck twelve years earlier in 1658, reads, JAMES BRIERLY I.M.B./OF OLNEY 1658. The reverse shows a pair of scales, a device common to all Olney pieces. Lace making was one of the most important industries in North Buckinghamshire and surrounding counties. James Brierly was the middleman supplying women at their cottage doors with the spinning wheel and roll of lace, buying the finished product and selling it to the drapers in Olney and nearby towns. Quaker records contain references to the deaths of several children of James and Mary Brierly, and of Mary herself on 19 April 1676. The burials took place on James' own land, a custom of the Society of Friends.

After Mary's death in 1676, James may have remarried, as a marriage is recorded of a James Brierly and Thomasin Knight, both of Olney, on 5 June 1676 at Sherington. If this is the original James Brierly, the token issuer, then he remarried within six weeks of his first wife's death, which seems unlikely. We do know that he died in 1691.

Let us now look at the tokens of the other Buckinghamshire Friends. Nicholas Steele's farthing (*W*106) reads, NICHOLAS STEELE OF/NORTH CRAWLEY N.M.S. A pair of scales is again featured on the obverse. He married Mary King on 5 February 1659, hence the intial M. The token was probably struck shortly after his marriage, judging by the early style. Steele died on 25 July 1683. His occupation is not known.

Thomas Burgess issued his farthing at Stony Stratford in 1657. It is no coincidence that the majority of tokens issued by Quakers seem to have been struck before Restoration Year. During the sufferings (1660–88) they would not have wanted to draw attention to themselves, especially to the fact that they were doing well in business. In 1611 Burgess was committed to Aylesbury Gaol for refusing to repair the steeple house there. He was a grocer and baker by trade; his token displays the Bakers' Arms on the obverse and its date of issue on the reverse, together with the initials T.A.B. The initial A represents his wife Anne, whom he married in 1627. She died in 1677, and Burgess himself died in February 1696. He was buried at Sherington, where he had worshipped alongside Thomas Brierley and Nicholas Steele, and the burial is recorded in the Stony Stratford parish register.

Another Quaker grocer who issued tokens was Edward Cooper of Newport Pagnell. He had three tokens struck, all of them post 1662. The earliest, a farthing, has both sides defaced and the reading NEWPORT PANNELL on the reverse. The second, also a farthing, features the Grocers' Arms on the obverse and the words NEWPORT PANNELL on the reverse, together with the date 1667 and the initials E.C. The third is an undated half penny with the initials E.E.C. The Buckinghamshire *Quarterly Meeting Digest of Marriage* provides a helpful explanation for the change in the initials. The first two tokens were obviously struck before he was married. The *Digest* informs us that his first marriage, to Susanna Walter of Linford, took place at Sherington on 25 January 1669. Unfortunately she died just a year later – in February 1670. Another marriage is listed in September of the same year between Edward Cooper of Newport Pagnell and Elizabeth Hootham. Thus Cooper's latest token, bearing the initial of his second wife, must have appeared after September 1670. Edward and Elizabeth had eleven children, most of whom died young. The grocer himself died in 1702, being buried, naturally enough, at Sherington.

John Thornton who described himself as a merchant of small wares issued an early undated farthing bearing a thorn bush, a pun on his surname. Thornton's name frequently appears in the Quarter Sessions records. As we have seen, he was sent to prison in 1660. Twenty years later John Thornton of Sherington was committed to Aylesbury Gaol for ten months for non-payment of tithes. I feel sure he is the same man. Again in 1686 he was sent to prison for a similar offence – this time for two and three quarter years. John Thornton married twice. His first wife Elizabeth, whose initial appears on the token, died in 1662. He married Susanna Arnold in 1664.

Tokens were issued by Quakers in other parts of the country, including two in Worcestershire. Ezekiel Partridge had a half penny struck in Stourbridge in 1665. Several dies are known, and Partridge half pence are quite common. The initials E.M.P. appear on the reverse. The Quaker *Digest Register of Burials* for Herefordshire, Worcestershire and Wales lists the widow of an Ezekiel Partridge of Stourbridge Mary, who died on 4 June 1706. John Noake records that this man was imprisoned in Worcester Gaol in 1663 on the evidence of Rev. Tristram, Vicar of Belbroughton. He was gaoled again at Worcester in 1674 for refusing to pay a church rate. Stourbridge, the home of Ezekiel Partridge, was a Constituent meeting place of Chadwick Monthly Meeting from 1668 until 1810. Stourbridge Meeting House, which still stands, was built in 1680. Partridge was an important member of the community, being elected overseer of the poor in April 1670 for the following year.

Edward Pittway was another Worcestershire Quaker who issued a token (*W2*): EDWARD PITTWAY AT THE (Lion Rampant)/RED LYON IN BENGWORTE E.F.P. Edward Pittway was married to Frances, buried in 1675, whose initial F is on the token. Pittway was elected Mayor of Evesham in 1648, but had to renounce his position as burgess upon joining the Society of Friends in 1655. When George Fox visited Evesham in 1655, he called at Pittway's house at Bengeworth, just outside Evesham, to find out whether stocks had been erected in the town for his benefit. In the evening they both joined a 'large and precious meeting of Friends'. The magistrates complained to Cromwell about their conduct, and twelve persons were fined, including Pittway himself, who received the heaviest penalty – £20. In 1674 he spent a period in Worcester Gaol with George Fox. He managed to persuade Justice Parker to order the gaoler to show him 'what lawful favour he could for the benefit of his health'.

Edward Pittway's token was issued at the Red Lion in Bengeworth, later the Northwick Arms, which still stands. It has always been assumed that the Red Lion was a tavern, and there is no reason why Pittway should not have been a tavern keeper, as abstinence from alcoholic beverages was more strongly advocated for Quakers in the nineteenth century. Fox himself often stayed at inns on his journeys. The diarist Samuel Pepys wrote on 2 October 1664, 'I entended to have seen the Quakers, who they say, do meet every Lord's Day, at the Mouth in Bishopgate but I could see none stay, nor was it fit to ask for the place'. Here we have a tavern actually used as a meeting house, but Pepys was slightly in error, as the Quakers actually met at the Bull and Mouth, Aldergate.

BAPTISTS

Buckinghamshire folk have always been noted for independent thinking and strong convictions. It is no accident that Amersham was a centre of Lollardry in the fifteenth century or that Buckinghamshire yeomen fought mainly on the Parliamentary side during the Civil War. Nonconformity had strong roots within the county so it is not surprising to find a rapidly growing Baptist community there shortly after the conflict, despite considerable persecution.

After the Restoration of 1660 the Cavalier Parliament was determined to ensure the permanence of the established Church by stamping out all forms of dissent. Everyone was expected to worship at their parish church whatever their private beliefs and faced fines or imprisonment if they refused. The Sectarians were particularly hit by the Five Miles Act and the Conventicles Act, which prevented them from even meeting as a group in their own homes. There is plenty of evidence that Nonconformists in Buckinghamshire, as elsewhere, were willing to risk imprisonment, the pillory or even death rather than submit to such legislation. The Clergy Returns of 1669 were required by

Archbishop Sheldon to show the extent of dissent in each parish, so that he could convince the government that more urgent legislation was needed, and throw considerable light on the way that Baptists were managing to meet and worship.

A random sample of these returns follows.

Wingrave: Middle and meaner sort of people, taught by Stephen Dagnall and William Smart.

Wycombe Magna: A 'holy town'. Numbers very great, and the persons very insolent; met at the house of Richard Harding, baker. Taught by mechanics.

Amersham: At the house of David Gimson. Taught by Robert Turner, malster, and Edward Edrepp, blacksmith. Also at the house of Sarah Grimsell, 'Jewes' taught by Nicholas Babb, weaver.

Olney: At the house of Widow Tears, 200 but decreasing. Taught by Gibbs, Breeden and James Rogers, lace buyers and Fenn, a hatter, of Bedford.

Swanbourne: At the house of George Deverell, yeoman, not above 20 mean people. Taught by William Giles, shopkeeper, and Hartnoll, a thatcher.

We have a picture here of ordinary working people – shopkeepers, lacemen, blacksmiths, housewives – meeting in each other's houses for worship and prayer, led by one of their own number. Three of the men mentioned in these returns issued tokens: Stephen Dagnall, an Aylesbury bookseller, William Bredon, an Olney lace buyer, and William Giles, a Winslow hatter. It is significant that all three were 'teachers', and interesting to note that the two Aylesbury men were teaching in villages several miles away from their home.

The Baptist Church, then as now, contained various shades of opinion in its doctrinal belief. The 'Jewes' meeting in Amersham were Seventh Day Baptists who celebrated the Jewish Sabbath as their Lord's Day. There were two main strands in the Baptist sect at this time – the General or Orthodox Baptists and the Particular or Strict Baptists. They had much in common, including lay leadership, the autonomy of each individual church, adult baptism and emphasis on prayer. The main difference was that Particular Baptists subscribed to Calvin's belief that Christ died for the 'elect', the chosen few. The General Baptists, on the other hand, were direct descendants from Wycliff's Lollards and, influenced by the continental Anabaptists, believed that it was God's will that all men should turn to Him and be saved.

By 1669, as the Clergy returns indicate, Baptists were meeting in towns and villages throughout Buckinghamshire. Yet all these widely separate groups were gradually being organized into five distinct churches of General Baptists. The first Assembly of these churches took place as early as 1654 and had representatives from Wing, Winslow, Aylesbury, Cuddington – Ford and Berkhamstead – Chesham – Tring. 'Messengers' were appointed to lead them; John Hartnoll, a thatcher from North Marston for the north of the county and Thomas Monk, a Bierton farmer for the south. Strangely enough, both men lived quite close to each other in the middle of the county. Their role was akin to that of bishop. Each church, however, elected its own leader or 'Elder', who was allotted a number of deacons to assist him. Stephen Dagnell was Elder of the Aylesbury fellowship. There was only one Particular Baptist church in the country at this time – at Haddenham, formed in 1653. This church remained quite isolated until other Particular Baptist churches were established at Chesham in 1701 and Princes Risborough in 1707.

No less than sixteen Buckinghamshire Baptists issued trade tokens. Each one tells a tale of courage and fortitude. One of the earliest was that of the Aylesbury Elder, Stephen Dagnall, bookseller, publisher and stationer. His token reads, STEPHEN DAGNALL S.I.D./IN ALESBURY 1655 and depicts a book. The initials are those of the bookseller himself and his second wife, Joan, whom he married in 1647, having lost his first wife, Eleanor, the previous year. The farthing is the only one of lead in the entire Buckinghamshire series.

Dagnall was a man of great influence in Baptist circles throughout the country on account of his publishing activities. One of his many enemies, Thomas Edwards, refers to him in 1646 as 'one Dagnall, a Bookseller, a man of errors, who to a godly minister denyed original sin and maintained many other wicked opinions'. In October 1650 Dagnall published a book attacking the 'Ranters', a wild sect whom John Bunyan claimed had no more religion than a wild bull. A year later he published a pamphlet of his own entitled *Several Proposals for the General Good of the Commonwealth.* Although a radical document, in some respects it shows the author to be surprisingly moderate. He advocates free schooling, the abolition of tithes and the election of parish priests by their own parishioners, yet he does not oppose tithes of honour or favour a widening of the Parliamentary franchise. In 1661 Dagnall published a book attacking the Quakers. Although the Baptists and the Quakers had a great deal in common, there was no love lost between them.

As a result of the Primary Visitation of Buckinghamshire by J. Robert Sanderson, Bishop of Lincoln, in 1662, demanding that church wardens supply information concerning anabaptists and other sectaries, Thomas Monk was denounced by the churchwardens of his own village and proceedings were taken against twenty-one Aylesbury Baptists including Dagnall. The County Gaol was so full of Dissenters that two annexes were used. Twelve of the Aylesbury Baptists were charged under an act of 1593 which stated that conventiclers could after three months imprisonment be declared felons unless they conformed or left the country. The prisoners included three token issuers: Dagnall himself, Thomas Hill, a mercer, and William Welch, a grocer and tallow chandler. Two women were also included in the twelve. They refused to conform and despite the fact that several magistrates left the bench in protest, the chairman sentenced all twelve to death. They were the last Protestants in England to be given the death sentence for their faith, but were pardoned after a public outcry.

Both William Welch's and Thomas Hill's tokens are undated. They bear the hallmarks of David Ramage in his pre-Restoration period – the mullet mintmark and the outer border of labels and lozenge shaped stops, so they were probably struck in the fifties, as were those of Quaker tradesmen. We know that Welch's piece must have appeared between 1657 and 1660, as it bears the initial of his second wife Joan whom he married in 1657. Strangely, he only put his initials on the token, which was unusual outside London. He describes himself as a TALLOW CHANNDLER and depicts a man dipping candles. Hill's token also states the issuer's trade MERCER and bears the Arms of the Mercers' Company. The only other known member of the Baptist Church in Aylesbury to have a token struck was Joseph Freer, another mercer. He obligingly dated his farthing 1652, well before the persecution.

Dagnall continued as Elder of the Church in Aylesbury after his release from prison, being supported in his work by his son Matthew. They both

14.1 The initials of William Giles and his wife Mary above the door of the meeting house at Winslow.

14.2 Half penny token of William Giles, hatter, of Winslow.

lived at Walton on the southern outskirts of the town. In 1684 they were indicted for being absent from church. Stephen died the same year, leaving his son to carry on the family bookselling business. Matthew does not seem to have shared his father's passion for the Baptist cause, for we find him rebinding the Bible of the parish church at Winslow in 1699, and actually being elected churchwarden at St Mary's Church, Aylesbury two years later.

Winslow, just ten miles north of Aylesbury, also had an active church which suffered persecution at the same time. Their meetings were usually held in a cottage belonging to a felt-maker named William Giles. We know this because the cottage still survives, and its porch bears the initials W.M.G. (William and Mary Giles) and the date 1695. These initials also appear on the two tokens which he issued, an undated early farthing and a halfpenny of 1666. Both pieces feature the contemporary broadbrimmed men's hat, significantly without ornamentation. A feather in the hat would have signified allegiance to church and crown!

The house is known as 'Keach's Meeting House' in memory of its celebrated Elder during the 1660s, Benjamin Keach. On 18 October 1664, Keach was indicted for writing a heretical book and summoned to appear before Chief Justice Hyde at Aylesbury Assizes. The book was in fact intended to be a children's reading book, but it incorporated 'dangerous doctrine'. There were several lively exchanges in court between the judge and the accused. Judge Hyde at one point commented, 'I have seen three creeds before, but I never saw a fourth until you made one . . . I know your religion. You are a fifth Monarchy man, and you would preach here if I let you'. He was quite right. Keach would have treated the court to one of his best sermons, given the opportunity.

The jury had the utmost difficulty in reaching a verdict, but Keach was found guilty and given a fortnight's imprisonment followed by two periods in the pillory at Aylesbury and Winslow respectively. Whilst pilloried at Winslow he had the humiliation of seeing his books burned by the common hangman. The house where the Winslow Baptists met in secret, conveniently tucked away along a little alley, is well worth visiting, being reminiscent of the Quaker Meeting House at Jordans in its plainness and simplicity. William Giles sold his hats on a stall in the market place close by. He lived to a ripe old age and was buried on 12 April 1713. He is maliciously referred to in the parish register as an 'anti-Christian Baptist'.

The only two Elders to issue tokens were Stephen Dagnall of the Aylesbury Church and Thomas Headach, Elder of the 'uphill' parts of the Cuddington and Ford congregation. Cuddington and Ford are tiny villages west of Aylesbury. Headach was a grocer at Monks Risborough, and probably had a shop at Princes Risborough too. His token, like Dagnall's, is a distinctive square shape (*W*115). It reads: THOMAS HEADEACH 1669/IN PRINSES RISBROW HIS HALF PENNY T.F.H. Before his period of office he was trapped by a 'spy' and accused of speaking treason. If he had been charged by the magistrates and found guilty like the 'Twelve Confessors', he too would have received the death penalty. Fortunately Poulter, the spy, was discredited.

Headach was elected Elder in 1689 at the age of fifty-three. He must have felt at times that his surname was very appropriate, for he was frequently allotted difficult and embarrassing tasks by his congregation. In 1701 he had to warn members not to worship with Edward Hoare and Thomas Norris, as they had formed their own Calvinistic meeting at Princes Risborough. A year later he had to exclude Hoare and fourteen other members of the Cuddington Church on account of their Calvinistic tendencies. Headach often had to warn members about their conduct in his capacity as Elder. He even had to administer an official warning to his own daughter, Mary, who married into the Delafield family, noted for their adherence to Calvinism. He is last heard of on 25 January 1716 at the age of eighty, visiting an erring sister King, who had married out of the fellowship. Baines sums up his character, 'he was a simple-hearted man, loyal to his church and creed, and implicitly trusted by his bishop and by fellow members. He deserved to have lived in quieter times'.

Dagnall, Headach and Giles were all present at an extremely important

14.3 Benjamin Keach in the pillory at Winslow.

meeting in Aylesbury on 30 January 1679, to sign the Fifty Articles drawn up by Thomas Monk to unite all orthodox Baptists against the heresies of the Kent and Sussex churches, led by their messenger, Matthew Caffyn, which were adopting anti-Trinitarian views current in the Low Countries. The establishment of the Unitarian Church was a consequence of this. There were fifty-four signatories of the Orthodox Confession at Aylesbury, five token issuers amongst them. Three we have met already. The others were William Norman, a grocer from Steeple Claydon, and John Rennals, a lace buyer from Buckingham.

Norman's half penny token (*W*117) was issued eleven years before he signed the Confession. It reads, WILLIAM NORMAN OF HIS HALF PENY/STEPELL CLADON 1668 W.I.N. The third initial stands for his wife Jane. Norman was excommunicated in 1662 for non-attendance at his parish church and was similarly indicted on a number of occasions in the 1680s. He was a faithful member of the Cuddington and Ford Church. Rennals, who probably belonged to the church at Winslow, issued his half penny in the same year as William Norman's token. There are three dies known. It shows a strip of lace, the symbol of his trade. He is probably the John Reynolds who is mentioned in the Clergy Returns of 1669 as preaching at Horne.

There is space only for a brief mention of other Baptists in the county who had tokens struck. Richard and Samuel Ware of Chesham, members of a well known Baptist family, issued early farthings. They were weavers by trade. William Childe, a Chesham brewer, had Baptist connections. His brother, Giles, was a prominent member of the Church at Amersham.

Finally mention should be made of two Wycombe Baptists, Thomas Harding and Thomas Taylor. They were great friends and used to worship at

14.4 Square half penny token of the Baptist elder, Thomas Headach of Princes Risborough.

Thomas Harding's brother Richard's house. Richard Harding, a baker, was frequently hauled before the justices for absence from church. Harding appointed Taylor in his will of 1674 as overseer to assist his wife. Harding's token, a farthing, appeared in 1668, whilst that of his friend circulated much earlier. Thomas Taylor's token,which is extremely rare, reads, THOMAS TAYLOR/IN WICOME T.E.T. and depicts a roll of lace. He was a lace buyer like William Bredon of Newport Pagnell and John Rennals of Buckingham. The initial E indicates his wife Elizabeth (*nee* Harding), whom he married in 1654. Thus there is a firm link between the two families. Thomas Taylor is remembered as being the only Baptist in Buckinghamshire to have his house licensed for worship under the Act of Indulgence of 1672. Most other Baptists were justifiably suspicious of the declaration, as the persecution continued until the firm Act of Toleration under William and Mary in 1688.

LOYALISTS

RATHER DEAD THAN DISLOYAL. These striking words appearing on a half penny token of a High Wycombe innkeeper and mayor, epitomized the attitude of the vast majority of English people to the Restoration of King and Parliament in 1660.

Sir George Clarke observes, 'the restoration of King Charles II released the English people from the fear and repression of nearly twenty years. All over the country maypoles were set up again, loyal toasts were drunk immoderately and Puritanism was repudiated and derided'. Most people were heartily sick of the petty social restrictions imposed by military dictatorship – even men like Samuel Pepys, once a staunch Cromwellian, but who had changed his views so radically that he had been a member of the delegation which invited Charles II in exile to return home to claim his kingdom.

Both Pepys himself and that other contemporary diarist, John Evelyn, describe in graphic detail the enthusiastic welcome which greeted the restored king on 25 May 1660. Evelyn estimated that more than 20,000 horse and foot accompanied the King, 'along ways strewed with flowers, the bells ringing, the street hung with tapestry, the fountains running with wine'. The diarist concluded his eye-witness account, 'I stood in the Strand and blessed God. And all this was done with not one drop of blood shed'.

London had, of course, supported the Roundheads and had witnessed the execution of Charles I with not a little joy, but the situation was now very different. Cromwellian rule had proved oppressive to all except extreme Puritans, and Cavaliers and Prebyterians alike had joined forces in bringing about the restoration of the monarchy.

A token-issuing publican actually took part in the King's coronation procession through the capital, as we know from Pepys' entry on 22 April 1661, 'Wadlow, the vintner of the Devil in Fleet Street, did lead a fine company, of soldiers, all young comely men in white doublets'. Wadlow's farthing (*W*3071) reads, AT THE D. AND DVNSTANS/WITHIN TEMPLE BARRE I.S.W. The obverse features Dunstan pulling the Devil's nose with a pair of tongs. John Wadlow took over the inn in 1640, remaining there until the year of the King's coronation, when he was succeeded by Jonathon Barford, who also issued a token. Meanwhile Wadlow took over the Sun Tavern behind the Royal Exchange, which he had rebuilt after the disastrous Fire of 1666. John Wadlow was the son of Simon Wadlow, who kept the Devil during the time of Ben Jonson (1607–27). Jonson refers to Simon thus, 'let your meat rather follow you to a tavern . . . at brave Duke Wadloe's . . . Simon the King will bid us welcome'.

Pepys also refers to a couple of Cheapside tavern keepers who demonstrated their loyalty to the monarch several months before his arrival in London. On 11 February 1660 we read 'And so we went to the Star Tavern (Monk being then at Benson's) where we drank, and I wrote a letter to my Lord from there. In Cheapside there was a great many bone fires and Bow Bells and all the bells in all the churches as we went home were a-ringing'.

The Benson referred to is Thomas Benson, innkeeper at the Bull Head in Cheapside, who had issued a farthing there ten years previously in 1650. Whitelock in his 'Memorial of the English Affairs' wrote on 12 February 1660, just a day later, 'Monk drew up his forces in Finsbury, dined with the Lord Mayor, had conference with him and the Court of Aldermen, retired to the Bull Head in Cheapside and quartered at the Glasshouse in Broad Street'. Monk and the Lord Mayor were obviously engaged in planning the details of the May procession. Whilst the general and the Lord Mayor were so engaged, Pepys was catching up with his correspondence in the nearby Star, where at least four tokens were struck by no less than three taverners. At the time of Pepys's visit in February 1660 it was probably in the hands of Francis Ringstead, who is mentioned in the diary in an entry of 1 December 1660.

To return to the High Wycombe piece with the words RATHER DEAD THAN DISLOYAL, this appeared ten years after Charles II's triumphant return to London. The half penny may be described thus: RICH LVCAS OF WICKHAM R.P.L./RATHER DEAD THAN DISLOYAL. A lion rampant appears on the reverse, advertising Lucas's tavern in the High Street (*W*169).

The issuer of this token is an extremely interesting character. He is by no means an ardent royalist and supporter of the Anglican Established Church, as one would assume; in fact he had been an enthusiastic Parliamentarian like most citizens of Wycombe. Certainly a dissenter, like other leading townsmen, he may be described as a Presbyterian rather than an Independent or Baptist.

Lucas was innkeeper at the Red Lion, which occupied a prominent position in the High Street opposite the Guild Hall. The inn was demolished about fifteen years ago, but the impressive Georgian frontage was preserved and forms an imposing façade for the Woolworth's store behind. Benjamin

Disraeli, Earl of Beaconsfield and a Member of Parliament for High Wycombe for many years, frequently addressed huge crowds from the balcony of the Red Lion at election time. Lucas himself played an active role in local politics. He was an alderman from 1649 to 1675 and was elected mayor on three occasions (1660, 1667 and 1672).

Where exactly does Richard Lucas stand? Later events seem to indicate that he was neither royalist nor anti-royalist; the slogan simply declared his loyalty to the government of the day. Although he did not belong to the 'establishment' party in High Wycombe, actively supporting church and crown, he was anxious that his support of the opposition party should not be construed as anti-royalist and disloyal.

The innkeeper-alderman must have found himself in many an awkward situation during the first decade following the Restoration, as he tried to walk a political tightrope. The Clarendon Code ensured that he moderated his Nonconformist views, yet he retained his friendship with more extreme Dissenters. Ashford comments on his delicate situation, 'the Presbyterians who had been so strong in the time of the Rump were perhaps more discomforted than other puritans by the effects of the Clarendon Code. They had regarded themselves as members of the Church of England which they had wished to reorganize on Presbyterian lines. Now they found themselves in the position of outcasts along with the Baptists and Independents, the sectaries they looked down on. In Wycombe some probably chose to remain in the Church and swallow the pill of Episcopacy with such appetite as they could. Others joined with the Independents and met with them in the house of Samuel Guy'.

Lucas almost certainly belonged to the group which remained within the Church, otherwise he would have lost his aldermanic status under the Corporation Act, as had Samuel Guy. Guy, dubbed by a contemporary as 'a forward man for the Rumpers Cause', had been elected alderman in 1656 and mayor the following year. Lucas' halfpenny was issued in 1670 when the Clarendon Code was in full operation.

The Declaration of Indulgence had given the Dissenters in the town new hope, when a Parliamentary by-election followed the death of Sir John Borlase in 1672. They chose the Dissenting Henry Bigg as their mayoral candidate. His royalist opponent, Nicholas Bradshaw, was elected on 26 September 1672, but died dramatically at the mayoral banquet within hours of his election, and Henry Bigg was selected in his stead. Bigg was forced to resign, however, at a public meeting on 6 December of the same year, because his political opponents sent a petition to the Privy Council claiming that he was ineligible for office as he had not received the sacrament.

The following day the burgesses of Wycombe met in the Guildhall and voted Lucas as their new mayor. Lucas had previously supported Bigg's candidature. Lucas would not have been chosen as mayor if he had been ineligible on the same ground as Bigg. Two of the five aldermen present, including Robert Whitton, Nicholas Bradshaw's son-in-law, opposed the election. Whitton drummed up support and at a rival meeting in the 'Catherine Wheel' – not the Red Lion! elected Thomas Gibbons mayor instead of Lucas. Thus on 6 December 1672 there were two mayors of High Wycombe simultaneously in office! Lucas had the official backing of the mace, charters and ledger book and possessed the majority support of the aldermen. The issue was finally settled during the campaign for the ensuing

Parliamentary election. Lucas wisely arranged that eighty-five burgesses be elected to ensure the election of his candidate Sir John Borlase, son of the late member for Wycombe. Borlase was duly returned by Lucas whilst Sir William Egerton was returned by the rival mayor. The House of Commons was petitioned by both groups and Sir John Borlase was declared the rightful member for Wycombe. Lucas' hold on the mayoral chair was thus confirmed.

His arch-opponent Robert Whitton was also an innkeeper – at the Antelope just a few yards from the Red Lion on the same side of the High Street. Whitton issued an undated farthing token depicting the sign of his inn and bearing the initials R.K.W. The K stands for Katherine Bradshaw, whom he married on 11 August 1656. She was the daughter of Nicholas Bradshaw, leader of the Royalist party in Wycombe. After the election of Borlase to the House of Commons in 1672, Whitton's Royalist and Church party remained in the background of local politics until 1688.

Whereas Richard Lucas's claim of loyalty to the crown may savour of political expediency, there are many examples of seventeenth-century tokens declaring unequivocal allegiance to His Majesty. A Monmouth half penny issued by Richard Ballard (*W*15) reads RICHARD BALLARD OF MONMOVTH HIS HALFE PENY FOR NECESARY CHANGE/GOD PRESERVE OVR GRACIOVS KING. The King's head crowned is featured above the date 1668 and the letters C.R.II.

Durham has traditionally been a Royalist stronghold, therefore it is not surprising that of the fifty-one Durham tokens listed in Williamson, no less than twenty-nine bear royalist marks. The King's head crowned appears on twenty-four Durham pieces, the crown on three and the Royal Arms on another. The words GOD SAVE THE KING may be seen on fifteen. Many of these coins are undated, but the majority of the dated ones were struck in 1666. The earliest is that of John Peacock of the George and Dragon (*W*36). His token reads, JOHN PEACOCK 1662 IN DVRHAM/GOD SAVE THE KING.

CHAPTER 15

THE ARMY

ARMY CANTEENS

Canteens have been an integral part of British Army life for the lower ranks since time immemorial. They certainly existed in the middle of the seventeenth century, being run by 'sutlers', who supplied the troops with food, drink and tobacco to supplement their meagre rations. Sutlers were civilians; the word is derived from the Dutch and means a small vendor or petty tradesman. An army ordinance of 31 December 1590 states, 'the Provost Marechal and Sergeant-Major at every garrison shall keep a perfect roll of all such English victuallers called in Dutch sutlers, petty merchants and other loose persons of the English nation'. They seem to have had a particular association with the guards' regiments; the *London Gazette* of 1701 refers to a Mr Wollaston, 'sutler at ye Horse Guards'.

Sutlers had an important role to play in the everyday life of the guards, as there was no such thing as an Army Service Corps until the end of the nineteenth century, and all the business of transport and supply was done by contract. In that old battleground of the Coldstream, the Low Countries, a contractor could always be found who knew the business thoroughly. But the contractor was concerned only with the bread and fuel. Everything else was a regimental matter conducted by the regimental sutler, which meant more stoppages, more financial regulations and more accounts. This arrangement must have been bad for discipline, for the soldier who had to pay for his ration of meat, had great temptation to lay violent hands upon every fowl, pig or sheep that came his way. Thus in the regimental sutler lay the germ of the regimental canteen.

Several sutlers' tokens are known. One of the more fascinating is that of Edward Lloyd, which gives his name and describes him as SVTTLER TO HIS MAIESTIES GARD OF FOOT. A barracks is featured on the reverse. The value of the piece is stated – HIS HALF PENY and the issuer's initials E.L.I., together with his wife's initial M. It seems that Lloyd supplied the physical needs of soldiers attached to the Royal Regiment of Foot Guards, formed in 1665 from Colonel John Russell's and Thomas Wentworth's regiments. The new regiment became known as the King's Regiment of Foot Guards and later as the First Regiment of Foot Guards. It was not until the overthrow of

15.1 Half penny of Edward Lloyd, Sutler to HIS MAIESTIES GARD OF FOOT.

Napoleon in 1815 that the term 'Grenadier Guards' was used to commemorate the victory of the Grenadiers over the French Imperial Guards at the Battle of Waterloo. Thus Edward Lloyd's customers were guardsmen who were forerunners of the Grenadiers. Several men bearing the name Lloyd are mentioned in the early records of the regiment, but Edward himself is not mentioned, as he had only civilian status. It is no coincidence, however, that the first quarter master was a John Lloyd, whose appointment was confirmed on 1 July 1665. What could be more natural than that he should employ a member of his family in the capacity of sutler? The quarter master and sutler together supplied a regiment's needs. During the years 1660–81, three commissioned officers named Lloyd served the regiment – William, Sir Godfrey and Charles. Thus five members of the Lloyd family were involved with the Grenadiers – Sir Godfrey and William as captains, Charles as ensign, John as quarter master and Edward as sutler.

Unfortunately Edward's half penny does not bear a date but its style of lettering suggests that it was struck in the middle sixties. It features a pierced cinq foil and a cable pattern inner circle. Morley and Pegg classify tokens bearing these features as Group K (1665–6), which coincides almost exactly with John Lloyd's appointment as regimental quarter master in July 1665.

Two sutlers' tokens, at least, are directly connected with the other contemporary Guards regiment, Monk's regiment of foot, which after the Battle of Dunbar had its headquarters at Coldstream on the Tweed. After the Restoration the men of this regiment were mustered on Tower Hill and ordered to lay down their arms. Within minutes they were instructed to take them up again, this time as the King's Second Regiment of Foot Guards. The men refused to accept their new designation, insisting that they were second to none! They were then ordered to take up arms as the Lord General's Regiment of Foot Guards. This remained the regiment's title until 1670, when it became known officially as the Coldstream Guards.

General Monk, newly created Duke of Albermarle, had been allotted the post of Lord General of all the forces in England, Scotland and Ireland by the House of Commons in February 1660. A sutler's token issued at the Tilt Yard actually shows a bust of the Duke of Albermarle on the obverse (*W*3150). Although the bust is not clear, its identity is in no doubt as the initials D.A. appear on either side. The obverse and reverse legends, if joined together as the engraver intended, read RICHARD WASHBOVRNE AT THE TILT YARD SUTTLER 1666 HIS HALFE PENNY R.A.W.

15.2 Farthing of the Sutler at St James's.

15.3 Half penny of Richard Washbourne, Sutler at the Tilt Yard, Westminster.

15.4 Half penny of Will Slidd, Sutler to YE GUARD (depicting the Duke of Albermarle).

In my view, Richard Washbourne provided a canteen service for the Lord General's Regiment of Guards under canvas in St James Park. At this time there were few permanent barracks; soldiers were either provided with tented accommodation or boarded out in private lodgings. Between 1660 and 1690 the major part of both Guards regiments were stationed at Westminster; it is no coincidence, therefore, that all five sutlers' tokens were issued in Westminster. The second of these pieces to be linked with the Duke of Albemarle's regiment was issued by Will Slidd (*W*2524), reading WILL SLIDD SVTLER TO YE GVARD Bust (probably of the Duke)/AT ST JAMESES HIS HALFE PRNY W.I.S. It is undated, but belongs to the period 1644–70.

The earliest token is a farthing which appeared in 1650 during the Roundhead occupation of the capital. The legend is simple and concise: THE SVTLER AT IAMSES 1650 R.M. The unknown issuer was clearly ministering to the needs of Parliamentary troops garrisoned at Westminster.

The final piece was issued by JOHN SCOTT, SVTLER AT YE COCK PITT and features a crowned cock on the obverse. Stowe mentions the Cock Pit in his description of St James' Palace, 'On the right hand be divers tennis courts, bowling alleys and a cock pit all built by Henry VIII . . .', and it also occurs in Pepys' diary.

One wonders if John Scott, sutler at Ye Cockpit, was ever asked to provide victuals for the Duke of Albermarle himself. It is far more likely that he supplied the needs of the non-commissioned officers and guardsmen. The fact that he was able to circulate his own token coinage, like four other sutlers, suggests his business was sound.

DISASTER AT SHEERNESS

Only one sutler's token is known to have been issued outside London – that of Richard Jones, who circulated a half penny to troops guarding the naval fortifications at Sheerness on the Medway in Kent (*W*522). It reads, RICHARD IONES SVTLER HIS HALF PENY/OF SHIRNESS 1667 R.I.

Charles II created the second standing army in time of peace, the first being the New Model Army raised by the Parliamentarians in 1645. He modelled his new army on the personal guard of Louis XIV. In the beginning it consisted of only four regiments: the Life Guard, the Royal Horse Guards, and the First and Second Guards of Foot. As we have seen, the last-named regiment belonged to General Monk and had not disbanded at the Restoration. Later in Charles's reign, new regiments were formed. Charles entrusted the administration of his new army to General Monk, newly created Duke of Albemarle, who took his post seriously and created a harmonious body of men.

Charles II also took a keen interest in his fleet. In his teens he proved a competent admiral, gaining a detailed knowledge of navel vessels. On his Restoration he appointed his brother Lord High Admiral. It was customary for successful army officers to be given high posts in the navy. Thus the Duke of York and the Duke of Albemarle were both involved in naval strategy, and their sea commanders also tended to be soldiers first and sailors second. The outbreak of the Second Dutch War on 14 January 1665 might have given Charles' new navy an opportunity of proving its mettle. Unfortunately a serious financial crisis meant that the greater part of the fleet was laid up when it was most needed. On the evening of 10 June 1667 the Dutch sailed up the Medway, virtually unopposed, seizing the *Royal Charles*, Britain's finest battleship, and destroying several others.

Samual Pepys, as Clerk of the Acts of the Navy Board, was personally involved in the events leading up to the Medway Disaster; indeed he was summoned before a Parliamentary Select committee to give an account of his part in the affair. His diary account makes fascinating reading. It is clear that the Medway Invasion was not entirely unexpected, as the following extracts show:

18 August 1665	To Sheerness where we walked up and down laying out the ground to be taken in for a yard to lay provisions for cleaning and repairing of ships, and a most proper place it is for the purpose.
17 February 1667	Up by candle light about six o'clock and by water down to Woolwich, I being at leisure this day, the King and the Duke of York being gone down to Sheerness to lay out the design for a fortification there to the river Medway.
6 March 1667	Great preparations there are to fortify Sheerness and the Yard at Portsmouth and forces are drawing down to both these places and elsewhere by the seaside, so that we have some fear of an invasion.

Richard Jones may well have been attached to one of the companies of the Foot Guards sent down to protect Sheerness and Chatham from invasion. His tokens would have been spent by the men to supplement their meagre army rations. Undoubtedly many of the troops at Sheerness were under fire from the Dutch. Pepys describes in detail a visit to Chatham at the end of June to inspect the batteries and gun emplacements. He criticizes the fact that defences had been made against a land force, but not against attack from the sea. Earlier in the month Pepys bemoans the fact that all the soldiers based on London have gone down to Chatham and Sheerness and that the trained militia has been called out.

After a sleepless night Pepys acquitted himself well at the Parliamentary enquiry on 22 October 1667, 'touching the safety of the River Medway and Chatham'. There were many angry exchanges, however. Lord Berkeley laid much of the blame on Sir Edward Spragg, saying to the House 'if the Offices of the Ordinance had done as much work at Sheerness in ten weeks as the Prince (Rupert) did in ten days, he could have defended the place against the Dutch'.

A gunner's token

Strangely, a gunner's token (*W*88) was issued at Chatham just ten years previously. It reads, IOHN ADAMS GVNER/IN CHATHAM 1657 I.S.A. A cannon mounted is depicted on the obverse.

Armourers

The end of the Civil War and the disbandment of the Militice led to a decline in the armourer's trade. One to remain in business was Peter Deale of Norwich, who issued a token in 1664 (*W*135), bearing his name and initials, and featuring a Roundhead helmet on the obverse. The issuer lived in Norwich from 1650 until his death in 1665, just a year after his token appeared. The initial A represents his wife Amy.

Gunsmiths

Several gunsmiths issued tokens, but refrained from specifically mentioning their trade on their coinage. Thomas Smith of Marlow in Buckinghamshire put crossed guns on his farthing (*W*89), THO SMITH IN/GREAT MARLO T.I.S. Thomas Smith put his practical skills to a number of uses, including repairing the church clock. The churchwarden's accounts show that he was paid in instalments.

(August 1643) Payd John More Sent to Thomas Smith towards the clock 10-00
(later in the month) Item Paid Tho Smith towards making the clock £2-10-0
(end of the month) Item pd to Tho Smith for the clock in full payment £10-15-0.

Smith maintained the clock and the church bells throughout the period 1641–52. He was born in 1605, married his wife Joan in the 1640s and died in 1662. His wife died a year later.

A ball and powder shop

Ammunition for firearms could be obtained at powder shops such as the one owned by Nevell Harwar in New Cheapside. His token (*W*1982) reads NEVELL HARWAR AT YE CIVET/IN NEW CHEAPSIDE BAL & POWDER SHOP. The obverse shows an African civet cat – an unusual trade sign. The fluid from its anal glands was used as a fixative in the manufacture of perfumes.

CHAPTER 16

GAOL

An intriguing token was issued at Newgate Gaol in 1669 for use amongst the prisoners (*W*2043). The prison had been very badly damaged in the Fire of 1666 and was in the process of being rebuilt when the token appeared. The building was finally completed in 1672. The Newgate half penny reads, BELONGING TO YE CELLOR ON THE MASTERS SIDE AT 1669/NEWGAT. An impressive view of the prison is featured on the reverse.

Newgate Prison originated in the twelfth century. The Assize of Clarendon (1166) empowered local authorities to provide gaols in all counties and in towns of borough status. The King's Courts at Westminster maintained their own prisons – the King's Bench, Marshalsea and the Fleet – which were almost entirely filled with debtors. Newgate, however, accommodated felons and trespassers. The celebrated Elizabethan historian, Stowe, quotes from a document of Henry III's reign, commanding the Sheriff of London to prepare the gaol of Newgate for the safe keeping of his prisoners, and assuring them that their expenses could be claimed on their account at the Exchequer.

Newgate was no respecter of persons; for example Robert Baldock, the King's Chancellor was incarcerated there in 1326. Conditions in medieval gaols were appalling, especially during plague years. It is reported that the gaolers of both Newgate and Ludgate died in 1414, besides a large number of their prisoners. Perhaps that is why Richard Whittington, known to posterity as Dick Whittington, a former Lord Mayor of the city, left monies in his will of 1422 to 're-edify the gaol of Newgate'.

Within two centuries the prison became dilapidated once more and had to be 'new fronted and new faced'. Soon after the completion of its restoration it was burnt down in the Great Fire, so rebuilding was again necessary – this time to a design of 'great magnificence'. Even Dick Whittington and his cat featured in the decorations. But, as Weinted and Hibbert observe, 'the sumptuousness of the outside only aggravated the misery of the wretches inside'. Prisoners perished through an inadequate water supply, complete lack of ventilation and gross overcrowding. The stench was overpowering, and it is little wonder that typhoid was rife. Henry Fielding once described Newgate as 'a prototype of hell'. A committee report of 1727 describes a typical ward measuring 16ft by 18ft by 8ft, 'here were sometimes 40 and never less than 32 locked up in George's Ward every night. The surface of the

16.1 Half penny token at Newgate Prison.

room is not enough to contain the number when laid down so that one half are hung up in hammocks, whilst the other half lie on the floor under them. Every night at eight of the clock in winter and nine in the summer the prisoners are locked up and from those hours until eight of the clock in the morning in the winter and five in the summer, they cannot, upon any occasion, come out. The stench is noise-some beyond expression'.

Newgate's more celebrated prisoners during the seventeenth and eighteenth centuries included Ann Askew, the Protestant martyr, William Penn, founder of Pennsylvania, Daniel Defoe and Titus Oates. In 1660, a Major Strangeway was pressed to death in the Press Yard, but it was more usual for prisoners sentenced to death to be hanged at Tyburn. Jonathan Wilde was one.

Newgate was rebuilt again in 1770, but was set on fire by the mob during the Gordon Riots. It is estimated that three hundred prisoners escaped. The prison was yet again rebuilt in 1780 and housed Lord George Gordon who was blamed for the riots. He actually died in Newgate of gaol fever in 1793, by when the place of execution had been transferred from Tyburn to Newgate itself. Large crowds thronged there to witness frequent public hangings outside the prison, which continued until 1868. Newgate had a terrible fascination for the novelist Charles Dickens, who visited the gaol on a number of occasions. It features in a number of his books, notably *Barnaby Rudge*, *Oliver Twist* and *Great Expectations*.

It took a very determined woman to change things. Elizabeth Fry devoted her life to prison reform and succeeding in transforming Newgate into a 'place of quiet study'.

A half penny token was issued at Reading Gaol by a John Thorp, who probably supplied provisions to the prisoners (*W*120). His token reads, JOHN THORP AT THE GOALE/IN READING 1665 HIS HALF PENY. The King's Arms are featured on the obverse.

Southwark was famed for its prisons, notably the Clink, the Cage, the Compter, the Marshalsea and the King's Bench. No tokens are associated with the notorious Clink, but an octagonal piece was issued in Clink Street. Similarly no tokens were actually struck at the Compter in Mill Lane, Tooley Street, probably the most dreaded gaol of all, yet the name of the prison appears on another octagonal token (*W*217), IOH WHEELER BEHIND THE/COUNTER IN SOVTHWARKE HIS HALFE PENY 1669. His device of three ropes and a bell indicates that he had a bell foundry.

16.2 Print showing the burning of Newgate Prison in 1780.

The Cage in St Katherine's is mentioned on a half penny of Thomas Houlcroft as the location of his business (*W*2617). The token reads, THOMAS HOVLCROFT 1665/BY Y^E^ CAGE IN ST. KATHERNS T.M.H.

The dreaded Marshalsea is thought to take its name from the marshals of England. Wat Tyler and his rebel mob broke into it in 1381 and beheaded Sir John Imworth, Marshal and governor of the prison. Bonner, Bishop of London, was imprisoned in the Marshalsea for ten years for refusing to take an oath of allegiance to Elizabeth I. He died there on 5 September 1569. Conditions were so appalling in the seventeenth and early eighteenth centuries that a committee of inspection was set up in 1729. As a result, Deputy Warden Acton was prosecuted for no less than five murders in the prison.

The half penny issued for the use of prisoners there (*W*305) reads, JOHN LOWMAN AT THE I.M.I./MARSHALSEY IN SOVTHWARK HIS HALFE PENNY. Williamson suggests that Lowman may have issued the piece at the gaol tap. John Howard relates that 600 pots of beer were supplied at the Marshalsea on a single Sunday afternoon.

The original buildings were destroyed in 1842, as a new prison had been constructed in 1811. Charles Dickens knew the later Marshalsea well, as he lived close by in an attic of a house in Lant Street, belonging to the prison, whilst he was working in a blacking factory. He used to have his breakfast at the Marshalsea with his family, who were prisoners there.

Several tokens were issued at the King's Bench, which was on the east side of Borough High Street, south of the Marshalsea. Stowe informs us that the rebels under Wat Tyler 'brake down the houses of the Marshalsea and Kings Bench and tooke from thence the prisoners'. Henry Prince of Wales, later Henry V, was incarcerated in the King's Bench for a time. In 1685, Richard

16.3 View of the Marshalsea Prison, which issued a token.

Baxter, the celebrated Nonconformist preacher, was condemned by Judge Jeffries, then Chief Justice of the King's Bench, for alleged sedition and confined in the King's Bench Prison. He lived there for eighteen months and managed to make his life reasonably comfortable. He and his wife kept house in a large room where they were as contented as at home 'though in a narrower room'. Baxter wrote, 'I had a sight of more friends in a day than I had at home in half of a year'.

The tokens circulated about twenty years before Baxter's imprisonment. John Poore issued an undated farthing depicting the Weavers' Arms (*W*282). He may well have made clothes for the prisoners. His token reads, IO POORE IN THE KINGS/BENCH SOVTHWARKE I.S.P. Robert Stonier issued a half penny in 1669, and Richard Hart a half penny two years later (*W*280). The latter reads RICHARD HART AT YE KINGS BENCH IN SOVTH/WARKE HIS HALF PENNY 1671. These pieces may well have been used to buy ale at the gaol tap. Williamson claims that five hundred butts were drawn in a single year at the common side. In 1771 the prisoners, suspecting that the beer had been diluted, destroyed fifty butts. The prison was set on fire in 1780 by the Gordon rioters and its prisoners set free.

The King's Bench eventually became the Queen's Bench for debtors, but ceased to function in 1860.

PRISONERS OF WAR

A trio of farthing tokens were issued at Chelsea College during the 1650s and 60s. The first, a tiny, insignificant piece, bears the words DANIELL DALTON IN CHELSEY COLLEGE and the initials D.D.E., together with a view of the college buildings. The piece bears the hallmark of David Ramage and was probably struck during the late 1650s. The second farthing, similar in design to the first, appeared at about the same time, in the name of John Stanforth, showing the issuer's initials J.S. and the first initial of his wife M. There is a similar view of the college. The final token is quite different in style, design and lettering and belongs to the post-Ramage era. This is confirmed by the date 1667 which appears on the farthing. The words CHELSEY COLLEDGE

16.4 A contemporary view of Chelsea College, which was used to house prisoners of war in the 1650s.

FARTHING are boldly displayed in four lines across the field of the obverse. The college buildings are featured on the reverse.

Chelsea College, the site of which is now occupied by Christopher Wren's Royal Hospital, was founded by James I in 1609 as a theological institution. The Gunpowder Plot of 1605 was fresh in people's minds, and leading churchmen were anxious to set up a sort of residential post-graduate university college and library to promote the cause of Anglicanism. Matthew Sutcliffe, Dean of Exeter, left money in his will for the foundation of 'a spiritual garrison with a magazine of all books for the purpose where learned divines could study and write in maintenance of all controversies against the papists'. The students would be particularly encouraged to produce cogent arguments refuting the doctrines of the Church of Rome. C.G.T. Dean suggests that Chelsea was selected as the site of the college rather than Oxford or Cambridge on account of its easy access from Whitehall and the City, and to avoid rivalry between the two universities.

There is no doubt that the college was originally a most ambitious project. S. Hooper's engraving of 1778 shows the college as it was intended to be on completion – an outer quadrangle was to consist of four storeys and the inner of two storeys. Such fine premises would have accommodated a large number of students. A particularly fine site was chosen, overlooking the Thames and its meadows and extending along the south side of the road from Westminster to Chelsea.

In the event the bold dreams of the planners were doomed to disappointment. Instead of accommodating a provost and nineteen fellows, as nominated by James I, as well as a large body of students, the college never had more than four fellows and a handful of students in residence at any one time. Only one wing of the projected building took shape – on six acres of land called Thame Shott – the southern side of the larger quadrangle, and of that only the central part was completed. Shortage of funds was the prime cause of the failure. The endowment proved inadequate and a great deal of money was wasted in law suits. King James provided the timber 'to be fetched out of Windsor Forest', but the Church could only find £3,000 from other sources. Thus the work soon came to a standstill.

Dean points out that a survey of 1652 described the building as a four-storeyed brick structure 130ft long and 33ft wide, comprising a hall, two parlours and a large kitchen on the ground floor, six large rooms and four closets on the first and second floors, and a long gallery on the top floor. Daniel Dalton's token of that date shows a crude representation of the College buildings as they then were. The building is shown to be of modest pretensions and about four storeys high; the brickwork is visible. A central arched doorway is clearly shown, but the only windows to be seen are in the two gable ends. Two typical Jacobean chimneys surmount the building, very similar to those appearing on the buildings of Hooper's engraving.

16.5 A farthing token of Daniel Dalton in Chelsea College.

It is little wonder that Chelsea College made little or no impact on the religious life of the day. It was dubbed 'Controversy College' by Archbishop Laud, whilst the Catholics derided it as nothing but an alehouse. As a theological institution it was destined for an extremely short life (*c.* 1612–51).

During the Civil War, the royalist Rector of Chelsea claimed possession of the college as provost, but his rights were contested by Lord Monsen, the Roundhead Lord of the Manor. In 1651 the college was taken over by the Council of State as a prison. It is known that French, German and Dutch prisoners were housed in huts beneath the college walls and, although the building was rapidly falling down, Spanish prisoners of war were confined in it in 1657.

It is extremely likely that the farthing tokens issued at Chelsea College by Daniel Dalton and John Stamforth were intended by the authorities to be used by the prisoners, who were permitted to purchase certain privileges and luxury items. It is perhaps surprising to find the term CHELSEY COLLEDGE used instead of CHELSEY PRISON, but after all it was but a temporary prison and old names die hard!

In 1660 a number of suggestions were again made for the possible use of the derelict college buildings and site, but no definite decision was made. Hartlib had suggested as early as 1650 that it should be converted into an Institute for Scientific Research, and later in 1652 that it should be made into a college for foreign Protestants.

Meanwhile in 1656 the building was patched up once more in order to house a fresh batch of prisoners of war, chiefly Dutch and Swedes, many of whom died of the plague and were buried in the college forecourt. The Chelsea College farthing of 1656 was probably used by these same prisoners to buy little extras from their guards.

In the following year (1668) the college was officially handed over to the Royal Society by John Evelyn the diarist, in his capacity as commissioner for the sick, wounded and prisoners of war. Dean informs us that Chelsea College proved of little use to the Royal Society and attempts to sell it failed, partly owing to objectionable smells issuing from a nearby glass works, set up by Prince Rupert, a Fellow of the Society. In May 1678, despite the fact that minor repairs had been effected, the roof collapsed. The Council of State ordered that 'the tiles and timber of Chelsea College be taken down and stored in some place near the same'. Sir Christopher Wren, who became President of the Royal Society in 1681, undoubtedly realized the wonderful architectural possibilities of the site overlooking the river meadows. The land was finally purchased 'to build a hospital for poor maimed soldiers'.

John Evelyn wrote on 14 September 1681, 'Dined with Sir Stephen Fox, who proposed to me the purchasing of Chelsey College, which his Majesty had some time since given to our Society, and would now purchase it again to build a Hospital or Infirmary for soldiers there, in which he desired my assistance as one of the Council of the Royal Society'.

Charles II laid the foundation stone of the Royal Hospital on 17 February 1682. The Hospital took eight years to build and in 1689, 476 non-commissioned officers and men moved in to live 'in a college or monastery' (*Evelyn*). Edward Hatton, a contemporary observer, noted that the Royal Hospital 'would be taken by strangers rather for the palace of a prince than a habitation of pensioners'.

HOUSE OF CORRECTION

A major feature of Elizabethan Poor Law administration was the setting up of houses of correction. Their main purpose was 'to receive and punish vagrants and homeless children, petty offenders and disorderly women'. Yet there was a positive side to them – hence their name, 'houses of correction'. Medical care was given to the ill and disabled, and work was provided for the 'undeserving poor'.

By the middle of the seventeenth century houses of correction and workhouses supplemented the common gaol in every part of the kingdom. They were commonly known as 'bridewells', named after the original Bridewell on the banks of the Fleet, adapted from Henry VII's palace. Bridewells were administered by local justices of the peace. Prisoners were sent to them for short terms only, and could expect to be flogged unmercifully. Public floggings took place twice a week at the original Bridewell in the forecourt of the prison. The prisoners were beaten on their bare backs by the junior beadle. It is known that Bridewell possessed both a ducking stool and stocks for recalcitrant prisoners.

Some attempt was made to provide for the present and future needs of orphaned children. They wore a blue uniform and when they reached adolescence they were apprenticed to local tradesmen for a period of seven years. By 1675 they were receiving a rudimentary education. Children at Bridewell were housed in the hospital, where an interesting token (*W*428) was issued in the 1660s, reading, THIS HALFPENY BELONGS TO YE/HOSPITALL OF BRIDEWEL LONDON. The City Arms are featured on both faces of the token, which unusually states its London location, probably in view of the fact that bridewells existed in many other towns. As bridewells were largely charitable institutions, the token probably had a similar use to the town pieces issued by overseers of the poor. All profits from its issue would be used to help the inmates of the hospital. It seems likely that the Bridewell half penny circulated in the years immediately following the Fire of London, which caused immense damage to the hospital buildings.

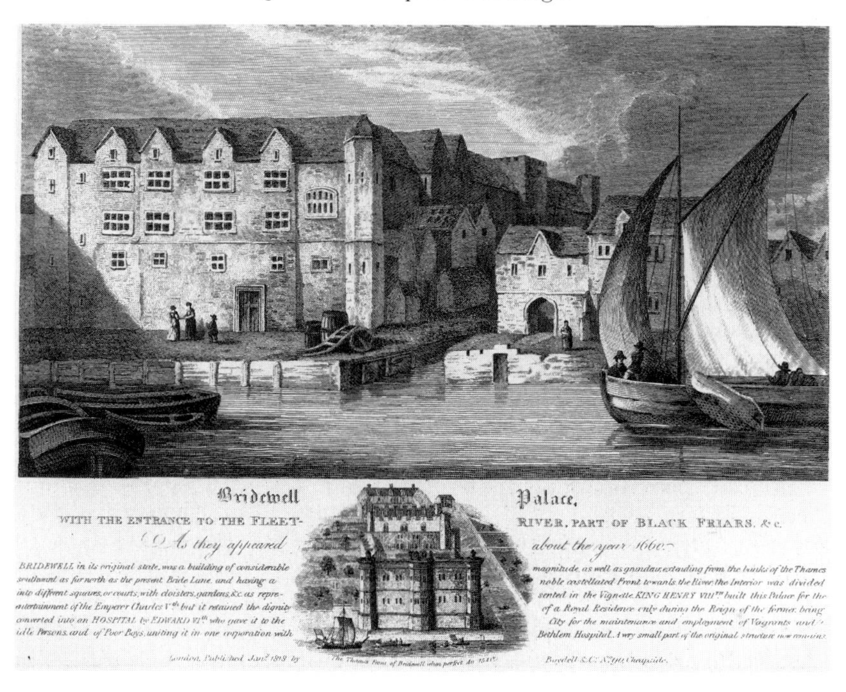

16.6 Bridewell Hospital as it appeared in 1660.

There were at least two other bridewells in the London area in the seventeenth century; one in Westminster and the other at Clerkenwell. Only one other bridewell is known to have issued tokens; that of Abingdon in Berkshire (*W*4). There are two dies, both reading, THOMAS GEAGLE AT THE T.G./BRIDWELL IN ABINGDON HIS HALF PENY. Williamson failed to identify the three objects featured on the obverse, which R.H. Thompson suggests may be bats or clubs used by marshals or gaolers.

It might be of interest to outline briefly the closing years of the London bridewell. A doctor was permanently employed there from 1700 onwards. By 1788 the prisoners were provided with straw for their beds – a most unusual privilege. Flogging was abolished three years later, and a system of weekly inspection introduced. The prison was taken over by the State in 1833 and finally closed in 1855. Both men and women prisoners were transferred to Holloway. The actual building disappeared in 1864, with the exception of its gateway constructed in 1802. A Unilever building now occupies the site of Bridewell Palace and Prison.

MASTER OF THE OXFORD BRIDEWELL AND RUG MAKER

The city council of Oxford made an eminently suitable appointment in making William Huntley 'Master of the Citty Workehouse', from about 1661 until 1688. It was not a permanent appointment, but a renewable contract, for which he was paid the annual sum of £20. He was a fully trained and qualified rugmaker and part of the agreement was 'to use his Best Endeavour for the Teaching and Instructing of the said six poore persons in Cording and spinning of such wooll as is convenient for the making of Ruggs'.

Thurlow Leeds provides us with many details of Huntley's service from the city records. He was sworn a Freeman of the city in December 1669 'provided he give a bond of fifty pounds to the weavers and fullers not to use their trade otherwise then as now he doth without theire consent'. Huntley is described in the articles of convenant as a 'ruggmaker'. He had originally practised his craft in Woodchester, Gloucestershire. In 1670 he issued a token (*W*147), which reads, WILL HVNTLEY RVG/MAKER IN OXON W.H. A woolpack appropriately appears on the obverse.

The terms of the Agreement make fascinating reading. Twelve 'poore persons' were to be sent to the Workhouse by the Mayor and Alderman. Huntley was expected to provide the 'wheels and tavournes, cards and other such implements' at his own expense. As soon as the original twelve had learnt to work by themselves he was to supervise their work in their own homes. He was also asked to train and provide wool and give work to thirty-eight other poor inhabitants of the city. Huntley or his deputy were also to receive into their custody 'all such vagrant, idle and desolate persons as the Mayor, Aldermen and Justices of the Peace shall send. They were to be given hard labour with stook, beateing of hemper otherwise'.

Huntley was permitted to live in the workhouse and house of correction 'situate without ye north-gate'. The Mayor, Aldermen and Assistants reserved the right to enter at any time in order to see that the inmates were being properly taught and kept to work, and Huntley had to give an undertaking to keep the workhouse in good repair. Huntley seems to have performed his duties efficiently, for in 1688 we read, 'in consideracon of the good service of William Huntly, Master of Bridewell, this house give him £5 and tenn pounds shall be given to Wm Huntly for his encouragement'.

He died unmarried in 1696, and his will refers to him as William Huntley of Oxford, Clothier. He left in trust 'my new erected Messuage in the parish of St Michael, Oxon in ye north streete of ye citty of Oxon on ye west side' and two acres of meadow in St Giles' Field. The new house was obviously built for his retirement from the workhouse.

Further Reading

GENERAL

BERRY, GEORGE, *Taverns and Tokens of Pepys' London*, 1978.
An investigation into the eighty or so token-issuing taverns and coffee houses frequented by the diarist. No less than thirteen of the tavern keepers are mentioned by name in the diary.

BOON, GEORGE C. (Ed), *Welsh Tokens of the Seventeenth Century*, 1973.
The notes on contemporary trade in Wales are particularly interesting.

BOYNE, WILLIAM, *Tokens issued in the Seventeenth Century*, 1858.
The first attempt to catalogue the entire series of seventeenth century tokens.

CAMPBELL, R., *The London Tradesman*, 1747 (reprinted in 1969).
An amusing and penetrating analysis of trades, crafts and professions in the early eighteenth century. Intended as a career guide.

DICKINSON, MICHAEL, *Seventeenth Century Tokens of the British Isles and their values*, Seaby, London 1986.
A complete revision of Williamson's standard work. Fourteen thousand tokens are listed, including pieces which are published for the first time. There is a clear and concise account of the historical background, and useful summaries of work on each county are also provided.

MILNE, J.G. (Ed), *Catalogue of Oxfordshire Seventeenth Century Tokens*, 1935.
The first serious attempt to examine seventeenth century tokens numismatically. Milne's classification system for borders on tokens is still widely used. The authors also realised the value of researching into the issuers' family backgrounds, using parish registers, hearth tax records, quarter session records, borough archives, and wills and inventories.

PRESTON-MORLEY, PETER, AND PEGG, HARRY, A Revised Survey of the Seventeenth Century Tokens of Nottinghamshire, *British Numismatic Journal*, 1981.
Using Milne's classification of borders, the authors devised a method of giving an approximate dating to a considerable number of the undated pieces.

SNELLING, THOMAS, *A View of the Copper Coin and Coinage of England, 1766.*
The earliest serious study of the series. The line drawings are particularly fine.

THOMPSON, R.H., Sylloge of Coins of the British Isles. The Norweb Collection. *Tokens of the British Isles, 1575–1750*, 1984 and forthcoming.
A comprehensive survey of the largest collection ever assembled in private hands, consisting of 13,000 tokens. Each token is minutely examined, accurately recorded and faithfully illustrated – a labour of love and a lifetime's endeavour!

WILLIAMSON, GEORGE C. (Ed), *Trade Tokens Issued in the Seventeenth Century*, 1889–91 (reprinted in 1967).
Has remained the standard work on the seventeenth century token series for almost a century. The Williamson numbering was retained in Michael Dickinson's recent revision (*see above*).

SPECIFIC

Sources mentioned in the general bibliography have been omitted here.

1 Inns and Taverns

BERRY, G., AND PRESTON-MORLEY, PETER, 'A Revised Survey of the Seventeenth Century Tokens of Buckinghamshire', *British Numismatic Journal*, 1973.
LATHOM, R., AND MATTHEWS, WILLIAM (Eds), *The Diary of Samuel Pepys*, 1970–76.
MANTON, J.O., AND HOLLIS, E., *Buckinghamshire Trade Tokens Issued in the Seventeenth Century*, 1933.
ROGERS, KENNETH, *The Mermaid and Mitre Taverns in Old London*, 1928.

2 London Coffee Houses

LILLYWHITE, BRYANT, *London Coffee Houses*, 1963.

5 The Skilled Craftsman

BEESON, C.F.C., Early Oxford Clockmakers, *Antiquarian Horology, Supplement to Vol. 1*, 1954.
BENDALL, S., 'Some Trade Tokens of Horological Interest', *Antiquarian Horology, Vol. 8*, June 1973.
COTTERELL, H.H., *Old Pewter, Its Makers and Marks*, 1929.
JACKSON, RADWAY, *English Pewter Touchmarks*, 1970.
LEE, CHRISTOPHER, *Goldsmiths and Silversmiths of England*, 1975.
LEE, R.A., *The Knibb Family of Clockmakers*, 1964.
LEEDS, E. THURLOW, *Oxford Tradesmen's Tokens*, 1923.
MICHAELIS, R.F., *British Pewter*, 1929.
REDDAWAY, T.F., AND WALKER, LORNA, *The Early History of the Goldsmiths' Company*, 1327–1509, 1975.
SICHEL, MARION, *Costume Reference 3, Jacobean, Stuart and Restoration*, 1977.
SWAN, JUNE, *Shoes*, 1982.
WRIGHT, THOMAS, *The Romance of the Shoe*, 1922.

6 Tobacconists and Pipe Makers

BERRY, GEORGE, *Seventeenth Century Tokens of Pipe-Makers, Tobacconists and Other Dealers in Tobacco and Pipes*. 'The Archaeology of the Clay Tobacco Pipe', *B.A.R. VII*, 1980.
OSWALD, ADRIAN, *Clay Pipes for the Archaeologist*, 1975.

7 Booksellers and Stationers

KEMPSON, E.G.H., *Wiltshire Seventeenth Century Tokens*, 1978.
MORGAN, P., *Early Booksellers, Publishers and Printers in Stratford-upon-Avon*, Records of the Birmingham Archaeological Society, Vol. 67, 1947.

PLOMER, H.R., *A Dictionary of the Booksellers and Printers who were at work from 1641–1667*, 1907.

PLOMER, H.R., *A Dictionary of the Booksellers and Printers who were at work from 1668–1725*, 1922.

MCKENZIE, D.F., (Ed), *Stationers Company Apprentices 1641–1700*, 1974.

8 The Clothing Industry

BAINES, ARNOLD, *The Signatories of the Orthodox Confession of 1679*, 1957.

BERRY, GEORGE, AND PRESTON MORLEY, P., 'A Revised Survey of the Seventeenth Century Tokens of Buckinghamshire', *British Numismatic Journal, Vol. 43*, 1973.

WRIGHT, THOMAS, *The Romance of the Lace Pillow*, 1924.

9 Mines and Mills

ASHFORD, L.J., *The History of the Borough of High Wycombe from its Origins to 1880*, 1960.

NEF, JOHN, *The Rise of the British Coal Industry*, 1932.

Papworth's Ordinary of British Armorials, 1874.

SHORTER, A.H., *Paper Making in the British Isles*, 1971.

TREVELYAN, G.M., *English Social History*, 1944.

10 Town Farthings for Ye Poor

ROWE, C.M., *Salisbury's Local Coinage*, 1966.

SLACK, P., (Ed), *Poverty in Early Stuart Salisbury.*

11 Medical Care

TREASE, G.E., 'Apothecaries and their Tokens 1648–79', *Pharmaceutical Journal*, 25 Sept. 1965.

WATSON, G.M., AND LEWIS, D.F., 'Apothecary Tokens', *Pharmaceutical Journal*, 15 Nov. 1958.

WHITTET, T.D., 'A Survey of Apothecaries Tokens Including Some Previously Unrecognized Specimens', *Pharmaceutical Journal*, 26 June, 1982 onwards.

12 Travel

BARRETT, MAVIS M., 'Bewdley Bridge', *Essays towards a History of Bewdley*, ed. L.A. Snell, 1972.

BURTON, J.R., *A History of Bewdley*, 1883.

QUENNELL, MARJORIE AND C.H.B., *A History of Everyday Things in England, Vol. II*, 1919 (revised 1960).

13 Sport

LEEDS, E. THURLOW, *Oxford Tradesmen's Tokens*, 1923.

MANNING, PERCY, *Sport and Pastimes in Stuart Oxford*, 1923.

14 Religion and Politics

ASHFORD, L.V., *The History of the Borough of High Wycombe*, 1960.

BAINES, ARNOLD, *The Signatories of the Orthodox Confession of 1679*, 1957.

BERRY, GEORGE, 'Benjamin Keach of Winslow', *Buckinghamshire and Chiltern Life*, April 1974.

BERRY, GEORGE, 'New Light on the Seventeenth Century Token Issuers of Chepping Wycombe', *Records of Bucks, Vol. XVIII*, 1967.

BESSE, J., *A Collection of the Sufferings of the People called Quakers*, 1753.

LOVEGROVE, D.W., *The Baptist Church in Mid Buckinghamshire*, 1965.

NOAKE, J., *Worcester Sects*, 1861.

SNELL, B.S., *The Minute Book of the Monthly Meeting of the Society of Friends for the Upperside of Buckinghamshire*, 1669–90, 1937.

WHITLEY, W.T., *The Church Books of Ford or Cuddington and Amersham*, 1912.

15 The Army

BERRY, GEORGE, 'Sutler to His Majesty's Guard of Foot', *British Numismatic Journal*, 1983.
DAVIES, G., *The Early History of the Coldstream Guards*, 1924.
HAMILTON, SIR F.W., *The Origin and History of the First or Grenadier Guards*, 1874–7.

16 Gaol

DEAN, C.G.T., *The Royal Hospital Chelsea*, 1950.

List of Illustrations

Index